Cognitive Analytic Therapy and Later Life

D0165492

Cognitive Analytic Therapy and Later Life aims to counteract pessimism and stereotypes associated with later life and guide us into creative and original ways of viewing older age in the future.

Experienced contributors illustrate how working with older people requires specialist skills and the need to share experience and theoretical developments in the 'hidden' developmental problems of later life. They include:

- The delayed effects of early trauma.
- The re-emergence of borderline traits and dissociative states.
- The struggle to maintain narcissistic defences in later life.
- The intricacies of severe depression and dementia.

The use of the Cognitive Analytic Therapy model offers a challenge to the child-centred paradigm of psychoanalytic theory, illustrating the value of recognition of the life-long development of the interpersonal.

Cognitive Analytic Therapy and Later Life is a fresh approach to working with older people. Clinical psychologists, psychiatrists, psychotherapists, nurses, social workers and occupational therapists alike will find this an illuminating and thought provoking book.

Jason Hepple is Medical Director and Consultant Psychiatrist to Somerset Partnership Trust. He is a Clinical Research fellow for the Peninsula Medical School and a CAT practitioner and supervisor.

Laura Sutton is a Consultant Clinical Psychologist and CAT practitioner and supervisor for Local Health Partnerships NHS Trust (Suffolk).

Cognitive Analytic Therapy and Later Life

A new perspective on old age

Edited by Jason Hepple
and Laura Sutton

Brunner-Routledge
Taylor & Francis Group

HOVE AND NEW YORK

First published 2004 by Brunner-Routledge
27 Church Road, Hove, East Sussex BN3 2FA

Simultaneously published in the USA and Canada
by Brunner-Routledge
29 West 35th Street, New York NY 10001

Brunner-Routledge is an imprint of the Taylor & Francis Group

© 2004 selection and editorial matter, Jason Hepple and Laura
Sutton; individual chapters, the contributors

Typeset in Times by Regent Typesetting, London
Printed and bound in Great Britain by T J International Ltd,
Padstow, Cornwall
Paperback cover design by Caroline Archer

This publication has been produced with paper manufactured to
strict environmental standards and with pulp derived from
sustainable forests.

British Library Cataloguing in Publication Data
A catalogue record for this book is available from the British
Library

Library of Congress Cataloging in Publication Data
Cognitive analytic therapy and later life: a new perspective on old age
/ edited by Jason Hepple and Laura Sutton.
     p. ; cm.
Includes bibliographical references.
 ISBN 1-58391-145-6 (hbk.) – ISBN 1-58391-146-4 (pbk.)
 1. Aged–Mental health. 2. Cognitive-analytic therapy. 3. Geriatric
psychiatry.
 [DNLM: 1. Cognitive Therapy–methods–Aged. WM 425.5.C6
C675 2004]
I. Hepple, Jason, 1964- II. Sutton, Laura.

 RC451.4.A5C615 2004
 618.97'89142–dc21

                                                    2003013898

ISBN 1–58391–145–6 (hbk)
ISBN 1–58391–146–4 (pbk)

Contents

List of figures, boxes and tables

Figures

Boxes

Tables

Notes on contributors

Editors

Jason Hepple is Consultant Psychiatrist to and Medical Director of Somerset Partnership NHS and Social Care Trust and a Clinical Research Fellow of the Peninsula Medical School, UK. He specialises in old age psychiatry and psychotherapy and has published work on attempted suicide in older people, ageism and CAT as applied to older people. He is co-editor of the manual *Psychological Treatments with Older People*. He is a CAT practitioner and supervisor and currently completing the CAT advanced training.

Laura Sutton is a Consultant Clinical Psychologist and CAT practitioner and supervisor, Local Health Partnerships NHS Trust (Suffolk), UK. She has been a leading figure in the theoretical development of CAT in later life, and gave the keynote address at the 1999 ACAT conference. She is a keen teacher and supervisor and has a broad overview of the diverse literature around the psychology of ageing.

Contributors

Peter Coleman Professor of Psychogerontology, University of Southampton, UK.

Mark Dunn Consultant Psychotherapist, Guy's Hospital, London, UK and Honorary Tutor in Psychotherapy, King's College London, UK. CAT supervisor and trainer.

Sally-Anne Ennis Consultant Psychotherapist, South of Tyne and Wearside Mental Health NHS Trust and Tutor in Mental Health Studies, King's College London.

Mikael Leiman Docent, Department of Psychology, University of Joensuu, Finland.

Madeleine Loates Clinical Psychologist and CAT Practitioner, Somerset Partnership NHS and Social Care Trust, UK.

Ian Robbins Consultant Clinical Psychologist, Head of the Traumatic Stress Service, St George's Hospital, London, and Professor of Mental Health Practice at the University of Surrey, UK.

Foreword

Peter Coleman

This is a particularly welcome book outlining the beginnings of a fresh approach not only to working with older people but also to conceptualising the nature of the human life course. The need for new ways of thinking is well illustrated throughout these fascinating and interrelated contributions which the editors have crafted together with much skill. Negative attitudes and low expectations about later adult life are so entrenched in Western culture that it is only too easy for the best-informed therapists and counsellors to collude with them. Even writing a book about ageing carries dangers of emphasising the old as a distinct and disadvantaged group within human society.

Although vital to lifting our sights to new understandings of what it is to be human, psychology alone can do very little to improve the circumstances of everyday life. Many of the problems older and younger people face are socially and historically conditioned, and therapists need to learn from the perspectives of sociologists, anthropologists, social historians and others working in the field of social sciences and humanities. But too often psychologists have been reluctant to engage in the demanding processes of dialogue, understanding and change required, too self-obsessed and fearful of what they might become through an excessive contact with society, its history and problems.

The concepts Erik Erikson developed to improve understanding of the psychosocial tasks of later adulthood are justly well known. To his lasting credit he emphasised reciprocity across the life course, that both old and young need each other if they are to flourish. But that the terms which he coined, like generativity and integrity, should be still, after 50 years, the only major conceptual tools available to those seeking to understand the meaning of later life, suggests a frightening level of neglect and avoidance of the subject matter.

This book is one of a number of recent signs of new life in understanding the developmental psychology of ageing as well as clinical psycho-pathology. It tackles some of the hardest issues of mature adulthood, including the lifelong consequences of early trauma, the emergence of treatment-resistant depression and anxiety, self-harm and withdrawal leading to states of 'pseudodementia', and narcissistic defences against the necessary losses of late life. Narcissism is a good example of the negative effects of modern society on adult development, resulting from an exaggerated focus on fostering achievement and talent rather than community and relatedness. Why is it that we find the elderly narcissist so unattractive? Perhaps because instinctively we expect something different from age, a letting go of the past self and an openness to others. What was once tolerable, a stage perhaps in self-discovery and a genuine celebration of the gifts of life, has become a dead hand preventing insight into truths of greater value to do with letting go, relationship, belonging and becoming.

The work of the therapists featured in this book shows that growth and development are possible in these difficult states so long as self-reflection is brought into dialogue with a genuine other person. It challenges the double pessimism about both old age and mental disorder. Cognitive Analytic Therapy (CAT) is now a well established approach to many of the most intractable problems in psychiatry, including the so-called borderline personality disorders. This book marks a further stage in its development, tackling the undervalued conditions of late adulthood. Much hopefully will come of this new dialogue. One contribution will be to diminish our tendency to categorise and separate: both persons, as individuals rather than persons in relationship, and successive stages of life, as discrete entities rather than parts of a continuous whole. Life comprises a set of experiences which we continue to learn from long after the event. Others can and should learn from us. Communicating and receiving this learning are true fruits of life well worth celebrating.

Acknowledgements

We would like to acknowledge the clients and relatives who kindly gave their permission to draw on their therapeutic work and all the older people who have inspired and changed us. Thanks also to the trainees, supervisees and health professionals who have road-tested some of our ideas and shared their experiences with us.

Particular thanks go to Dr Anthony Ryle, for his support, encouragement and comments on the manuscript, and to Dr Mikael Leiman, for his theoretical contribution in the opening chapter and for the clarity of his thinking. Our gratitude is due to all the contributors to this book, especially Madeleine Loates, for her support and hard work, Janet George, for her patience and dedication in preparing the manuscript and Sue Kuhn, for her expert supervision.

On a personal level we would like to mention Graham Parley (for his patience and for cooking Laura so many dinners), Mark Dawson, Denise and George Hepple, Elsie Lombard and Andrew (Gus) Neesom for their inspiration, continuing support and tolerance!

JH and LS
November 2003

Abbreviations

ACAT	Association for Cognitive Analytic Therapy
CAT	Cognitive Analytic Therapy
CBT	Cognitive Behavioural Therapy
DBT	Dialectical Behaviour Therapy
MSP	malignant social psychology
ORT	object relations theory
PPW	positive person work
PSM	procedural sequence model
PSORM	procedural sequence object relations model
PTSD	post-traumatic stress disorder
RRP	reciprocal role procedure
SDR	sequential diagrammatic reformulation
SORT	semiotic object relations theory
TPP	target problem procedure
ZPD	zone of proximal development

Introduction

Jason Hepple and Laura Sutton

The germ of the idea for this book first appeared at a meeting of the Association for Cognitive Analytic Therapy (ACAT) special interest group – older people, held in 2000. Those present had a breadth of experience of working psychotherapeutically with older people, many being familiar with the CAT model. Although hard to formulate at that time, the group felt a need to communicate to a wider audience the essence of their work with older people. Immediately a trap appeared. How can one write a book about working with older people without beginning the project from an ageist position? A title such as 'CAT and the Elderly' seemed to encapsulate all that we were trying to avoid. While working with older people does call upon particular skills and adaptations to technique, and sharing experience in this area must be desirable, it was not the differences between the age groups that the group, intuitively, wished to emphasise. Working with older people is both the same and different. A difficult message to get across.

When considering ageism further, it became clear that a way out of the stereotypes and fears to do with ageing and death needed a reconnection of old age to each individual's life and development. Existential issues such as 'the meaning of life' and 'what happens after I'm dead' are common to all people, irrespective of age. To work effectively with older people needs a lowering of the distancing and denial-based defences of ageism and the development of a person-to-person emphatic dialogue around the existential issues surfacing at the time. To achieve this requires both a giving of the self to the therapeutic process (in a way that can be exposing, frightening as well as rewarding) in addition to the need to develop a psychotherapy theory that arises from, and can communicate with, later life. This is a challenge to the child-development centred theories of psychoanalysis and the intrapsychic individualism of information-processing and cognitive theory. CAT seemed in a good position to bridge the gap between therapy and later life, in terms of both the therapy relationship and the underlying therapeutic model being employed. Mikael Leiman's integration into CAT theory of the concepts of sign-mediation and dialogue seemed timely as a way of beginning the extension of CAT theory, already unashamedly interpersonal in nature, into later life.

With this in mind the book formed itself into two parts. The first: 'Ageing, ageism and CAT: the theoretical and psychological context of psychotherapy with older people', covers the theoretical ground mentioned above as well as critically addressing 'ageism' and the concept of 'elderhood' as the context to work with older people. This part puts forward, above all, the position that older people are 'the same' as anyone else.

In Part II, 'The developmental conditions of later life from a CAT perspective', it seemed necessary to point out some of the differences in work with older people. Due to the effect of ageism on the development of psychotherapy theory, it is yet to be adequately described how concepts core to psychotherapeutic work with younger people (narcissism, borderline personality traits) manifest in later life, as well as describing in interpersonal terms the way that severe disability, depression and dementia affect the thoughts, feelings and behaviours of older people and those they relate to. Later life is seen as a testing part of development where not only do old dilemmas, reciprocal roles and idealisations resurface, but where also an individual can face, for the first time, terrifying threats to the integrity of the self. To try to help in this area needs both personal strength (developed through self-awareness) and a theoretical approach that is flexible enough to begin this dialogue with later life. We very much hope that this book is a valuable contribution to this important area.

Part I

Ageing, ageism and CAT

The theoretical and psychological context of psychotherapy with older people

Introduction

Jason Hepple

In the first part of this book we hope to consider the context within which psychological work with older people is grounded. This takes in, first, the way that psychological theory has developed, with particular reference to CAT, and how both an individual's chronological age and personal life story, generational and cultural identity have been and can be viewed in the context of an interpersonal theory of mind and behaviour. Second, we consider the changing place of older people in Western society, around the concepts of 'ageism' and 'elderhood'.

Negative societal views of old age have had a detrimental effect both on the development of a satisfactory psychological theory that can 'speak to' later life with meaning, and on the way that psychotherapy services have, or have not, evolved. To improve matters it will be necessary to develop the psychotherapy theory of later life in parallel with services. More personnel alone will not alter the dominance of the biological model and the way that professionals, often unwittingly, can play out society's ageist views in the way that work with older people is approached. Awareness of the context of their work with older people, developed through formal training, clinical teaching and supervision based on a theory that is designed for and arises out of work with older people, may be a positive way forward.

In Chapter 1, Laura Sutton and Mikael Leiman provide a sweeping overview of the evolution of CAT theory by a retrospective analysis of four key papers by the founder of CAT, Anthony Ryle, spanning the years 1975–91. Apart from being of great interest to the CAT student who may have struggled with the conceptual leaps bounded by these papers, the theoretical developments described take us more and more into the realm of the interpersonal and the need to find the shared meaning between the individual strangers in the space of a CAT therapy. To deal with the necessary jargon: the theoretical journey of CAT begins with information-processing and cognitive theory (the Procedural Sequence Model – PSM), the integration of object relations (Procedural Sequence Object Relations Model – PSORM) and on into the role of 'sign media-tion' (semiotics is the study of signs) to produce a Semiotic Object Relations Model (SORT). Mikael Leiman, based in Finland, has been highly influential in the integration of the Eastern European tradition of developmental psychology (loosely arising from Activity Theory) with particular interest in the role of signs and the creation of consciousness and self-awareness through the internalisation of the signs created when two individuals relate. As Ryle puts it, sign mediation is the 'hyphen between nature-nurture'. This hyphen can be seen to bridge the gap between the individual and the collective and allow object relations to become transformed into truly dialogic (from dialogue) events, taking into account the past (history), the present (the therapeutic relationship) and the future (the open 'voice continuing to be heard'). It is hard to over-estimate how different is his view compared with the 'demonology' of object relations and the linearity and lack of other in information-processing models. Laura and Mikael argue a powerful case for a theo-retical position where constantly evolving and unwinding interpersonal meaning is the essence of psychotherapy. This is a perspective that allows individual culture and historical differences to be fully participative in the therapy and one that is naturally adaptable to work with older people, as they demonstrate through case material.

In Chapter 2, Jason Hepple traces the concept of ageism through both Western society and Western psychotherapy theory. Negative views and stereotypes about ageing and older people are deeply ingrained in both. The question as to what extent contemporary ageism can be seen to be a backlash against the more powerful elderly cohort of the past, with a modern demise of the role of 'the elder' in society, is extended in Chapter 3. Perhaps ageism has been slow to establish itself as an identifiable form of oppression, in comparison with racism and sexism for example, due to the fact that it concerns itself with a universal occurrence: ageing and dying. Psychological defences based around denial are needed to maintain an ageist position and to place older people in the category of 'them' that is distinct from 'us'. Seen from the point of view of a CAT 'snag', ageism can be viewed as a short-sighted attempt to avoid dealing with existential reality, which generates hostility, fear and unhelpful escape fantasies (unnecessary cosmetic surgery for example). Ageism can be seen as an interpersonal and reciprocal phenomenon that is replayed both intrapsychically and intergenerationally. Awareness of ageism in health and social care settings (and its reciprocal role partner 'reverse ageism' – or the contemptuous dismissal of the young by the old) can illuminate both individual and group work. In addition, a psychotherapy theory that moves away from the linearity of Erikson's stages (ending in old age with the unattractive struggle between 'ego integrity and despair'), and towards one in which interpersonal and existential challenges permeate development and adaptation throughout life, may be a better way to approach work with older people.

In Chapter 3, Mark Dunn takes a wider cultural and sociological view of elders and 'elderhood'. He contrasts being chronologically old with being psychologically and socially elder and looks at what needs to happen in order for the young to want to grow old. From the disillusionment with elders in contemporary times, especially in Western cultures, he draws on examples from pre-modern societies and Jungian analysis to examine some of the processes involved in becoming psychologically and socially elder, illustrating these in contemporary context (in business, family life and psychotherapy). From a CAT perspective he draws on the notion that psychological and social development links to increasing one's repertoire of reciprocal roles, oriented ultimately in elderhood to the continuation of community, rather than to the more restricted aim of ego-strengthening alone, as is the emphasis in most therapies with their traditional middle-age, youth and childhood rather than old-age orientation. This begins also to develop the notion of transition, from adulthood to elderhood, alongside that from childhood to adulthood, as a process not of sequentiality in a linear 'leaving behind' of previous ages, but of successive reflection and integration of periods in life where the person, as in notions of elderhood in traditional communities, can draw flexibly on different life experiences timely to the developmental struggles of those to whom they attend.

Finally, in Chapter 4, Madeleine Loates offers an introduction to the practicalities of using the CAT model with older people in a clinical setting. This chapter aims to prepare the ground for Part II of the book, where CAT is applied to a range of specific and severe psychological problems that arise in later life (narcissism, trauma, borderline traits, involution and dementia). This chapter offers an introduction to the CAT tools and terminology used in this work with older people, and gives an overview of the type of patients who may most benefit from a CAT approach. Through case material she shows how CAT can help an older person 'manage the unmanageable' in dealing with traumatic memories and, through the therapeutic relationship, allow reconnection with the return to 'being in dialogue' with the self and others.

Chapter 1

The development of the dialogic self in CAT

A fresh perspective on ageing

Laura Sutton and Mikael Leiman

Working as a therapist to older people helps the practitioner to see the need for cultural-historical context in the very concepts that are developed to guide practice and scientific inquiry. Part of this is the multiple layers of meaning that are encountered. For example, in order to convey the nature of human relatedness, CAT involves the concept of a 'reciprocal role'. An example of a more damaging reciprocal role is 'criticising to crushed', conveying the unrelenting feel of such related experience. The word 'criticising' however has a modern tone to it, in contrast to the word 'chiding' that a client in her early 70s used. This word was unfamiliar to some younger therapists, yet conveys a sense of moral admonishment linked to the contexts of the day. Thus, Knight (1996) talks about cultural differences, but over time, rather than geographical distance. He discusses this need to be sensitive to word usage, especially with those he refers to as 'earlier born cohorts'. He comments on the lack of methodological sophistication in studies of memory, where most studies are cross-sectional and so confound the issue of 'age' differences with such cohort effects; studies that use cohort-appropriate words for instance have shown better learning. Working with much older clients makes it easier to see how words speak profoundly to collective discourse. Indeed clients themselves comment upon social, economic and political change which is not easily accommodated in conventional therapy theory.

The story of the development of theory in CAT over its last twenty years and more is intriguing in this regard, because it has adopted analytic and cognitive concepts in light of their historical underpinnings; and through dialogue with other concepts in other settings in other times, for example from child development and semiotics, has transformed them from their individualistic bases into notions of shared activity mediated through dialogue. It is this longevity of perspective on meaning which matches the longevity of perspective of older clients, with its potentially transformative qualities if allowed to be in dialogue. More intriguing still is CAT's notion of the dialogic self, or, more properly, dialogic-self processes, because these processes are considered to continue throughout life, from its very beginning to its very end, making the self permeable throughout life. It upholds the need to 'be in dialogue' throughout life for the self to continue to be constructed, reconstructed and sustained. Because these processes are important, whatever one's age, and are not attached to any one chronological age in particular, the dialogic self is in a sense an 'ageless self'.

Intrigued by this, Laura Sutton approached Mikael Leiman to see if it would be possible to write a chapter to present CAT theory to gerontology and psychogerontology. Our resultant chapter aims to orientate the reader to the process of the development of theory in CAT, both to show how the notion of the self as dialogic process came about, and to explain what this is. It aims to be a general reader in this respect, offering a reading of, and commentary through, four landmark papers over CAT's development, in order to stimulate debate about the implications of this approach to theories of personal development in later life. We begin with some contextual issues surrounding CAT's current position.

Contextual issues

Cognitive Analytic Therapy – CAT – is showing an ever diversifying practice within a relatively coherent conceptual framework. There is now 'standard CAT', very brief interventions, and long-term CAT. There are couples and group versions and specialised approaches to different patient groups (Ryle and Kerr 2002). This variety in practice raises an interesting question: What holds the approach together? Here there seem to be two developmental directions. One emphasises professional unity by creating codes of practice, norms for appropriate CAT delivery and so on. The other aims at developing flexible and high-order concepts that can function as analytic tools in various practical contexts. The former endorses professed codes of practice, for instance recommended ways of using the CAT tools, such as the 'reformulation letter' or 'sequential diagrammatic reformulation' (the 'SDR'), or a faithful adherence to the PSORM (procedural sequence object relations model, below) as the final explanatory model. In contrast, the latter sees the most important unifying task as developing the basic concepts (the reciprocal role, procedural sequence, self state) further through empirical inquiry.

This is an interesting sociological issue. Professionalistic tendencies in

psychotherapy are closely tied with the market economy and its regular-
ities. Basically, professional boundaries function to restrict influx to
limited markets, regulated by codes of practice and modes of gaining
expertise, which then bring the spirit of 'doing it properly and according
to accepted standards' to the field. Thus professionalism has an inherent
tendency to conservatism and different therapies are positioned so as to
compete. Innovation easily becomes looked on as though it is 'deviation'.
A tendency to standardise practices by setting criteria for adequate delivery then, ironically, starts to counteract scientific development and cross-
fertilisation. This is of course happening not only in psychotherapy, but

---

Dilemmas, traps and snags represented the first mode of formulating recurring and problematic action patterns.

1. *Traps* – Negative assumptions generate actions which
    produce consequences seemingly reinforcing the assump-
    tions. For instance, in the placation trap, feeling uncertain
    about himself, a person tries to please people by doing what
    they seem to want. As a result he ends up being taken advan-
    tage of by others, which makes him angry or depressed and
    reinforces his uncertainty.
2. *Dilemmas* – The person acts as though available action or
    possible roles were limited to polarised alternatives (false
    dichotomies) usually without being aware that this is the
    case. An example of an interpersonal dilemma, prescribing
    for the person two contrasting, and equally costly, ways of
    relating might read 'either a ruthless bully or a compliant
    martyr'. Personal dilemmas, similarly, represent polarised
    options with regard to one's own activity e.g. 'either I keep
    feelings bottled up or become vulnerable, out of control and
    make a mess', a common dilemma often leading to rigid
    self-control.
3. *Snags* – Appropriate goals or roles are abandoned (a) on the
    (true or false) assumption that others would oppose them, or
    (b) independently of the views of others, as if they were
    forbidden or dangerous. The individual may be more or less
    aware that he acts in this way and may or may not relate this
    to feelings such as guilt.

Box 1.1 First formulation of target problem procedures (Leiman 1994) generally in these times of evidence-based medicine. Here there is a tension between evidence-based practice and practice-based evidence (Mace *et al.* 2000). In the latter, scientific concepts are open to development when they are combined with practice in different developing settings with dialogue between therapies able to establish common important therapeutic processes, for instance the importance of the quality of the therapeutic relationship to outcome.

In his papers at the end of the 1970s, Anthony Ryle, founder of CAT, clearly regarded high-level conceptual integration as a basis for developing psychotherapeutic practices as an alternative to narrow professionalism. This spirit of innovation and non-dogma was a key feature of CAT's early stages where the main aim was to help those who work with difficult cases to do better psychotherapeutic work in practical settings with many limitations. The conceptual tools (the 'dilemmas', 'traps' and 'snags' – Box 1.1) and the practice of reformulation were combined with whatever therapeutic skills were available in order to improve the quality of the work that was done anyway.

After all, the majority of people are treated in institutional settings that still do not know anything about the most basic psychotherapeutic orientation and skills, which very much includes such settings for older people. The spirit of innovation and non-dogma remains a vital part of CAT alongside the recent professionalist tendencies, as understanding the theory and practice of CAT via a thorough professional training enables the practitioner to offer this kind of supervisory and consultative work. For the purposes of this chapter, in order to convey the evolution of understanding the self as dialogic process, we shall concentrate on the conceptual level.

The 'A' and the 'C' story in CAT

In CAT, object relations theory in psychoanalysis provided the original model that Ryle wished to translate into cognitive terms. From the PSM (Procedural Sequence Model, Box 1.2) to the PSORM (Procedural Sequence Object Relations Model, Box 1.3), CAT is now consolidating in 'semiotic object relations theory' (Ryle 2001). We shall refer to this as SORT. This is very new, so it would be inappropriate to try and 'box' it, but it is a fascinating conceptual journey with some interesting landmarks, namely Ryle's papers: 'Self-to-self and self-to-other' in 1975, 'A common language for the psychotherapies' in 1978, 'Cognitive theory, object relations and the self' in 1985, and 'Object relations theory and activity theory: a proposed link by way of the procedural sequence model' in 1991.

1.   Define aim (maybe in response to external event).
2.   Check aim for congruence with other aims and values, i.e. for personal meaning.
3.   Evaluate situation, and predict one's capacity to affect it, and the likely consequences of achieving the aim.
4.   Consider the range of means or roles (sub-procedures) available and select the best.
5.   Act.
6.   Evaluate (a) the effectiveness of the action and (b) the consequences of the action.
7.   Confirm or revise (a) the procedure and (b) the aim.

Box 1.2 The Procedural Sequence Model – PSM (from Ryle 1990, p. 10)

In 'Self-to-self and self-to-other' in 1975, the concept of reciprocal roles was introduced to replace the concept of internal object relations in psychoanalysis. The story of the development of the concept(s) of 'object relations' in psychoanalysis is a complex one, with different and conflicting views between analysts over time and lineage, indeed with such conflicts within individual analysts' writings, such as those of Freud and Klein. How this was engaged with in terms of re-articulating their notions in a more accessible way is at the heart of the early evolution of CAT, the 1975 paper being an early, and 'pre-cognitive', example. From the point of view of our chapter, a key distinction lies in being able to see 'monologic' and 'dialogic' positions. For example, Freud's classical drive theory is 'monological' whereas his notion of 'superego' is a forerunner of the 'dialogical' line. This is because his concept of the 'superego' (conscience) entails the need for another person: the superego is the type of concept that is representing the idea that a part of our self is derived from an other. In contrast, the notion of 'drive' is representing the concept of an unconscious and innate instinct as motivating: there is no 'other' in this – hence, 'monological' (from 'monologue' rather than 'dialogue'). The 'self-to-self, self-to-other' paper can then be positioned as representing an early freeing from an over-reliance on the monologic (and archane) aspects of psychoanalysis, in the direction of the interpersonal aspects on the way to the dialogic, in between which is the 'cognitive' part of the story in CAT.

As Ryle has emphasised, the main cognitive influence in CAT is from personal construct therapy, where the use of repertory grids in research on therapy process led to the articulation of the 'traps', 'snags' and

1. On the basis of inborn attachment behaviours and using sensorimotor intelligence the infant contributes to the development of 'role procedures' for relating to his or her mother ('mother' is used to indicate other caretakers also).

2. Early role procedures are based on only parts or aspects of the mother and precede the infant's ability to discriminate self and other.

3. Unlike a procedure for manipulating a physical object, a role procedure requires the infant to predict the other's response to their action. Thus, the infant learns two aspects, namely that derived of their own accord (self-derived) and that derived of the other (other-derived). The term 'reciprocal role procedure' underlines this point.

4. In time, the infant not only predicts and elicits the mother's role but enacts it, for example, mothering a doll or teddy bear.

5. Later, as evident from early speech, the child enacts the maternal role towards her/himself. This internalisation of the mother's role is the basis for a capacity for self-care, self-management, self-consciousness and also a liability to internal conflict.

6. The dependent infant can only control the environment by way of communication with the mother. Hence one's sense of the world, of oneself, one's capacity to express and control feeling and to act upon the world, are all first acquired within the mutual relationship(s) of infancy, experienced through primitive conceptual processes.

7. A major task of early childhood is the integration of these part procedures into complex, whole-person procedures.

8. This integration depends upon the mother's capacity to provide a safely predictable environment appropriate to the child's temperament and developmental level. Separations, deprivations and more severe disturbances of parenting will interfere with this process and the capacity to unite contrasting, polarised part procedures that convey opposing emotional implications may be damaged. This, rather than defensive splitting and projection, is seen as the origin of poorly integrated adult personalities.

9.   The persistence of non-integrated part procedures will be manifest in splitting (as persistent polarised judgements) and in projective identification, so that one pole of a poorly integrated reciprocal role procedure is elicited from the other person.

Box 1.3 The Procedural Sequence Object Relations Model (PSORM) (from Ryle 1991, pp. 308–9, slightly abbreviated)

'dilemmas' noted above (Box 1.1). From there, in the early development of the PSM, Ryle experimented with notions from information- processing, but because of its 'monologic' nature this was abandoned (Ryle, personal communication). The problem was how to keep the notion of 'sequentiality' (one thing leading to another in our actions) *and* the notion of 'structure' (as in a 'self state') *without* losing sight of the role of the other, or more precisely without losing sight of the relational (in time, the reciprocal). For instance, if there is only a sequence, how could separate states ever be linked? And, how do you do that without losing sight of the 'other'? It is this sense of the 'other' that would be lost in a 'cognitivising' of analysis: the PSM was primarily a concept of sequential, not reciprocal, action. 'Traps' and 'snags' are primarily sequential concepts, whereas 'dilemmas' are closer to reciprocal roles, that is, potentially having a reciprocal structure. For instance, the CAT dilemma 'If close, then smothered' indicates a position without, however, explicating the reciprocals (to either 'close' or 'smothered'). In other words, many dilemma formulations in effect outline a sequence of two reciprocal roles by naming the position with which the person identifies and leaving the reciprocal (e.g. 'nurturing-to-close', and 'smothering-to-smothered') out.

Our reading of 'A common language for the psychotherapies' of 1978 shows how the sense of the other can readily disappear in the force of monologic theory. In this paper, the general line of argument proceeds on solidly conventional cognitive grounds, linked to information-processing views of schemas and developmental psychology. On the one hand it illustrates nicely how experimental research in psychology on the development of concept formation in children can be used to re-construe the failure of mental development as viewed from psychoanalysis. On the other hand, over the course of the paper the dominance of this individual-istic (monadic) cognitive psychology has the effect of occluding the 'other' from view. Traces are still visible, as with 'restricted range of potential role relationships' and 'confused boundaries of self and others'.

We offer our reading of this paper to illustrate how, taken in isolation from CAT's conceptual journey as a whole, a 'monologic' presentation of CAT could happen.

Continuing with CAT's development, 'Cognitive theory, object relations and the self' in 1985 then represents the third conceptual shift, still attending to this problem of how to keep sequentiality (the influence from cognitive theory) *and* structure (the influence from object relations) *in* relational or reciprocal frame (i.e. not defaulting to monologic presentations of self). This paper represents early foundations for the multiple-states model for those with severer disturbances of self-development (Ryle 1997). Ryle's paper 'Object relations theory and activity theory: a proposed link by way of the procedural sequence model' in 1991 represents the start of the fourth period – featuring semiotics – which took ten years to mature within the PSORM. The 1985 and 1991 papers also signal Leiman's involvement. This is the role played by the introduction to CAT of the work of Vygotsky within the traditions of Activity Theory.

Psychoanalysis and activity theory had been in methodologically separate camps since the 1920s. Psychoanalysis for decades had been considered a bourgeois ideology in Soviet psychology, and activity theorists were not interested in the different analytic traditions, and their affinities remained unexplored. Because of its geopolitical situation, Finland (where Leiman is) was in a good position to take this up, a strong interest in the cultural-historical school of psychology, which had been originated by Vygotsky, having arisen there at that time, in the 1970s. This was important because in the therapies there had conversely been no theoretical base which could hold the cultural and historical in self-development. Activity theory represents the concept of a collective, rather than individuals in interaction (linking to the distinction made by Ryle and Kerr 2002, and others, between 'relational intersubjectivity' and 'monadic intersubjectivity' respectively). Leiman gives the example, from Leon'tev, of the primitive hunting team. Hunters had different tasks that, as such, would have been irrational (as for instance chasing the prey unless there were somebody waiting behind the cliff with his bow). 'Activity', then, represents a set of coordinated actions (originally in collective forms). How this is translated to an individual use remains problematic in activity theory, but an adequate theory for therapy needs to be able to explain this. This needed Leiman's work on semiotics via Vygotsky and Winnicott, and later the Bakhtinian concept of the dialogic voice. From a CAT perspective, 'procedures' or 'procedural sequences' are deeply dialogical events. Box 1.4 gives an example of how a 'dialogic procedural sequence' is derived, involving 'chiding'.

Jean came to her twelfth (of 16) sessions saying that she had been very unwell this week, very anxious, not sleeping. She had an upset stomach. She felt tired and exhausted. She apologised to me (LS) because she said she always said this to me. She did not know whether it was to do with the 'flu going round, or whether it was because of all the people who had moved on lately (her son having moved area, her neighbour having moved out of area, her CPN leaving, her daughter now living abroad). There was no warden at her warden controlled flat at the moment (one had left and another was awaited) when she needed them to read her mail to her (she was suffering macular degeneration). She said she just felt like going to bed and hiding. She had to force herself to get up and to do the things she needed to do that day.

In this sequence, Jean began by telling me her symptoms, like a child might tell her mother she has an upset stomach. In other words, Jean was relating to me as if appealing to me to offer her a caring response, i.e. expecting care – see her 'SDR' (Sequential Diagrammatic Reformulation – see Chapters 6, 8 and 9 for other examples) below. However, her next response was to apologise to me as she said she always said this to me, namely, how bad she felt. In other words, rather than offer to herself a caring response in the face of her need, she was self-apologetic: part of herself apologised for another part. In short, she 'chided' herself. 'Chiding' was the term she used to describe her sense of unremitting admonishment from her mother. It was as though Jean did not know how to recognise her own need, rather knowing only/having learnt to admonish herself for expressing neediness. It was as though in chiding she was simultaneously self-neglecting: part of her self neglecting or ignoring her expression of her neediness.

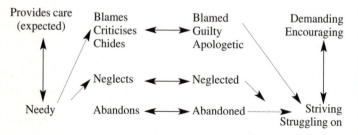

Dotted arrows bring the sequence forward. The two-head arrows represent the reciprocal role patterns.

Jean started to self-reflect a little: part of her self reflected on another part, to ask whether she felt ill because she had the 'flu or whether it was because of all those who had left her. It was hard for her to 'stay with' her self-exploration. Instead, she speaks of those who have left, with a sense of abandonment. She then talks about the warden who should have been there to read to her. It is as if for Jean there is no-one there in the face of her need for attention, she is finding it hard to sustain her ability to give herself attention, i.e. to self-reflect. However, when we were exploring her sequence together, written in the form of the above diagram, this reminded her of her father, and second husband (who had died). She described her father as wonderful and that when she was little he was the only place she could go to get away from her mother and her frequent chidings. She said her father would take her interest-ing places, and I got the impression that he made her feel she was of interest and special. She felt this was also the role fulfilled by her second husband, whom she described as kind, in contrast to the cruelty she expressed of her first husband with his chiding and neglect of her too.

It was as though Jean felt abandoned now, with no-one to distract her from her unremitting gloom, part of which was sustained through her self-chiding and self-neglectful response to virtually any self-expression of neediness. In response to this chiding neglect she wanted to go to bed and hide but forced herself to get up and do things. So here another 'dialogic voice/position' is evident, in her striving response to a self-encouraging/self-demanding voice.

In her therapy, her 'exits' to her 'dialogic procedures' were, first, a period of learning to recognise when she did feel needy: she was not used to noticing this. Then, learning to give herself a caring response and special attention in the face of her now gradually forming ability, warming to a self-recognition of her neediness, rather than to admonish herself. Her response to her diagram and the idea of developing these new ways was moving, feeling that this could help her move through her grief and establish more of a balance in her life with her friends and family. It was as if the SDR was relevant to her in a genuinely helpful way, and enabled her to extend her ability to sustain her self-reflection. This links to the influence from Winnicott in CAT and to the attention paid in CAT to understanding the interpersonal origins of self-reflection, i.e. the need for the other as a necessary condition for becoming mindful, and therefore the role of the therapist and the therapist's tools in this (below). Ryle and Kerr (2002) comment: 'Motivation is not a separate faculty, it does not depend on a motor being wound up and it is not something which can be simply taught; people will proceed to involve themselves in a task when the task makes sense to them' (p. 77).

Comment

Jean's chiding and neglecting herself simultaneously shows that it is possible to be psychologically in two positions at the same time. Her example also raises an interesting point not currently well developed in CAT. When we describe reciprocal roles we do not pay attention to identifying from whose perspective they are defined. Often we use our 'outsider' perspective and mix it with the client's subjective perspective, although this should not be done. 'Expecting care' tried to capture something in neutral terms (rather than for instance the term 'perfect care'), because there is not enough information at this point to grasp her position as she experienced it. Also 'neglecting' describes mother's response as seen from outside. Now the interesting question for therapy is how she saw her mother. The quality of neglect is her experience of it, and that should go into an 'accurate' description of the counter-positioned role.

Jean's dialogic procedural sequence also illustrates how the concept of 'procedure' involves perception, memory, others and so on (see text) and so is different from the concept of 'schema' or a mental representation of some kind. It is possible to see how the internalised dialogic positions speak to many encounters with others, with traces from many, and speak to the embodiment of discourses of different times and ages.

Box 1.4 Tracking Jean's dialogic procedural sequence (cf. Leiman 1997)

Ryle and Kerr (2002) define 'procedure, [and] procedural sequence' as 'The basic CAT unit of description required to understand the persistence and possible revision of problematic behaviours and experiences. Combines mental, behavioural and external events and other people in a sequence (and hence not equivalent to the cognitive concept of a schema)' (p. 220). Here, Still and Costall (1991) point out that the dominant frame within psychology for socio-historical reasons came to view people's 'actions' in terms of narrow delineation of behaviours as the output from inputs, for instance, schemas, overshadowing earlier social conceptions of action of even strict behaviourists such as Skinner. Ryle's concept of 'procedure' is closer to complex notions of 'action', in wider psychological traditions, than the concept of behaviour as came to be understood more narrowly in relation to cognition. The term 'procedure', then, conveys more than only linearity, and conveys more of a sense of 'patterns internalised' or 'sequentially linked patterns of action' (in time, reciprocal). However, the force of 'monadic (one-person) behaviourism' wipes out insights of patterns of activity. CAT then needed the PSORM to re-establish these more structural aspects of relating: procedural sequences being reciprocal roles (in extension from object relations theory) which have operational or sequential effects which are different at the different poles of the reciprocal role and which together serve to maintain the relational structure.

The question then arises as to how such 'procedures' are acquired. Is it from the infant's innate capacities ('nature')? Or from parenting styles ('nurture')? Or from culture and society more generally? This is where the semiotic aspects of CAT come in, representing the cultural-historical voices that mediate the 'hyphen between' nature-nurture. Ryle and Kerr (2002) review different evidence bases in respect of the 'nature-nurture' debate in personality development to clarify how this has been largely resolved, as it is now the 'hyphen' that is theorised and empirically investigated (for example in the work of Stern, Trevarthen and colleagues and others). The 'hyphen' symbolises the mediating link, which needs 'semiotic' devices in order to operate, language being a particularly powerful such device, or 'tool', in human relating. This is particularly important when it comes to self-reflection and the interpersonal origins of an internalised trustworthy (or untrustworthy) inner commentary, as language forms the basis of decontextualised thought, including the ability to make ourselves the object of our reflection and commentary. This becomes more important the more disturbed the person is, with increasing degrees of personality fragmentation, as the need for an integrating voice is paramount. This aspect of CAT theory and practice is one of the distinctive contributions to therapies.

Vygotsky developed work on the internalisation of speech, Bakhtin on the dialogic voice, Winnicott developing the notion of the 'transitional object' which is also a semiotic device. Ryle and Kerr (2002) suggest that the absence of emphasis on language(s) in theories of self-development in therapy risks a repeat of the neglect (speechlessness) that people have experienced in their lives. They suggest that this attention to language, in powerfully mediating nature-nurture, is needed if theory and practice in relation to personal development is to be fully humane, that is, linked to cultural-historical communities (the semiotic devices holding meanings over times and generations). In old age, this links to the idea of how the person's voice will continue to be heard, in transformed ways, once they have died; even what kind of ancestor to become. Equally, we are born into cultures of such 'voices'.

So, 'semiotic object relations theory' is used to contrast with the more usual 'non-semiotic object relations theory' in psychoanalysis, and represents the bringing into CAT the aspect of language in mediating sociocultural activities, so that procedural sequences represent trans-formed object relations as deeply dialogic events. Our reading of, and commentary through, the four papers attempts to point out how this happened and how current development is represented by SORT, within the PSORM.

Introducing reciprocal roles – 'Self-to-self, self-to-other': the world's shortest account of object relations theory (Ryle 1975)

In this paper Ryle aims to show how commonsense psychology helps an understanding of psychological theory, namely psychoanalysis. His central observation is that many of our interactions in everyday life are organised in a way that leads to a narrowing of attentional processes and to predictability in our actions. His examples include the interactions between a traveller-to-ticket collector, shopper-to-fishmonger and patient-to-doctor. These roles are already 'scripted' so to speak and we play the various parts. We expect the ticket collector, shopper or doctor, and they expect us, to behave in some ways rather than others. There is the degree of 'reciprocity'. 'Reciprocal' can be defined as 'both given and received' (Hawkins 1988), hence, 'reciprocal roles' in CAT. In order for us to play our part, out of the infinite possibilities for behaving consistently or inconsistently with this, we need to be able to be selective as to what to attend to; there is this narrowing of focusing of attention. We have decided our aim, plan how to get there, take steps and adjust as necessary to achieve it. All within the reciprocal role, indeed contributing to its stability. So there is a degree of predictability in the sequence the person proceeds with, with a degree of boundedness to the role as well as a degree of unboundedness if someone acts contrary to it; by definition in opposition to it, so, ironically, not wholly free from its influence. This presents us with a dilemma. From the point of view of the reciprocal role, it is as if our options for acting are restricted, *either* to being consistent with it (i.e. compliant) *or* rebelling against it. This dilemma is to anticipate not only 'reciprocal roles' in CAT but also the linking of this to sequences, or 'procedures' in joint activity: with initial formulations in the 'procedural sequence model' or 'PSM' for short.

Meantime, in this paper Ryle aims to look at how these reciprocal processes can be understood in everyday life. In everyday life people can be talked about as 'lazy' or 'kind' or 'stupid', and so on. These can be seen as traits of the individual. If accurate, these descriptions represent, as it were, what the person has become. They give little room for manoeuvre however because they do not help us know how to help someone change. That is, they do not help us with the question of how to help someone *become* otherwise. British psychology since the 1950s has concentrated on the study of 'traits', as with the development of personality inventories and so on, with the so-called 'big-5' perhaps the best known (neuroticism, extraversion-introversion, openness to experience, conscientiousness and agreeableness, cf. Ryle and Kerr 2002, p. 26). Elsewhere in Europe, such as with the work of Vygotsky, the emphasis has been more on what the person is yet to become. In this paper Ryle suggests that more helpful to us are other ways in which we express in everyday life what we know of someone. His examples are phrases such as 'he is hard on himself', 'he is self-indulgent', 'he is sorry for himself', 'he drives himself', 'he admires himself', 'he neglects himself'.

These ways of speaking imply that there are two parts within the person: first, the 'part' that isn't named as such but that is doing the regarding, and second the part called the 'self' that is being regarded. There is this first 'part' who is looking 'hardly' 'indulgently' 'sorrowfully' on the 'self'; that is 'driving' 'admiring' 'neglecting' towards the part that is the 'self'. The former may have a parental quality, the latter more a childlike quality. This gives some clue as to the origins of these ways of regarding one's self in one's inner world which others are now observing from the outside: the reciprocal roles – in their re-frame from classic object relations theory as 'inner objects' – that the person appears to be responding to still, and creating dilemmas for them, or trapping them, or snagging them up, so that they are less able than others to move and to thrive, and to change. These ways of becoming more aware of how the self is talked about in everyday life, with questions about how this comes about, suggests Ryle, have subtle and more far-reaching implications for our experience of the person with whom we must relate.

Ryle looks at how psychoanalytic psychotherapists draw out the connections between one's outer and inner worlds in more detail. If a person 'neglects himself', there is the part that is not named as such but which is 'neglecting-to' his 'self'. Where – or from whom – did this person learn this way of responding to his own needs? This is thought to be internalised from the way another responded to their needs initially. What if, though, this person had a parent who tended to their every need? How could the parent be said to be neglecting originally? It may have been that, in caring for everything, in reality this was smothering and prevented the child from connecting to his or her own capacities. In this situation, the parent may have been out of touch with their child's own experience and needs for exploration, so the person goes into the world out of touch with this too. This may indeed be so. There is also another possibility, that we draw conclusions from our experiences with others from the earliest, and these conclusions do not necessarily correspond one-to-one with what happened originally. In object relations theory, the internalised 'object' is created by such conclusions, and that is why it can be much harsher than the original person. Klein accounted for this phenomenon by her example that when a baby is left alone it is not alone but left with terror. The absent mother may turn into a monster in the baby's experience. This aspect is important in order to save CAT from crude interpersonalism (such as the Neo-Sullivanian tradition in the United States).

Ryle then refers to the concept of the retention of 'dual images', effecting a repeat of either neglect or over-care (or fantasy-care) in subtle and sometimes profound ways. The notion of 'fantasy care' is the ORT (object relations theory) notion that we can create internal responses (in fantasy) to externally induced role positions: the real story was neglect, but the cycle of expecting perfect care and always being disappointed again shows that we do not copy exact role patterns but can create our individual responses to the position that the other has brought us into. Here we find an early example in CAT of the notion of how roles can be replaced: response shifts. Such response shifts are different from the formal concept in CAT of 'state' shifts. A response shift would be for instance shifting one's response from submission to defiance in response to control. If dissociation is involved then the response shift also brings about a state switch. In the former, the person maintains their sense of themselves as continuous and coherent while in the latter this breaks. Thus in some of these early ideas can be seen the first steps to the formulation of the sequentiality of reciprocal patterns, anticipating the multiple self-states model.

As the child grows up, they may now offer to another such suffocating care, unable to tune in to that person's own capacities. This is what is meant by having internalised or learnt *both* poles of the reciprocal role. It is not, Ryle suggests, that the person is fated to repeat over and over exact parent-to-child relationships, but rather that not knowing *as yet* otherwise they are for the time being more or less restricted to being, in this example, at one or other pole of a 'neglecting parent-neglected child' or 'dependable adult-dependent child' relationship, acting towards others in this way too. Ryle writes,

> In this way, the fight against a harsh parental bit, or the search for the ideal parent bit, or the caring for the dependent child bit, or the attack on the rebellious child bit, takes place in relation to other people. Thus, the pain of accepting disregarded aspects of the self is avoided and inner conflict reduced.
>
> This, however, can only be achieved at the cost of disallowing others the possibility of being more than the 'bit part' allocated to them, and from this arises much interpersonal conflict.
>
> (1975, p. 13)

If others are more than the 'bit part' allocated to them, however, so is the person in question. Ryle explains that people are commonly never entirely dominated by these remnants of early 'dialogic relations' and are able to break free as they move through life with new experiences. Some people's sense of self is, however, he says, too weak or beleaguered to do this. The therapist's job is then to be able to offer adequate 'holding'. The term 'holding' is often used in psychotherapy and needs some articulation. Here it is used to denote a specific form of non-reciprocation. First, the therapist resists the pull or pressure to adopt the expected 'role'. In response to this non-reciprocation the client may become anxious, for instance because of the lack of certainty (for example, for a client in her late sixties who commented, 'It makes me feel I'm floundering'). So, second, the therapist is alert to how the person responds to this lack of certainty and resultant anxiety. They might make their own conclusion that they are not wanted, for instance, so take themselves off in some way, for example by becoming silent and withdrawn, maybe finding it hard to return to therapy (this client became despairing, saying in a plaintive, whispered voice, '. . . but what else is there?' – she could not, as yet, comprehend there was any other way to be in relation to me). Or they might take the defiant rather than submissive route, as one client, again in her late sixties, did, saying, 'you professionals are all the same' and become angry, or storm off.

These may be repeats of past patterns – for instance, taking themselves off to their room, now figuratively speaking, when once they had been told, 'go to your room', in response to which they had either complied or stormed off. The therapist offers a non-reciprocating response to this too, naming and tracking this 'procedure' with them too. The therapist's job is to offer the 'observing eye' to all of this, so as to bear with the person through the anxiety and depression of becoming aware and changing or letting go of past ways. Here the therapist represents the 'true otherness' while establishing an intersubjective connection to the patient's experiential world. This defines a 'containing' relationship, and represents a special form of transference. So, says Ryle, this is not necessarily about providing a long therapy, but is about being able to stand by the person and offer some interpersonal safety while these differences are faced. In the absence of a holding relationship or some such safety interpersonally elsewhere in life, it also gives some insights into why it is so difficult for some people to bear the initial uncertainty of change, who therefore abandon efforts early.

Ryle says that these observations of reciprocities help us approach questions like, 'Why does this kind person (doctor, social worker) have such difficulty in allowing those he helps to manage anything for themselves?', or 'Why does this man spoil every relationship with a girl by becoming impossibly demanding?' or 'Why does this woman marry a second husband who seems to hurt and undermine her as much as the one she has just divorced?' (1975, p. 55).

Thus, this paper represents the beginning of Ryle's reformulating object relations theory in terms of reciprocities , formalised later as the notion of 'reciprocal roles' in CAT, with no need to infer archane inner drives and innate conflicts of classical analysis. He had identified the possibility for a common language for the therapies, suggesting in his paper in 1978 that this could be the language of cognitive psychology.

The 'cognitivising' of psychoanalysis – 'A common language for the psychotherapies' (Ryle 1978)

In this paper Ryle says that there is a need for better theory in therapy, especially a theory of mind as it relates to behaviour in relation to self-preservation. He presents a brief résumé of behavioural-cognitive psychology and then looks at how it may be applied to phenomena observed in psychoanalysis.

Ryle explains that behaviourism was changing. While the stimulus-response reflex arc was a sufficient explanation for some very simple aspects of behaviour (in which behaviour – 'output' – is reflexly the effects of a stimulus stimulating the senses, i.e. with no higher order processing in between), this was being recognised as inadequate as an explanation for the complexities of human behaviour or action. The behaviourists were re-turning to thinking, that is 'cognition', as mediating between stimulus and response. In short, the behaviourists had begun to reformulate behaviourism cognitively. Ryle cites Bandura for example as suggesting that the mechanism of change in behavioural therapies was cognitive, via improved 'self-efficacy'. Ryle considered that a similar reformulation could be done with psychoanalysis. He thought that simply translating one theory into the language of another would have little point, but if two theoretical traditions could be restated using the same language then the project becomes more interesting, especially if it reduced theoretical confusions. Here, behaviourism and psychoanalysis have both become the targets for cognitive reformulation, and in this we can see an early step to the idea of semiotic mediation as a common language (below), Ryle comments:

> there is a need for a better theory to guide us in choosing and evaluating the effects of our interventions, and there is a need for a theory that does not, subtly or obviously, deny aspects of the humanity of those we set out to help.
>
> (Ryle 1978, p. 585)

Ryle then outlines 'cognitive theories of man [woman]', highlighting four principal issues: the issue of how 'cognition' and 'affect' are construed; 'passive' and 'active' models of cognition; the issue of mental representations in the relationship between conceptual and biological development; and how verbal and non-verbal processes are viewed. He gives examples from classical psychoanalytic theory to illustrate how it may be better understood in these terms.

First, he touches upon some divergences and the ways in which 'cognition' has been understood in cognitive psychology. In some arenas 'cognition' is treated as though it is separate and distinct from 'feeling', as though there can be 'pure rationality' and then 'pure emotion'. For Ryle though the word 'cognitive' as used here does not carry the implication of 'as opposed to affective' (Ryle 1978, p. 585). Yet, he continues, 'Cognitive processes are those whereby meaning is accorded to experience, and hence they are inseparably linked to affects. Our cognitions of events are derived from sense perceptions and their relation to our memories, feelings, needs and intentions' (p. 585). In other words, Ryle repeats the cognitive tenet of 'ascribing meaning to experience' but adds immediately the requirement of affectivity and, further, blurs the boundaries by taking on board memories, feelings, needs and intentions (this, later, required the introduction of the PSM to sort out the components).

He next draws out the contrast between passive models of cognition and active ones. In 'passive' models, input from the environment (which includes the senses) is transferred into memory storage in a passive way. The first and briefest memory store is that of 'iconic memory'. This is the first perceptual store, as with still seeing the afterimage of the light from a lightbulb if you have just looked at it. From there it is transferred to a short-term store of some kind, and then into a long-term memory store of some kind. The person is seen here largely as a passive recipient of information from the world. As work in cognitive psychology developed, this changed and people came to be seen as active information-processors. In the more general cognitive traditions, Ryle explains, others have emphasised the active nature of exploration and meaning-building that is typical of humans, for example Kelly's work on personal constructs. These cognitive theorists are saying that as experience is built up so are mental understandings of these experiences – or mental 'structures' or 'schemas' or 'personal construct systems'. These organised mental structures or schemas, or personal construct systems, are themselves open to modification by new experience.

Meantime, in developmental psychology, conceptual development was being understood as building up from the infant's awareness or consciousness of bodily states or emotion, the meaning of which is derived in complex ways from complex social interactions with others. In this way the person's history determines the construction of events, including the construction of one's 'self', when neither this history nor the mental structures or schemas are necessarily accessible to awareness. Ryle's suggestion was that the importance of early infantile experience which the analysts write extensively about is best understood not in terms of instincts and drive theory but in terms of the elaborations of concepts and conceptual tasks:

> We do not have to accept that babies have the terrifying time described in Kleinian theory to recognise that unresolved conceptual tasks from infancy may indeed determine the form, of formlessness, of fears or furies experienced later.

(1978, p. 588)

Ryle then considers how non-verbal and verbal processes are viewed in psychoanalysis, linking these respectively to Freud's distinction between primary process thinking and secondary process thinking. For Freud 'primary process' thinking was the thinking of the unconsciousness which we have access to in dreams, symbolism, art, impulsivity, and so on. He regarded this as more primitive than 'secondary process' thinking. Citing Noy, Ryle suggests that this idea of primary process thinking as being more 'primitive' than secondary is misleading because this type of thinking offers an integrating function throughout life. Thus Ryle has a more positive view of primary process thinking, encouraging the exploration of this thinking through image and fantasy. He links this to notions in cognitive psychology in Bartlett's distinction between thinking in terms of images and thinking in terms of words, explaining that Bartlett looked at images as combined on the basis of emotion and interest rather than separation in space and time, whereas what he called the 'thought word' method of thinking was that of reason and inference. He cites the cognitive psychologist Neisser, for whom primary process thinking was 'omnipresent' and comparable with the pre-attentive processes of perception, and only when it is elaborated by some executive process does it become important. Finally, he cites Paivio, who suggested that images and verbal memory commonly interact and that images are particularly important in matching current impressions with past stores.

From this brief exposition of some of the cognitive theories of man [woman], Ryle then looks at how the classic psychoanalytic terms, focusing on the concept of defence, could be restated in such cognitive terms where he emphasises,

> The central role of conflict in psychoanalytic theory is accommodated in . . . [a] . . . cognitive account of the defences, but not in terms of simple oppositions between mental institutions.

> (1978, p. 590)

In psychoanalysis, the concept of 'defence' is a military metaphor to describe the conflicted relationship between the id, ego and superego. For Ryle, analytic notions such as 'repression', 'denial', 'disassociation', rather than representing simple oppositions between such mental institutions, instead cognitively represent examples of selective perception in respect of the personal construct system for the individual. Analytic notions such as 'reaction formation', 'a turning against the self', 'sublimation' (the classical defence mechanisms) and so on also then cognitively represent examples of selection of certain programmes and plans of actions for the self. For example,

> plans elaborated to avoid diverse consequences may continue to
> dominate behaviour and thinking and prevent the testing out of
> alternative plans
>
> (1978, p. 589)

Thus, 'defence mechanisms' can be reformulated in terms of restricted
constructions of events leading to restricted ways or options for acting in
the world which thereby exclude alternative interpretations and options
for acting (i.e. 'traps', 'snags' and 'dilemmas'). A lot of neurotic behaviour can be explained this way, Ryle considered, in terms of the individual being trapped by specific restricted perceptions, views which he says
can often be identified as false dichotomies, or polarised thinking. His
examples are: women (and men) who construe femininity and achievement as polar opposites; or men (and women) who see masculinity
and brutality as necessarily correlated. With these positions there is no
comfortable self- (or other-) definition available. These ideas moreover
are amenable to empirical testing, unlike those of psychoanalysis, which
makes the latter non-scientific for Ryle. In repertory grid studies, for
instance, Ryle found that the hypothesised restricted ways of construing
did indeed map out that way in participants' personal grids.

More tragically, though, the primitive defences described by the
analysts as 'projection' and 'projective identification' and 'splitting' could
be taken, from a cognitive point of view, as confused boundaries between
self and others, potentially as failures of conceptual development during
these early years. This may be further compounded by restriction in the
range of potential reciprocal role relationships that were available to the
individual. Ryle gives the example of a repertory grid study of a married
couple in conjoint therapy. In psychoanalytic terms the husband was
using 'projective identification, as he had to keep up his good spirits by
"putting his bad feelings into his wife" who remained depressed and ill
until they separated' (Ryle 1978, p. 590). The repertory grid work
showed how this could be reformulated as:

> the husband could only see the dyadic relationship in terms of one
> being competent, active and caring and the other being depressed.
> Given this view the only way he could remain well himself was to
> cling to the competent role and be nasty enough to keep his wife in
> the depressed one
>
> (1978, p. 590)

Thus Ryle uses cognitive psychology to re-view classic psychodynamic
defences. He accounts for these not in terms of oppositions between

warring internal drives and conflicts, but now in terms of restrictions in thinking/construing or conceptualising which lead to limited perceptions and limited options of behaving. What Ryle aimed to bring to cognitive psychology in return are the insights from analysts into the preservation of the self. For instance, it would be necessary for the husband in the above example to continue in these ways because there are no other options for him so far: were he *not* to take up these different positions he may be faced with a too confusing and fragmented view of himself. In this sense 'narcissism' (Chapters 5 and 6), suggested Ryle, could be re-viewed as a normal process involving cognitive processes which are needed if we are to maintain a sense of self as integrated and continuing. Ryle mentions the work of Stolorow, who suggested that pathological narcissism could reflect the failure of such processes, with an over-dependence on sources outside themselves, with rage and panic resulting from the failure of these resources (Chapters 5, 6 and 9 for examples).

In this way, Ryle illustrated how some of the central concepts of psychoanalysis could be re-viewed more clearly in the language based on a model of cognitive processes. He points out that there have been many developments within psychoanalysis which move away from notions of biological reduction (accounting for mental life in terms only of instincts and drives) into much more interest in meaning. He argues that because of their obscure language the important insights that the analysts have to offer psychology generally have remained sadly isolated from the rest of the psychological world. By restating psychoanalytic terms in cognitive terms Ryle aimed to bring to cognitive psychology ways of comprehending the self in terms of preserving integrity enough to survive in the face of potential or threatened fragmentation and disassociation.

However, in this paper, in the presentation of cognitive psychology these insights were overshadowed. The clarity of reciprocity was gone, even if traces of it were evident (for instance in the example of the repertory grid study of the husband and wife). This shows how the power of the one-person ('monologic') view in cognitive (and behavioural) psychology can wipe out earlier insights as in the 1975 paper. Our third paper sees the reintroduction of 'the other' more clearly.

Reintroducing 'the other' – 'Cognitive theory, object relations and the self' (Ryle 1985)

Ryle says that the clinical usefulness of object relations theory in psycho-analysis is unquestionable, and in this paper he re-addressed the issues introduced in the first ('Self-to-self, self-to-other'). In between is the conceptual development in CAT inspired by cognitive views. There the emphasis had been on the sequential nature of activity, which tends to overshadow reciprocal or structural concerns. Here Ryle reinstated the structural.

Ryle's main point of critique in this paper is the persistent reification of intrapsychic processes by psychoanalysts. The *Chambers Twentieth Century Dictionary* defines 'to reify' as 'to think of as a material thing: to convert into a material thing, to materialise' (Chambers 1972). So, this pertains to what has materialised for us in our inner worlds. Klein's unconscious phantasies are for her very vivid internal imagos that do things within the psyche ('phantasy' was indexed with a ph to denote it as a strictly technical term, different from, for instance, day-dreaming). It was this form of materialising that Ryle objected to, seeing it as a form of 'demonology' (that is, linked to the classical religious doctrines of evil spirits). Ryle suggests that such archaic demonology presents a barrier to clear thinking. He wished to offer a clearer account of the mental processes that the object relations theorists talk about, and where they come from, so as to make their insights into the human condition accessible to general psychology and to overcome the isolation of psychoanalysis.

Freud conceptualised the 'id', the 'ego' and the 'superego' as mental agencies. Melanie Klein, explains Ryle, developed this further, particularly taking it to earlier stages of life than Freud had. She brought in two aspects, namely the Oedipal triangle and the development of a primitive superego, to a much earlier developmental stage than Freud had proposed, and incorporated polarised versions of both parents, defining relations with parts of self. For Klein the 'object relations' were, however, purely internal from the beginning. They represented the instinctual forces, particularly the attacks of the death instinct, in the form of unconscious phantasies. For example, the infant's experience of sustenance through the breast was said to be taken by the infant in a rudimentary way as something good: re-presented (represented) in the mind, or 'remembered' as the 'good object'. If the mother or the feeding were unavailable for some reason then the infant was seen as being deprived temporarily, which would trigger the infant's persecutory anxiety state: the depriving breast re-presented itself internally ('represented' or 'remembered') as a 'bad object'. Actual experience was not however focused upon; rather it was the infant's phantasies about it that was considered the focus for analysis. From being whole initially, due to his or her innate life and death instincts drawing conclusions of their own from infantile experience, the infant's psyche is now split and populated by 'friendly and hostile demons'.

Fairbairn began to release the infant from the over-reliance on the idea that her or his mental life is effectively largely a product of her or his phantasy as a result of the conflict between her or his base instincts. He saw the infant as 'seeking relation' (needing relationship). This stemmed from his critique of 'impulse psychology' which Freud's and Klein's views of instinctual forces represented. Fairbairn modified the libido theory by stating that the libido is primarily object-seeking, rather than pleasure-seeking. Consequently the infant needs real objects in order to develop. This was an important idea for Fairbairn because of the conceptual shift, from dynamic structures as independent mental agencies (for Freud and Klein) to dynamic structures understood as the internalisation of actual objects (albeit through quite a complicated process for Fairbairn).

For Klein, splitting represents a primitive defence of keeping the good and bad internal objects separate, lest bad objects destroy the good. With Fairbairn's conceptual shift, it now meant that splitting could also be viewed as a primitive way of coping with unsatisfactory or frustrating events in the infant's ways of finding his or her objects. For Fairbairn, curiously, only 'frustrating objects' were internalised, not 'providing' ones. Frustrating objects were inherently ambiguous because they could be viewed as both 'exciting' and 'rejecting' (for example, tantalisingly withheld). Fairbairn saw their infantile internalisation as having to be split in order for the infant to be able to bear this, so deriving a 'split' world of inner frustrating objects, of those that were 'excitatory' and those that were 'rejecting'.

Ryle, however, considered that all experience is internalised, that is, not only frustrating others/objects but also providing others/objects from parents and others. This makes Ryle more socially minded than most, without subscribing to a simplistic interpersonalism. He brings in the work of Herbert Mead at this point, for whom the self is essentially a social process. Mead did not subscribe to the concept of the unconscious as it was understood in psychoanalysis. Avoiding the 'either/or' dichotomy, of either inter-personalism or intra-psychicism, Ryle's contribution involves the two, linking social processes of which we are more or less aware (the distinction of 'I' and 'me', originally from William James in 1899) with intrapsychic ones of which we are not aware, for instance in understanding the 'other-derived' aspects of the self founded on what was, 'first learnt at a stage of life when the ability to conceptualise self and other, and their separateness and relationship was elementary' (Ryle 1985, p. 3). From there, Ryle introduced a more general understanding that unintegrated experiences cause unintegrated mental processes, via his concept of 'reciprocal role procedure' (Box 1.5).

The procedures governing a person's interaction with another will incorporate a capacity to predict and adapt to the reciprocating acts of the other, and may be called reciprocal role procedures (referred to as RRPs). Such procedures will be acquired from the early family experiences and from the more general culture in which the person grows up. They will operate largely unconsciously. This does not necessarily imply the 'dynamic unconscious': as repertory grid studies show (e.g. Ryle 1975) people may be able to describe a series of individual relationships without being aware of the patterns of assumptions and expectations expressed in these individual judgements. The construing of relationships in terms of one's individual RRPs will lead to behaviours intended to elicit the appropriate reciprocations. Non-reciprocation may lead to modification of the procedures but is often met with attempts to force the other to play the expected role.

In acquiring RRPs a person must learn the essential rules governing both his own and the other's roles, for roles are defined in terms of interaction. In this sense, two role procedures are learned in each interaction (Ryle 1985).

Box 1.5 The concept of reciprocal role procedure (RRP)

Ryle's starting point is neither the mother nor the infant but their *relation,* because 'roles' exist only relative to a position in a relation. So 'relationship' is primary: adult and infant have agency alike and differential conceptual developments. In their dyad, normally the parent recognises the infant's own expression of their need reliably enough to meet that need, in such a way that the infant's sense of safety is maintained. Sometimes the infant will be deprived or thwarted in her or his demands. Different reciprocal roles are being learnt, for example 'caring-to-cared for', 'depriving-to-deprived' or 'controlling-to-controlled'. This shows Ryle's 'Fairbairnian' slant, with the important difference that all qualities of early caregiving are internalised.

In most cases, Ryle suggests, there is a sufficient meeting of need for the infant to learn that they can be effective in their worlds: they can get their needs met when they ask, and can tolerate frustration enough to wait for rewards in due course. Because the parent is offering an integrated-enough experience then the infant also internalises this – is able to offer themselves a good-enough integrating voice or inner commentary ('I may be anxious now {you are gone} but that will soon pass {because you will be back soon} and I will feel better again'). However, some young children might find that their needs and impulses are too harshly suppressed or too loosely contained. Then there is less coherence, so there is less coherence in the way that the different reciprocal roles develop. There is less integration by the parents, so their infant or child would be less able to integrate their different experiences. With more adverse or malign experiences still, little or no integration is offered by the more powerful other. An experience of caretakers who can be very different at different times means that the infant or child becomes very different at different times. The lack of any integrating function by the parent, moreover, means that the infant or child has not developed their own capacities here either and so has no integrating voice to hold these sudden (reciprocal) shifts in experience and action in the world, so the shifts become 'split off' from their reciprocal origins, the person unable to connect them.

All of this has implications with future relationships, both in terms of one's experience of one's self and also what one makes of and achieves in relationships. For example, if one partner is playing the more parental role and the other takes up the more childlike role they may run into conflict if the one playing the parental role now feels in need of more care from the other or if the one in the more childlike role starts to gain or seek more autonomy. More difficult still would be those relationships in which the main patterns are based on unintegrated or partially integrated reciprocal role procedures. The relationship can appear to be stable until split-off reciprocal roles emerge (Box 1.6).

This also makes sense of why people resist changing. From a cognitive point of view 'resistances' are normal, and important, processes in maintaining the self. However, the cognitive view does not need to postulate a dynamic conflict such as 'resistance' at all, for instance, because of the propensity for 'procedural memory' to carry on tasks as before – circularity being the other aspect of maintaining processes – and this was very important in the concept of procedure. Roles, however apparently painful and costly they are to the person, are not roles in an abstract or 'mentalist' sense: roles are not something the person 'has' but 'is'. Ryle suggests,

> As long as the therapist is seen to comply, whether to an idealised, persecutory, persecuted or other role, or as long as the therapist does not seek to connect up the fragmented patient's contradictory role assignments, the patient's known self is validated. But the moment the therapist insists on a different understanding or evolution of

relationship, which is the heart of interpretive therapy, the patient may feel threatened, and may resist change.

(1985, p. 5)

This is because these define one's early and continuing existence, however fraught. Ryle says that a demonology adds nothing to this and can even obscure the fact that all the procedures of the person are historically justified or comprehensible but often no longer necessary or appropriate.

In this way, this paper moves away from the formal reification of cognitive or mental processes in object relations theory to a more cognitive, but 'procedural' rather than 'monologic', view of issues surrounding the preservation of the self and the role of the other in this creatively, benignly or malignly. This is in terms of mental processes serving to organise contradictory strands in the person's experiences and actions, rather than these having 'agency' in themselves. The role of the 'other' was once again visible and productive. How to continue to sustain the cognitive language without the re-individualising or 're-monologising' of mind then needed the introduction of 'activity theory', represented by our fourth paper.

Activity theory – 'Object relations theory and activity theory: a proposed link by way of the procedural sequence model' (Ryle 1991)

Ryle had now taken object relations theory out of an over-reliance on the intra-psychic aspects, particularly rejecting traces of archaic demonology, and into description in terms of relational procedures, and extended the theory to include the internalisation of all experience as the person's repertoire of reciprocal roles so far. He had extended these understandings into a more general model of how unintegrated experiences cause unintegrated self-states, given a lack of an integrating other. In this paper he draws out parallels with developments in activity theory.

Ryle observes that neither psychoanalysis nor cognitive psychology has been free from serious reductions in attempts to account for people's states of mind and development. Psychoanalysis reduces the complexity of influences from others to an internal drive economy, and this to biology. The role of culture is then not attended to. This too is a 'restricted procedure' operating at the level of theory and therapy discourse, instantiating (internalising) the restricted procedures of culture (see Chapter 9 for examples from Kitwood's work on cultures of care in dementia). In cognitive psychology the metaphor of mind as computer has come to dominate, which de-personalises and de-contextualises human minds. It too can be seen as instantiating a sociohistorical discourse in the 'mechanising' of human thinking so is a re-enactment of a sociohistorical procedure that restricts attention to 'other' (Still and Costall 1991). Thus neither psychoanalysis nor cognitive psychology was able to offer an approach that does not, effectively, re-enact a diminishing of states of mind and states of development. In addition, the cognitive account envisages a 'single-voiced' person, who assigns meanings to incoming information and responds to it according to internalised schemas. As noted, the role of the other as a special and reciprocal agent shaping our mental processes is not recognised.

In this paper, Ryle points out that Leiman had earlier noticed the similarities between the procedural sequence model and Activity Theory, and that this paper arose following discussions with him. For Ryle, Activity Theory offered a model that locates individual experience within the broader cultural setting, and Vygotsky's work is part of it. Although new in clinical arenas, within educational psychology and the psychology of work it is quite widely applied and is intensively studied. The notion of 'activity' is not easily translated into English. The corresponding German word is *Tätigkeit*. This conveys the 'subject-oriented' or human nature of 'activity' much better than the English word that is completely abstract. Ryle reiterates that the concept of activity is not readily translated into English, but concerns

> a high-level, motivated thinking, doing and being of an individual in a given social context. This is the chosen focus of the theory within which, and only within which, the traditional categories of psychological investigation (perception, cognition, memory, feeling, etc) may be studied and understood.
>
> (1991, p. 312)

This is important because even the categories of perception, cognition, memory, feeling, and so on, have come into being through social processes and been studied in restricted ways. There are lower levels, such as a specific action, in terms of setting a goal in specific circumstances. It was this distinction of levels which Ryle thought useful when considering the different therapies. For instance the level of specific action might be appropriate for those people with a reasonably circumscribed phobia, which is most effectively approached using behaviour therapy. Similarly, people suffering from 'type 1' traumas are most effectively helped with cognitive-behavioural therapies (see Chapter 7).

However, these evidence bases do not encompass those who have experienced complex traumata or prolonged privations, wherein there are complex disturbances. Then there is a need for a more complex theory of self- and other-determination. Thus, Ryle was seeking a theory that could offer an integrating voice for the un-integrated array of different therapies: a common language (understanding) at this level. It is this extended conceptual level that CAT as an 'integrative' approach pertains to.

Activity theory, suggests Ryle, is in fact a thorough-going object relations theory in that Vygotsky's central interest was in how inter-personal experience is internalised to become individual experience, as the root of what is specifically human in human psychology. Vygotsky (1896–1934), Ryle explains, came from a cultured Russian Jewish family with an interest in non-dogmatic Marxism in post-revolutionary Russia:

> Marx saw man's [woman's] ideas as being the product of historical activity; in transforming nature, social man [woman] had evolved tools, language and concepts which served in turn to transform man [woman].

> (1991, p. 311)

Whereas Piaget's research on child development, and so concepts of their minds, was founded on their manipulation of *physical* objects (a general observation in the orientation to the study of cognitive function, such as memory, in mainstream cognitive psychology, cf. Middleton and Edwards 1990), Vygotsky's starting point was how *interpersonal* activity, in the form of tools, language and concepts, is internalised; that is, in how cultural (human) artefacts enable thinking, direct our perceptions and shape our actions in the world (in sum, mediate thought). Such tools, language, concepts are 'signs'. Human development, including mental, conceptual and self development, is then essentially the development of 'sign-mediated activity'. Vygotsky was very much a social theorist: one of his slogans was that the infant is 'maximally social', thus contrasting his view with Piaget, who shared the psychoanalytic idea of a pleasure-seeking infant. Internalisation creates individuation for Vygotsky.

The role of speech is central in this. For Piaget the so-called 'ego-centric' speech noticed in pre-school children represented an individual and pre-social form of speech. In contrast, Vygotsky proposed that what is taken as 'ego-centric' was in fact a derivative of original external and social speech which is now beginning to go 'underground' (be internal-ised). In other words, outer speech becomes inner speech which is 'thinking'. Because pre-school children tended to use 'egocentric' speech in novel problem-solving situations, Vygotsky regarded it as a mode of 'thinking aloud by talking to oneself', so 'thinking' is 'quasi social' dialogue. So, 'This dialogic nature of thought is the basis of our capacity to make ourselves and our thoughts the objects of our thinking' (Ryle 1991, p. 312). In other words, these processes are the roots of our 'decontextualised' thought, which is our ability to think abstractly rather than only 'be in' our participation in the world (cf. Abrams 1996). In CAT this includes our ability to self-reflect and other-reflect rather than only be 'in' these states and relations.

Vygotsky worked a lot with children with learning disabilities, where his notion of the 'zone of proximal development' was important. He applied the concept originally to shed light on the concept of 'mental age' that was prominent in the intelligence testing of the time (the 1920s). He observed that attaining the same score on these tests might relate only to independent performance, because, of two children who had attained the same test level, when under guidance one of them might be able to advance three or four levels whereas the other might not be able to do this. This difference in benefit from joint activity related to their 'zone of proximal development' (ZPD). The ZPD then is the gap between what a child is able to do on his or her own, compared with what he or she can do with a more capable peer or adult. This was taken further by several educational psychologists such as Cole (1998) and Rogoff (1991). Here, the teacher needs to be ahead of development, leading the child to his/her potential areas of development, introducing tools or concepts as needed and transferring responsibility to the child steadily. For Ryle then,

> Vygotsky was concerned (in a way Piaget was not) with the 'highly charged experiences of intimate relations' of the child because of the emphasis he placed on the adult's role in the process of intellectual growth through internalisation, and he was interested (in a way psychoanalysts are not) in the absolute importance of object relations (*i.e. sign-mediated joint activity*) for culturally shaped cognitive development.
>
> (1991, p. 315, our emphases)

Elsewhere, in the context of psychoanalytic therapy and paediatric practice, Winnicott effectively looked at the early unity and slow separation of the infant and the mother, via the concept of the 'transitional object' – the 'security blanket'. Winnicott listed some other things that could get this function. In addition to the blanket and other objects, a musical sequence, even the baby's own gesture, could signify the presence of the other in their absence. It is not just that the baby makes a sign which the mother takes as meaningful so the outcome is a shared transitional object which is symbolic of this process. The birth of a transitional object does not originate in the baby's signifying act, whether as a 'gesture' or an 'act-of-mind'. Winnicott is very explicit about the idea that transitional objects can receive their symbolic power only because of the presence of the mother. If she is absent too long, the object loses its quality as a transitional object. Winnicott claimed that the transitional object is the baby's first 'not-me possession'. It exists externally but at the same time it is under the baby's 'omnipotence' (again Winnicott's term). Thus, it mediates a peculiar mode of action which cannot be accomplished without the other's psychic presence, although the baby can perform it as a 'gesture' (i.e. something that is in his or her possession). Obviously the meaning of the object gets richer in use, but the initial quality of its emergence has a peculiar character of a dyadic, or dialogic, act. This links to the notion of the 'dialogic sequence' in CAT, in so far as the 'other' is present in all of our actions either by having shaped the sequence or by reappearing in the objects and artefacts that constitute the means of our actions (although this aspect of theory is not really developed yet and belongs to the as yet unexplored field of studying the implications of semiotic dialogism for CAT; compare below).

CAT needed Winnicott to make the link of its processes of internalisation to culture from the very earliest times of life, because Winnicott, like Vygotsky, had shown how object relations are mediated by signs. As Ryle notes, Winnicott believed that the presence of an integrating parent, one who can provide a reasonably consistent acceptance of the full range of procedures and affects, was essential. Then for Ryle,

> In many ways the PSORM could be regarded as an extension of the developmental theory of activity theory to earlier ages (with a bias towards abnormality). One aspect of its contribution could be epitomised by rephrasing Vygotsky's statement [what a child does with her mother today, she does on her own tomorrow] as follows: 'what the adult *cannot* let the child do or know today, the child *cannot* let herself do or know tomorrow'. It would seem to be important for educators as well as for therapists to recognise the potential effects of damaging early internalisation, and of how they may inhibit later entry into the (intellectual and emotional) zone of proximal development.
>
> (1991, p. 313, Ryle's emphases)

part of the integrating function of the parent may include providing an accurate account of what is enacted between parent and child. The inconsistent or damaging parent may also provide a distorted account, leaving the child with a mistrust of self and other and an untrustworthy inner commentary.

(1991, p. 314)

This idea, of a mistrust of self and other and an untrustworthy inner commentary, links back to Vygotsky. Taking Vygotsky further, there is a need for an integrating external voice, if there is to be an inner integrating voice. In this regard, Ryle comments on how quickly many clients can make use of the CAT tools such as the SDR, which suggests to him that it is not the intensity of their procedures or experiences that makes progress difficult for them: it has been the absence of an integrating commentary or 'voice'. This voice needs its 'tools' in order to be operative, and the active use of reflective tools, like the reformulation, diagrams, diaries, etc. – in the dialogic presence of the therapist – accounts for the some-times rapid development that we may observe with even severely dam-aged clients.

In all, there have been two main implications of the introduction of the concept of semiotic mediation to CAT. The first, as already discussed, is to overcome the separation of the inner and outer – the nature-nurture – through the concept of the internalisation of cultural tools (like language): which at the same time bridges the gap between the individual (a total intrapsychicism) and the collective (the 'maximally social') in human mental, emotional and self development. The second, also discussed just above, is to conceptualise therapy as a developmental process by which the client learns to employ new tools for self-observation and self-reflection with the help offered by the therapist, that is, within their 'zone of proximal personality development' (Ryle and Kerr 2002).

SORT within the PSORM

So, in object relations theory, Ryle was objecting to the traces of an archaic demonology which he felt was in part maintaining the isolation of their powerful and often moving relational insights into someone's development, emotionally, intellectually and personally, and how they worked with this transferentially and countertransferentially. He showed through personal construct research how these could be more clearly articulated in a way that was open to empirical test. Taking this further he drew on research in developmental psychology to show how some of what the analysts talked about in terms of accounting for someone's damaged development could be re-construed, for instance in terms of failures of early conceptual development in damaging or depriving environments.

He explored the new information-processing ideas that were emerging as part of the contemporary developments in psychology, but this proved too limiting because of the occlusion of the 'other'; that is, the lack of a concept of the special and reciprocating role of the other in our mental, emotional and self development. This speaks to the long 'monadic' (one person) tradition in psychology, since Descartes and Kant (Still and Costall 1991; Leiman 2002a) which has importantly influenced scientific concepts in mainstream psychology. Over this period of CAT's development there is potentially a sense of loss, of the founding insights from the object relations analysts. Here there is a risk of the 'monologising' of the concept of 'procedure', when this concept is more aligned with more general psychology traditions in terms of patterns of activity, than with the more narrowly defined range of what came to be presented as behavioural psychology. Jean's example (Box 1.4) shows how important it is to retrieve and sustain the relational, through the concept of the dialogical, as opposed to the monological, sequence. Tracing her 'dialogic procedures' (both structural and sequential) explained why it was hard for Jean to sustain her capacity for self-reflection (to give herself sustained/sustaining attention), and how the ability of the therapist to show her what seemed to be happening enabled her to join in her therapy, to bear to become interested in this. Then it is possible to see how, as Ryle and Kerr (2002, p. 77) observe, 'Motivation is not a separate faculty . . . people will proceed to involve themselves in a task when the task makes sense to them.' This challenges a 'monadic' view of 'motivation', individual differences making sense in terms of different spheres or 'zones' of proximal personality development (ZPPD) within a dialogic relation: the 'more competent other' helping their development.

So, this takes us up to the 'PSORM' (Box 1.3): the object relational, re-stated as reciprocal roles, formed in the earliest times of life; now articulated with the clarity of behavioural and cognitive sequential description (rather than in the interpretive analytic language); without however defaulting to their 'one person' view of cognitive development. This signals the introduction of the dialogic rather than in 'single voiced' approach to human developmental processes. This is the introduction of research that addresses the internalisation of interpersonal activity, rather than activity in relation to physical objects. This then permits the linking of the individual to cultural-historical activity (Chapter 3), mediated by signs, such as language: SORT within the PSORM, represented as the 'hyphen between' nature-nurture, which is as relevant to old age as to any age.

The significance of the introduction of SORT to the PSORM is perhaps most clearly evident with those who may not have experienced the integrating voice of another, so may not have had any way of holding their reciprocal shifts. As one client, who was in her early seventies, described it, and who experienced confusing states switches, she had felt in a 'zombie state' all her life and was 'waking up' now (Box 1.6). The formulation of the dialogic concepts have effectively enabled this arena, which includes the capacity for self-reflection, to be conceptualised and thereby thought and talked about and researched.

These processes are the same in later life as in earlier life stages, with the addition that ageist discourses may make it harder for this to be permitted. So many people come to therapy in later life pessimistic about change 'at their age'. Hepple (Chapter 2) discusses ageism in detail, drawing out the fruitless cycle that is being replayed intergenerationally in this respect, conceptualising 'ageism' as a dialogic act, enacted in terms of a CAT snag, and which prevents the person from progressing. Coleman (1999) in his review of research in gerontology on 'identity management' in later life and old age, explains that the emphasis so far on the notion of the stability of the self is now being questioned, and considers that a changing self is potentially more adaptive, gerontology now becoming interested in these processes.

Fawkes considers that the persistence of personality traits into old age may be explained in part by the absence, from a Vygotskian perspective, of new forms of mediation in the self (personal communication). In Jean's case (Box 1.4) the persistence of her personality trait, of melancholia, may have been in part because there had been no new form of 'mediation' of her 'dialogic self': in Patricia's case (Box 1.6) the key absence seems to have been the lack of an integrating commentary to her 'split off' states in relationships. Sutton (2002) suggests that old age is approached too often as if 'all is said and done' on the self. CAT's dialogic perspective on the self, within its semiotic object relations theory, has supported a new challenge to this, with a refreshing way of looking at the beginning of a developmentally informed and clinically useful model that is located not only in childhood and younger years:

> replacing, 'I think therefore I am' with, 'We engage and communicate, therefore I become'. Dialogue continues throughout life, both

Patricia, in her early seventies, who was referred because she had attempted to cut her wrists, was afraid for her future, with unstable relationships. In the early sessions she looked suspiciously towards me (LS). She was extremely tense, and would hold one of her arms over her head, so that her hand would reach for her hair, to curl some strands around her finger repetitively. She spoke in a child-like voice as if she had just been told off, as if whimpering in protestation. From a CAT point of view, she was 'looking sus-piciously on' to me as the 'other' and in response to this made a self-soothing gesture: part of her self (her hand) soothed another part of her self (her hair). Thus, her gesture was a '*semiotic*' '*object-relational*' device.

Patricia had come to depend on an old friend after her husband had died. It was a few years ago when he had been admitted to hospital, where he died, Patricia never visited him. Her daughters were said to be extremely critical of her for this and broke off all contact. Patricia sold up the family home and moved in with her divorced friend. All was well until her friend decided to remarry. Patricia realised she may have to find a place of her own. She became increasingly jealous of her friend's relationship, going into sudden rages if she were not included in their events, screaming at her friend, only then to go to her room, returning some time later, acting normally as if nothing had happened, seeming not able to remember. She increasingly threatened suicide. Eventually, Patricia went into respite care in order to give her friend a break. It was there that she attempted to cut her wrist. She was being considered for a permanent residential place in a sheltered accom-modation complex where she very much wanted to go. However, she was afraid she would break down completely.

Patricia's mistrust of me contrasted with her view of her relation-ship with her friend on whom she had come to depend so badly. It looked as if, in response to her feared rejection or feared abandon-ment, Patricia had 'cut out', either in the form of numbing after her 'Screams' or in attempting to cut her wrist in respite care. I won-dered how she would relate to me. Meantime, in her therapy, we came to reformulate her difficulties in terms of a dilemma between 'trust and mistrust' (drawn as an SDR): 'feeling desparately (sic) in need of someone to trust, I seek someone I can trust completely –

all is well – until they are unreliable in their care – I become mistrustful, suspicious and paranoid – rageful, I attack them ("blow a gasket" – scream) – I am terrified of rejection or abandonment – so I try and numb the pain by shutting out (go to my room), numbing or cutting (become a zombie)'.

Over the course of her therapy, Patricia learnt quickly to divert her 'Screams', by beginning to recognise the feeling of rising tension and walking away. This initially caused concern to her carers, who wondered what was wrong; it also repeated her procedure of taking herself off if she felt she had done 'wrong'. However, this was an important first step, Patricia remarking that she was 'beginning to think rather than react'. She moved into her permanent residence about then. Gradually, Patricia started to be able to talk with her new carers more directly; for example, when one had not come to give her a bath, rather than give in to her feelings of despair (she lived with chronic pain from a degenerative spinal condition and the water and bubble bath were soothing), she was able to bring this to their attention. To her surprise, she found that they were not critical but said sorry and, indeed, became more reliable in their care of her.

Her friend continued to visit her. Patricia began to reflect that she had 'clung' to her. This seemed to signal a period of mourning. She felt utterly alone, without anyone who cared for her. She also reflected of her jealousy and sense of betrayal in the face of everyday disappointments that 'it seems so real'. She began to tell me more of her life, which she had been scared of doing lest going over her distant trauma would overwhelm her. Initially I heard only about her early years, she only much later telling me about her middle years in an unhappy marriage. She remarked of her youngest that she was aggrieved to think they had been so close when she was growing up, not at all like mother and daughter, but close friends, only for her to betray her. As she said this she looked across at her SDR. We were thinking the same thing: that she had lived out her trust-mistrust dilemma with her too. She went on to let me know of the lack of her bonding with her elder daughter from the time of her birth, because of tragic family circumstances, and we started to comprehend a little of her distancing rejection of her (cutting out to the pain she represented).

Patricia said she was dreading the end of therapy and said she didn't want to think about it. Just before the end, transport was unreliable and neglected to pick her up one day. At the time we should have met, I wrote to her to say that I was thinking of her at this time when we would have met, when she had been let down at a time when she was finding it hard to think about our not meeting again. She returned the following week, having been comforted by this, as she had been struggling with blaming herself for her absence. I wondered with her whether we might have also seen her struggle with her 'trust-mistrust' dilemma in our relationship, and I invited her to think about how she wanted to construe her abandonment by me, in the end of her regular sessions.

Although dreading finishing, by the end of her therapy Patricia was pleased to be feeling 'more normal', and more able to 'mix more normally', which had been her specific aims so she could secure her placement. In other words, she was able to mix with other residents and relate to her carers (to ask to have her needs met) without either 'blowing a gasket' too much or numbing too unduly. She was on the residents' committee. At follow-up three months later, she had maintained her progress, was still on the residents' committee, and was now able to walk into the lounge without having to say to herself, 'I am entitled to exist'. Her old friend remained her friend, often popping in.

What neither of us had expected was that her daughters had each made an attempt to re-establish contact. At follow-up she said that she and her youngest had met up again. Her daughter wanted a family reunion, but Patricia felt she needed time to get to know her. Her elder daughter, of whom she had been particularly critical, had telephoned her. Patricia tried hard not to 'blast' or switch off to her, but she wasn't sure if she had managed very well.

*

At the outset of her therapy, Patricia had been terrified of contracting Alzheimer's Disease, as her abusive father had had and whom she had to nurse until his death. Coleman (1999) summarises research which shows that 'fear of future self' is a mediator of depression in later life, including when there is physical and mental frailty (Patricia, as well as suffering chronic pain, had slight memory problems after a slight stroke). In Patricia's case her fear of future self was of becoming in the image of her father, perhaps hating to care for him: her fear was 'dialogic' (mediated by her imaginative capacities). Now, there was a sense of an unknown potential future in the new developments in her relationships with her daughters, and her residential home to her was indeed a felt 'home'. Patricia described herself as having 'grown up' a little in therapy: I had not seen her self-soothing gesture in many months, and her voice was less childlike. In other words, her maturing self may be viewed as a deeply dialogic (*semiotic and object relational*), and continuing, intergenerational event.

Box 1.6 SORT within PSORM

external dialogue with others and the internal dialogue representing the transformed conversations of early development. Our ability to keep these internal conversations private, combined with the intensely individualistic ideology accompanying the development of capitalism in Western Europe during the last few centuries, supports an intense conviction in the centrality of the 'I' which, for many people, is as hard to abandon as was the belief that the world was the centre of the cosmos. In the dialogic view, however, the self remains permeable throughout life, generating and responding to other selves directly and through accumulated words and other artefacts.

(Ryle 2001, p. 4)

References

Abrams, D. (1996) *The Spell of the Sensuous*. New York: Vintage Books.

Chambers Twentieth Century Dictionary (1972). Edinburgh: Chambers.

Cole, M. (1998) *Cultural Psychology: A Once and Future Discipline*. Cambridge, MA, and London: Belknap Press.

Coleman, P. G. (1999) Identity management in later life. In P. G. Britton and R. T. Woods (eds), *Psychological Problems of Ageing: Assessment, Treatment and Care*. Chichester: John Wiley.

Hawkins, J. M. (1988) *The Oxford Minidictionary*, 2nd edn. Oxford: Clarendon Press.

Knight, B. G. (1996) *Psychotherapy with Older Adults*, 2nd edn. London: Sage.

Leiman, M. (1994) The development of cognitive analytic therapy. *International Journal of Short-Term Psychotherapy* 9(2–3): 67–82.

Leiman, M. (1997) Procedures as dialogical sequences: a revised version of the fundamental concept in Cognitive Ananlytic Therapy. *British Journal of Medical Psychology* 70: 193–207.

Leiman, M. (2002a) Rigs, reciprocal roles, working models and semiotic positions. *ACATNews* 17: 10–13.

Leiman, M. (2002b) Toward semiotic dialogism. *Theory and Psychology* 12: 221–35.

Mace, C., Moorey, S., and Roberts, B. (2000) *Evidence in the Psychological Therapies: A Critical Guide for Practitioners*. London: Brunner-Routledge.

Middleton, D., and Edwards, D. (1990) *Collective Remembering*. London: Sage.

Rogoff, B. (1991) *Apprenticeship in Thinking: Cognitive Development in Social Context*. Oxford: Oxford University Press.

Ryle, A. (1975) Self-to-self and self-to-other. *New Psychiatry* (April): 12–13.

Ryle, A. (1978) A common language for the therapies. *British Journal of Psychiatry* 132: 585–94.

Ryle, A. (1985) Cognitive theory, object relations and the self. *British Journal of Medical Psychology* 58: 1–7.

Ryle, A. (1990) *Cognitive-Analytic Therapy: Active Participation in Change. A New Integration in Brief Psychotherapy*. Chichester: John Wiley.

Ryle, A. (1991) Object relations theory and activity theory: a proposed link by way of the procedural sequence model. *British Journal of Medical Psychology* 64: 307–16.

Ryle, A. (1997) *Cognitive Analytic Therapy and Borderline Personality Disorder: The Model and the Method*. Chichester: John Wiley.

Ryle, A. (2001) CAT's dialogic perspective on the self. *ACATNews* 15 (Autumn/Winter): 3–4.

Ryle, A., and Kerr, I. (2002) *Introducing Cognitive Analytic Therapy: Principles and Practice*. Chichester: John Wiley.

Still, A., and Costall, A. (1991) *Against Cognitivism: Alternative Foundations for Cognitive Psychology*. New York: Harvester Wheatsheaf.

Sutton, L. (2002) Introduction: contemporary views – a duel with the past. In J. Hepple, J. Pearce and P. Wilkinson (eds), *Psychological Therapies with Older People: Developing Treatments for Effective Practice*. Hove: Brunner-Routledge.

Chapter 2

Ageism in therapy and beyond

Jason Hepple

What a long and painful road it has been. I feel my life has been wasted, I could have done more, become more, and given more. What a sad waste of time it has all been. I find it difficult to see myself as I really am. Have I lost the art of living, and like a worker just toil away at what needs to be done? . . . At least I am (now) trying to see and question. Thank you again for your great help. It has been indispensable to me. I was a 'no hoper'. I will try to repay what has been invested in me. By helping my fellow creatures all I can and by being kind and understanding to the less fortunate. I will miss our sessions.

The man who wrote this was ending a CAT therapy. He was sixty-eight at the time and had found the therapy both challenging and transforming. He had experienced much doubt as to whether he deserved the therapy and the commitment of a younger person (myself) in an endeavour that he feared was too little too late. He questioned whether he was being self-indulgent and self-pitying in his old age; struggling to find some meaning in the 'long and painful' journey he had travelled seemed to raise doubts that such a catharsis was both unnatural and undignified. Yet, from 'no-hope' he had found self-reflection and the kernel of his self-esteem, but this gift, he felt, needed to be repaid rather than accepted. He could not relinquish the despair that seemed the inevitable conclusion to (his) life. To do so would be to deny the existence of death and, somehow, deprive the young of their chance.

Despair expresses the feeling that the time is now short, too short to attempt to start another life, and to try out alternate roads to integrity.
(Erikson 1963, p. 294)

It is difficult working psychotherapeutically with older people. Ageism is deeply ingrained in modern Western society and is inevitably represented in both therapist and client as a series of negative stereotypes, unchallenged assumptions and unconscious reactions which exert a profound influence on therapeutic work. So difficult has it been to see the wood for the trees in this area; the theoretical models underpinning modern psychotherapies themselves providing some of the most glaring examples of ageism around. To top even this obstacle is a medical and psychological model of ageing where increasing age and decline in function are synonymous and inevitable and where there can seem no alternative but to chart deficits and monitor deterioration rather than measure strengths and encourage adaptation and development.

In this chapter I will attempt to tease out some of the complex issues related to working psychotherapeutically with older people in an ageist context. I shall begin with a discussion of the nature and construction of ageism from a sociological perspective and suggest how ageism may serve as a psychological defence against the realities of ageing and death. Next I shall discuss the presence of ageism in psychotherapy theory and how this has been reflected in the provision of psychological services for older people. Finally I shall look at ways of working therapeutically with older people in this ageist context, both individually and in groups, and suggest means of challenging ageism and organising services so that the provision of psychological therapy services is based on need and effectiveness rather than age.

The nature and construction of ageism

Ageism is a term used to describe a societal pattern of widely held devaluative attitudes and stereotypes about ageing and older people. Like racism and sexism, ageism is presumed to be responsible for social avoidance and segregation, hostile humour, discriminatory practices and policies, and a conviction that elderly individuals are a drain on society.

(Gatz and Pearson 1988, p. 184)

What are these stereotypes of older people? In an interesting paper, Miller *et al.* (1999) chart the evolution of stereotypes of older people from 1956 until 1996 using the medium of advertisements in magazines in the USA. They define elderly stereotypes as follows:

stereotypes of the elderly have been described as generalisations and over-simplifications of characteristics of elderly individuals that

Table 2.1 Stereotypes of older people from Miller *et al.* (1999)

Negative Stereotypes	
'Despondent'	Sad, lonely, neglected.
'Severely Impaired'	Senile, incoherent, slow-thinking.
'Vulnerable'	Afraid, victimised, worried.
'Shrew/Curmudgeon'	Complaining, selfish, prejudiced.
'Mildly Impaired'	Tired, fragile, dependent.
'Recluse'	Timid, naive, lives in the past.
Positive Stereotypes	
'Golden Ager'	Active, independent, fun-loving.
'Perfect Grandparent'	Wise, grateful, trustworthy.
'John Wayne Conservative'	Patriotic, nostalgic, determined.

produce ridiculing and demeaning portraits of the group (negative stereotypes) or sanitized portraits and idealized images (positive stereotypes).

(Miller *et al.* 1999, p. 321)

In reviewing the literature on elderly stereotypes they describe clusters of characteristics that emerge from previous studies and form them into six negative and three positive stereotypes (see Table 2.1).

The clusters show remarkable consistency across the various studies reviewed, and give a flavour of the nature of ageism in the latter half of the twentieth century in Western culture. The negative stereotypes create an image of an incompetent, sad, dependent older person who has only the defences of hostile counter-attack (Shrew/Curmudgeon) or dissociation (Recluse) as pathological ways of avoiding the awful reality of age-based decline. The positive stereotypes create an idealised elder who either proves that 'age is all in the mind' by the triumph of will over physiology or, with allusion to a slightly devalued 'wise old man', knows their place but may be called upon for guidance as needed by the powerful young. It can easily be imagined how a positive stereotype applied to an individual may flip into a corresponding negative one when the illusion of immortality or perfection is shattered by poor health or the assertion of the needs of the older person over the demands of the young. In CAT terms the transition is from an idealised reciprocal role to one based on contempt or despair (see Figure 2.1).

The CAT formulation in Figure 2.1 demonstrates how stereotypes can lead to polarised (or split) views of older people that lead to unsustainable ways of relating that can reinforce the stereotypes themselves. Already

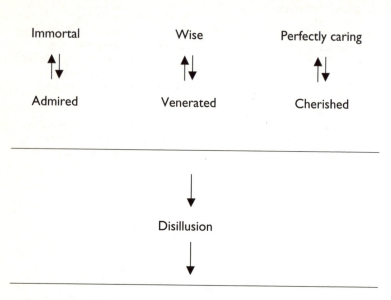

IDEALISED ROLES

NEGATIVE ROLES

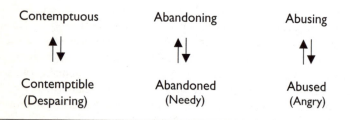

Figure 2.1 Positive and negative stereotypes of older people as reciprocal roles

there is a sense of the nature of ageism as an interchange between the 'young' and the 'old' – an interpersonal phenomenon, not a series of prejudices in the minds of the persecuting young alone, but more of this below. Miller *et al.* (1999) go on to show a trend towards increasing negative stereotypes of older people in the four decades studied (from 0 per cent of ads in 1956 portraying negative stereotypes to 13.3 per cent in 1996, with a corresponding decline in positive stereotypes from 80 per cent to 60 per cent over the same period). The rise in negative stereotyping was particularly in the portrayal of older people as impaired, dependent and incompetent. There was a marked decline in the positive image of the wise, strong, 'John Wayne Conservative' cluster that seems to represent positive, useful elderhood (as discussed in Mark Dunn's chapter), rather than the illusion of sustainable youth and vigour.

In the second part of their definition of ageism, Gatz and Pearson (1988) describe ageism as it is generally conceived – the latest in a long line of prejudices that have surfaced into the collective consciousness of Western society. Negative beliefs and stereotypes fuel prejudice and discrimination, and an individual seems to be judged by a single quality (age, sex, race) rather than on the basis of the whole range of individual differences that make them who they are. This is an interesting model that may help provide an overview of ageism in comparison with its near neighbours sexism, racism and the rest. If one considers the history of '-isms', it is possible to see some patterns emerging over the last handful of centuries. Prejudice and oppression on the grounds of race, gender, sexual orientation and disability have all embarked on a journey that begins with a position of collective denial and ends (theoretically any-way) with a position of acceptance of diversity and legislated equality. I will leave the reader to consider how much progress has been made in each area of discrimination, but it may be possible to describe stages of the journey that each has in common.

To begin with, the beliefs around an -ism are so widely held (often as strongly by the oppressed as the oppressors) that they are not consciously linked to the effects they have on the oppressed group (*The phase of denial*). Then follows a dawning moral awareness, in the oppressed group or in their altruistic advocates, where the oppressed group establishes both an internal and an external identity – the identification of a peer group and the awareness in the wider society of the existence of this group, which is usually a minority (*The phase of identification*). Next is the establishment of a political agenda for change around the construct of equality, and the campaigning begins (*The phase of reaction*). Eventually, the wider society (or at least an influential minority within it) decides to protect the human rights of the oppressed group in practice and statute (*The phase of equality*). Theoretically at least, a further task lies ahead where remaining prejudice gradually fades as pluralism for that particular difference becomes established in society's consciousness and prejudice dwindles in the group unconscious (*The phase of pluralism*) (see Figure 2.2).

This final phase may, of course, be an unachievable ideal, as it is difficult to think of any '-ism' that has truly become extinct. (Consider

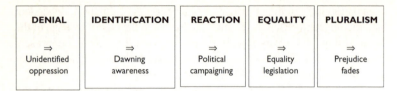

DENIAL	IDENTIFICATION	REACTION	EQUALITY	PLURALISM
⇒ Unidentified oppression	⇒ Dawning awareness	⇒ Political campaigning	⇒ Equality legislation	⇒ Prejudice fades

Figure 2.2 The demise of an '-ism' in Western society

prejudice against left-handedness as an example. While discrimination on the grounds of this difference would generally be thought to be unacceptable and not tolerated in statute, left-handed people will tell you that 'sinisterophobia' is still alive and thriving in isolated pockets such as corkscrew manufacturers and musical instrument makers, and jibes of 'kak-handedness' are not extinct.)

Now, where is ageism in relation to this journey? It is probably in the early stages of the phase of Reaction, with some indications that limited legislation may not be too far off in some Western countries. For a prejudice based on a universal quality (getting older and eventually dying), it appears to be lagging behind all the '-isms' I have listed, which is, on the face of it, surprising. I can see two possible explanations for this: either '-isms' have a rise and fall within cultures over time and Western society is currently on the crest of an ageist wave or, perhaps, it is the very universality of the quality ageism seeks to deny (ageing and death) that has caused this mass procrastination. The two explanations are not mutually exclusive, and I shall discuss each in turn.

As is discussed in Mark Dunn's chapter on elderhood, prejudice towards older people is not universal to all cultures and is likely to change with time within a particular culture. The historical model of '-isms' discussed above, therefore, may be limited by its assumed linearity. In Western society, it may be that ageism has something about it that does not fit in with the trend from oppression to pluralism that seems to fit the other '-isms' listed. The difference may be around the concept of elitism. The other '-isms', which seem to fit the model better, have in common the evolution of rights for a group of people that have never held an elite position in society. Women, homosexuals and racial minority groups, for example, have not held privileged status in Western society. There has been no fall from grace. Oppression has been the historical norm and the linear model described above seems to represent some commonality in the acknowledgement and reversal of prejudice on these grounds. Ageism may have a different quality about it, as it is likely that older people did have higher status in the past than they do today. Ageism may be representative of a group of '-isms' where a society, due to changing demographics, or values or priorities, 'turns against' a group that previously held higher or elite status.

From this perspective, it may be possible to spot how some new '-isms' may be created as favoured groups take the fall. Groups of men have been seen campaigning against the Child Support Agency in the UK and have felt themselves the victims of oppression by a society that they see as having gone too far in the direction of gender equality – a new reverse sexism? Other possibilities include previously powerful religious groups (the debate over the role of Christianity in a multi-faith society), and perhaps even the beleaguered academic classes have begun to feel the pinch in a society that no longer seems to value scholarship and scientific method over pragmatism and capitalism. With an awareness of the possibility of fluctuations in the fortunes of a particular group over time, it may be that twentieth-century Western society has all the factors present to generate a wave of ageism that has only begun to be seen for what it is in the last few decades.

Traxler (1980) considers there to be four roots to ageism in Western society: (1) The fear of death and dying (and association with old age). (2) The Western culture of youth and beauty. (3) Emphasis on productivity. (4) Research bias. It is likely that the valuing of youth, beauty and productivity above wisdom and experience is a relatively modern phenomenon. Factors that may have influenced this change include an ageing population, the industrial and IT revolutions and the development of state-provided health and social services paid for by general taxation. An ageing population clearly puts more demands on the taxpaying younger population, and confirms stereotypes that associate 'older' with 'useless', 'burdensome' and the ubiquitous 'bottomless pit'. As Mark Dunn describes, in Western society, the early part of the twentieth century saw the beginning of a move away from equating wisdom and the right to political power with older age and a growing distrust of elders as leaders and policymakers, particularly after the huge losses of younger men in the First World War at the command of distant, older generals.

New technologies and e-commerce have undermined the established order which valued seniority, experience and wisdom – qualities typically correlated with age. There seems no reason not to climb the ladder several rungs at a time or even bypass it all together in the quest for extraordinary shorter-term profits. Older people, in this new IT-driven world, can be stereotyped as 'slow', 'stupid' or 'conservative' and are unlikely to gain employment over the 'happening' young. How all this will pan out in the longer-term is open to debate, but, as Mark suggests, the absence of wisdom and a longer term perspective, particularly in business and politics, may soon become apparent. Perhaps in the next fifty years, with the growing power of the 'grey dollar', we will see the tables turned on the technologised young as companies, and their older backers, decide that older people have more of the qualities needed for longer-term growth and stability. It will be interesting to see what happens.

The second explanation for the robustness of ageism in Western society is noted by Traxler as the association of death and dying with older age. Ageing and eventually dying is something that we all can expect to experience. This is another quality of ageism that marks it out from the other conventional '-isms' discussed above and may account for its relatively slow progress along the path to the ideal of pluralism. It is easier to be sympathetic (or indeed patronising) to an oppressed group if one is confident that one will never be 'one of them', but much more threatening to the self-concept when one knows (at least unconsciously) that the negative stereotypes will one day be applied to the self, if one makes it that far. It is likely to be the very universality of ageing and the myriad of negative images associated with it that has induced the need for a powerful shared psychological defence to guard against the basic existential angst in everyone. This defence has taken the form of a mass denial and the invention of a construct (ageism) that separates 'them' (the old) from 'us' (or more importantly 'me').

> Ageism reflects a deep seated uneasiness on the part of the young and middle-aged – a personal revulsion to and distaste for growing old, disease, disability; and a fear of powerlessness, 'uselessness' and death.
>
> (Butler 1969, p. 243)

> Ageism allows those of us who are younger to see old people as 'different'. We subtly cease to identify with them as human beings, which enables us to feel more comfortable about our neglect and dislike of them . . . Ageism is a thinly disguised attempt to avoid the personal reality of human ageing and death.
>
> (Butler 1975, p. 893)

To Butler's definitions of ageism there needs to be added something about the presence of ageism in older people themselves, toward both their peers and the 'young' ('reverse ageism'). It is common to find older people who decline the opportunity for peer group support on the grounds that 'I don't want to sit there with a lot of old people', or as one 89-year-old said to me recently: 'It was shocking, some of them could barely walk, I discharged myself immediately.' Even when faced with overwhelming evidence that one's peer group consists of individuals whom one would not hesitate to label 'old', there often remains a remarkable resistance to allowing the self to be re-categorised as 'one of them'. This is perhaps not surprising. It is a mark of the strength and prevalence of the ageism defence that makes it so hard to give up. It is a terrifying prospect, in full awareness of the persistence of one's own individuality, character and experience, to be banished to the twilight world of the 'poor old souls'; a place one avoided in one's younger imagination by expressing the wish that death would come suddenly, mercifully and perhaps a little magically when the entrance to the twilight world was reached. This bleak world, of course, is largely populated by the ghosts of negative parts of the self that have been projected over the years to maintain the equilibrium of a denial-based immortality. It is not the other older people that are the source of the fear, grief and rage – it is the self's *seeming* failure to process the existential uncertainties before reaching this point that fuels the ageist reaction.

'Reverse ageism', or the contemptuous dismissal of younger generations by older people can be understood as a defensive reaction to negative stereotypes of older people and an attempt to diminish the threat of the persecuting young. Jean Anouilh's character Madame Desmortes, in the comedy *Ring Round the Moon*, is an amusing caricature of this:

CAPULET: Well, the Ball has really got going now, hasn't it madam ?

MADAME DESMORTES: It can get going and go, for all I care. It bores me until I don't know whether to yawn or yelp. I was never fond of dancing, and since I've been screwed to this chair, it looks more than ever like the hopping of kangaroos . . . Look at them twirling and twiddling. They think they're enjoying themselves, but all they're doing is twizzling their vain little heads.

(From *Ring Round the Moon*, Anouilh / Fry 1976)

The presence of reverse ageism shows some acceptance of transition of the self from young to old, but again the negative emotions derived ultimately from the uncertainty of existence are projected out onto the unsuspecting young, and their ridiculing or rejecting reaction is seen as further evidence of their guilt. The basis of the negative reciprocal roles is described in Figure 2.1.

Ageism does not reside exclusively in the young or indeed the old, but in the psychological relationship between the imagined two. Ageism is a mass ego defence; a projection and introjection of negative beliefs and fears about ageing and death in an attempt to escape the reality of the human condition. Cognitive Analytic Therapy uses the concept of 'Snags' to describe patterns of feelings, thoughts and behaviours that profoundly sabotage an individual's chances of success and happiness. As Ryle and Kerr (2002) define: 'Snags: A form of problem procedure in which legitimate and appropriate goals are abandoned either because of the assumed attitudes of others or because of irrational guilt.' It may be possible to describe ageism as a Snag. The core belief that needs defending against has both the component of the fear of others' reactions (contempt of the old) and irrational guilt (that one's life has failed to find ultimate meaning). The ageism defence leads on to negatively reinforcing consequences that further generate fear and anxiety. The procedure may run along the lines of:

> I feel uncertain about the meaning of (my) life and anxious about the future. It seems as if there is no escape from the fact that we all grow old and die without finding meaning to our existence and with others abandoning and ridiculing us as our physical and mental faculties decline. If I am to avoid being preoccupied with fruitless rumination about death, which causes depression and stasis, then I must get on with life. There seems no alternative but to put off the acknowledgement of my own ageing to a point in the future when I am old(er) by using defences based in denial ('You are only as old as you feel', plastic surgery, idealisation of the power of medical science, etc.). This leaves me disconnected from my self, my life and my development and vulnerable to life events that shatter the illusion of immortality and provide glimpses into the seemingly inevitable despair that lies ahead. As time goes on I must try harder and harder to hold it all together. This ends in exhaustion, anxiety and despair about the future and the futility of my past.

The point of restating ageism in the form of a CAT Snag is to allow some overview of the fruitless cycle that is being played and replayed, and to identify 'Exits' from the procedure. I ask the reader to ponder on this, but as far as I am able to see, an Exit from this Snag is likely to have something to do with an awareness of the existential reality (as opposed to denial) and a facing up to, working through or acceptance of, as Erikson put it, life's final dilemma: 'Ego integrity versus despair' (Erikson 1963), *before* it seems to be too late. More of this later. I shall now move on to consider how ageism has been present in and affected the development of psychotherapy theory, so that Erikson's work can be seen in context.

Ageism in psychotherapy theory

The attitude of traditional psychoanalytic theory to the value of psychotherapy in later life is summarised in this much quoted pronouncement by Freud (which bears repeating):

> Near or above the age of fifty the elasticity of mental processes, on which the treatment depends is, as a rule lacking – old people are no longer educable.
>
> (Freud 1905, p. 257)

He could be criticised for short-sightedness given that he was forty-nine at the time of writing. Perhaps he did not feel that this general rule applied to him, a common justification for prejudice in all its guises, putting him in the category of ageist coined as 'The Exceptionalists' in an entertaining editorial on ageism:

> These elders consider themselves the fortunate exceptions to society's negative view of old people. While they think of themselves as vigorous, productive and useful to society, they imagine most of their peers to be in bad shape, useless and boring.
>
> (*GeriNotes* editorial 1996)

Despite the influence of Freud, twentieth-century analytically orientated psychotherapists have, however, had mixed views on the value of psychotherapy with older people. Karl Abraham (1919) took the view that the age of the neurosis was more relevant than the age of the patient. He and other psychoanalysts who did work with older people, for example Eliot Jacques who wrote the well known paper 'Death and the midlife crisis' (Jacques 1965), tended to think of later life as somewhere between thirty and forty where existential issues were first confronted and where progress could be made before real old age set in. Hanna Segal conducted an eighteen-month analysis on a 73-year-old man. She wrote: 'This analysis has illuminated for me the problems of old age. It has altered my views on the prognosis of analysis at an advanced age' (Segal 1958).

Hildebrand (1982) pioneered brief psychoanalytic therapies with people over sixty beginning in the mid-1970s at the Tavistock Clinic in London. He states in a lecture in 1989:

> Psychoanalysis can make a major contribution to our understanding

of the dynamics of later life . . . No other theory can account for feelings of abandonment and despair, intimacy and isolation, arrogance and disdain, stagnation and creativity as each of us struggles with the developmental task of the third age.

(Hildebrand 1982, quoted in Hunter 1989, p. 250)

Hildebrand describes how early object relations can have much relevance to understanding maladaptive ways of coping with the losses and challenges of later life. The unconscious, as Freud pointed out, is timeless, and it is certainly the experience of those working analytically with older people to find repressed trauma surfacing in the eighth and ninth decades of a person's life with undiminished force. It is clearly a challenge to ageism to continue to use psychotherapeutic insights derived from theories of early development, and ultimately child analysis, to understand distress in later life. In Chapter 8 I will explore the concept of the resurgence of borderline personality traits in older people using the CAT model. Although it is clearly desirable to treat older people to all the benefits that object relations theory has to offer, and this may be substantial when the individual has abuse or trauma in their past experience, it may, however, require something more to work successfully with older people as a whole. This something else is likely to have something to do with the future as well as the past.

Carl Jung wrote of a ' psychology of life's morning and a psychology of its afternoon' (Jung 1929, quoted in Garner 2002, p. 128), and opened up the concept of continuing development throughout the lifespan, with different tasks being relevant at different life stages. His notion of individuation as a journey towards self-understanding and exploration of the self archetype mark a move away from a child-centred view of psychodynamics with the emphasis on early object relations and parental relationships. As Garner (2002) points out, however, Jung wrote less about the 'Senex' than the other archetypes and she muses that the adjective 'wise' may have been added to 'old man' more as a defence than as an acceptance of ageing. Erikson clearly acknowledged the progression of dilemmas throughout the life cycle, where developmental challenges present both obstacles and opportunities for progression and resolution. In his well-known 'Eight ages of man', he describes eight polarities relevant in a sequential fashion throughout the life cycle (see Table 2.2). (After his death, Erikson's wife discovered and developed notes which alluded to a ninth stage of development in a person's ninth or tenth decade, where further 'transcendency' may be achieved, although this stage is not named as a polarity.)

Table 2.2 Erikson's eight ages of man

VIII	Maturity	Ego integrity	vs	Despair
VII	Adulthood	Generativity	vs	Stagnation
VI	Young adulthood	Intimacy	vs	Isolation
V	Puberty and adolescence	Identity	vs	Role confusion
IV	Latency	Industry	vs	Inferiority
III	Locomotor-genital	Initiative	vs	Guilt
II	Muscular-anal	Autonomy	vs	Shame, doubt
I	Oral-sensory	Basic trust	vs	Mistrust

While this developmental approach acknowledges the continuing need for adaptation and change beyond childhood and adolescence and validates the existence of psychological conflicts in adults and older people that exist in the present and future and not just the past, it is still inherently ageist. The model suggests a linear progression through the stages and a lack of awareness of what challenges there are to come when immersed in the trials and tribulations of one's current phase. The core existential dilemma, stage eight, is reserved for the end of life. The 'final conflict' if you like. The wise old man in dialogue with the universe; with all the attendant imagery of Sir Alec Guinness and George Lucas's *Star Wars*. This is, as explored earlier, the whole basis of a psychological understanding of ageism. A denial of the need to consider the question of meaning until one is at the nearest point to death. It is the putting off of this conflict that generates the phenomena of ageism and the separation of older people (them) from us (the rest). The exits from the ageism Snag described above must surely involve awareness of the reality of ageing and death at an earlier stage in life so that, if nothing else, older people can be seen as individuals struggling with exactly the same fears and uncertainties as the rest of us.

As Jacques (1965) points out, existential anxieties often force their way to the surface in early midlife and can be usefully explored in the fourth and fifth decades, but why stop there? This line of argument is in danger of sounding as if there is an answer to existential uncertainty and that doubt and fear can be removed by early psychotherapeutic intervention. This is to give psychotherapy undue powers and adds weight to the spurious claim that 'psychotherapy is the new religion'. As described in the ageism Snag, the whole procedure is initiated by two profound beliefs: that others will abandon and ridicule you when you are old, and that the purpose of life is to find meaning and that failure to do so is somehow your failure – as the man in the opening extract of this chapter concludes: 'What a sad waste of time it has all been.'

The exits are now perhaps becoming clearer. An awareness of the commonality between old and young will make it harder to divide the world into 'them' and 'us' and tend towards older people being treated as individual human beings by the young and their peers alike. The primary task that the old and young share is the quest for (and guilt at not finding) meaning. There is no need to separate out the task into further stages appropriate for the young and old to go about separately and at distinct times in their lives. We are all in it together. Whether one believes there is true religious or spiritual meaning to the universe or that, as Camus (1973) describes so eloquently in *A Happy Death*, the only truth to be discovered may be the absurdity of the quest for meaning itself, makes no real difference. It is our shared journey that validates our lives. The ability to communicate, react, love and hate each other is the basis of our interpersonal psychological reality.

From here we move into the development of object relations theory via CAT that has been pioneered by Leiman and Ryle based on the work of Vygotsky and Bakhtin. At the start of this book, Laura Sutton explores some of these developments in a dialogue with Mikael Leiman (see Chapter 1). An interpersonal model of psychotherapy, with an emphasis on life story and the need to find shared meaning within the cultural, historical and personal context of client and therapist, is likely to be particularly suitable for working with older people. As Ryle puts it:

> Personality and relationships are not adequately described in terms of objects, conflicts or assumptions, They are sustained through an ongoing conversation with ourselves and with others – a conversation with roots in the past and pointing to the future. In their conversation with their patients, psychotherapists become important participants in this conversation and, CAT, I believe, fosters the particular skills needed to find the words and other signs that patients need.
>
> (Ryle 2000)

Ageism in psychotherapy services

The ageism in psychotherapy theory that has been so slow to fade is reflected in the twenty-first century in both the quality and quantity of psychotherapy services for older people. Siobhan Murphy did a recent survey of one hundred psychotherapy departments in the UK (Murphy 2000). Of the respondents, 87 per cent felt that the services they offered to older people did not match up to those provided for the under-65s. While only 13 per cent of departments had an upper age limit for referrals, much of the paucity of provision was accounted for by the low referral rates of older people. Although the over-75s accounted for over 8 per cent of the population, they were represented by less than 1 per cent of referrals to departments questioned. Although respondents were aware of the unmet need, they felt themselves unequipped both clinically and financially to deliver an effective service even if higher rates of referrals could be generated. Many respondents cited the fact the older persons' services had been separated off into different organisational structures (Trusts in the UK) which presented contractual difficulties when trying to provide psychotherapy services across the whole adult age range. These findings emphasise the fact that the older peoples' services have tended to be seen as separate and of low priority compared to services for younger people, and have been formed in a culture of lower expectations where sub-standard services seem an inevitable reality; part of the 'geriatric' legacy. It was interesting to note that old age specialists in medicine and psychiatry referred their patients for psychotherapy less than their colleagues who dealt with patients of all ages. A reflection, perhaps, on the internalisation of institutional ageism by those working most closely with older people.

Collins *et al.* (1997) present an interesting survey of the attitudes of General Practitioners in the UK to the referral of older people with depression to psychological therapy services. Again, there was an open-mindedness to the use of psychotherapy with older people, with 93 per cent of respondents saying that they would consider a referral, although only 44 per cent had actually ever referred an older person for psychotherapy. The respondents expressed confusion as to the indications for particular types of psychological therapy, generally favouring counselling over more formal psychotherapy interventions, and the authors suggest that more education and training around the role of different types of psychological therapies with older people would be useful.

So it seems clear that although many working with older people are open to the use of psychotherapy, they are hindered in the development of services by lack of training and structural hurdles that support the status quo where older people's services are separated off into the nether world of 'psychogeriatrics', where the rules and priorities seem to have always been different. It is interesting to note that the use of developmental or systemic theories to formulate a client's distress decreases across the three age bands found in typical mental health services. Child and adolescent psychiatry is well known for use of the psychodynamic and systemic family therapy models. As adulthood is reached, a client's chances of receiving a developmental or systemic formulation reduce as the 'medical' or biological model becomes predominant, and distress is more likely to be framed as illness or linked to recent life events rather than deeper personality-based antecedents. As later life is approached it is a rare exception to find anything other than the biological model of decline and multiple pathology applied to an individual older person. This is confirmed by the low referral rates by old age specialists in Murphy's survey above. Older people in hospital settings often find themselves lost in a hostile environment where their identity, let alone their context in terms of their life story and experience, is at risk through stereotyping and a failure to *think* outside of a 'geriatric' context where bed pressures, waiting lists and arbitrary categorisation are the norm. It is this inability to think about later life that is at the root of the problem. To use Freud's words, the lack of 'elasticity' is clearly not in the older people who, despite tremendous hurdles, often manage to adapt to the 'geriatric obstacle course' with inventiveness, skill and dignity. As anyone who has tried to counter ageism in health services will testify, it is not the old who appear ineducable.

Working with older people in an ageist context

In the final section of this chapter I will discuss ways of working positively with older people in the context of a society and its health services that are historically and institutionally ageist. On a personal level, a practitioner can become aware of their own ageist preconceptions that impinge on their work with older people and use insights gained from this reflection in their understanding of transference and counter-transference issues in their therapeutic work. In a group or therapeutic community setting, ageism is often a source of resistance to growth and development and needs to be incorporated into whatever theoretical model is being used. On a broader level, it will be important for the future to introduce all health and social care workers to the concept of ageism and to try to break down the defences that encourage the view that older people are somehow different from the rest of us and can be satisfied by lower-quality care.

In individual therapy, it will be important for the therapist to think about their views and beliefs around psychotherapeutic work with older people. Due to the lack of referrals to and structural hurdles around psychotherapy services for this age group, many therapists will have had little or no experience of working with older people. Therapeutic nihilism may be present as a defence against an imagined onslaught from 'the bottomless pit' if referrals are encouraged, and may also cover up a degree of doubt in the therapist that they are up to the challenge of working with an age group that have different cultural and generational contexts. The higher level of disability in older people, especially sensory deficits, may put off a potential therapist. There can be fear that the therapist will look stupid or incompetent in their attempts to enable a client with disability, and also a nasty superego voice representing the rest of medicine and psychiatry that has always looked down on those working with older people to a similar degree to which it displays contempt to the older people themselves. Failure to acknowledge one's own fears of death and dying may be converted, using the ageist defence, into disgust or ridicule of older people and a reluctance to take seriously the need for therapeutic help.

Many psychoanalytic writers have described how the nature of the transference relationship with older people can be as powerful and varied as that with a client of any age. Arden *et al.* (1998, p. 62) point out: 'The therapist or staff member is seen as child or grandchild, parent or grand-parent, lover or partner, as well as an authority figure.' Martin Berezin (1972, p. 1487) discusses how the main energy behind the transference is the persistent character style and unconscious drives of the older person: 'Transference by definition is unreality; it is unconscious and not time orientated.' He discusses the fact that many of the younger trainees he has supervised go into a therapy with an older person expecting a transfer-ence relationship where they are as a child or grandchild. This is often not the case and a needy client will project a parental protecting figure on to the therapist or powerful erotic transferences will see the therapist as a peer or lover.

Such transference relationships are often unexpected and difficult to process for inexperienced therapists. The perceived neediness of the client may leave the therapist feeling an inadequate and neglectful parent who will either be paralysed and deskilled, or resort to looking for 'magic' or unrealistic solutions to some of the problems of ageing. The therapist may fear the dependency of their needy patient and feel trapped or unable to terminate the relationship appropriately. Pity (or covert sadism) may stem from an unequal power balance between a young, able therapist and a disabled, frail client. The therapist may enjoy the client's voyeuristic appreciation of the therapist's sexuality and vitality while being unable to acknowledge the client's own sexuality and covert envious attacks. Occasionally, a therapist may find, in their client, an idealised parent or grandparent figure and may use the therapeutic relationship to explore their own insecurities, putting the client in the role of wise protector, so negating the older person's own needs and fears. It

goes without saying that good supervision is the key to successful practice. The main point about individual psychotherapeutic work with older
people is that it encounters the whole range of transferences, countertransferences and resistances found in work with clients of any age, but
that therapists may be taken by surprise by the power and timeless nature
of the unconscious role-play being re-enacted in the therapy.

An awareness of ageism is also useful in therapeutic group work with
older people. In my experience of working in a day hospital setting with
therapeutic groups for older people designed to help process their experiences of ageing, depression and loss, there is always the need to get
beyond ageism and reverse ageism, in that order, before real communication, support and healing can take place. To start with there is resistance
to becoming part of a peer group of older people – particularly older
people with mental health problems – and many fail to engage in the
therapeutic work at that stage. The contempt at this stage is towards the
other older people, who are seen as 'beyond help' and deserving of pity.
To join this group would be an admission of failure and an irreversible
step towards despair. Even when the need for help outweighs the reluctance to join this stigmatised peer group, and the person begins to engage,
there is often a prominent reliance on the mental health professionals in
the groups to 'save' the new individual; to make them better quickly so
that they can take a step back into the 'normal' world. In the groups, this
anxiety takes the form of a dominating medical model, where doctors and
nurses in the group are asked for specific medical advice on personal
diagnosis and treatment or where individuals ask, in the group, to be seen
individually immediately after the group for a 'consultation'. So dominant can be this rather infectious stage that the work of the group can be
paralysed in the absence of a doctor, there being no seeming point to any
peer group discussion or support. Using a prison analogy, attendance is
seen as 'doing time', whereas real progress can only be made in the court
of appeal or in front of the parole board (in the doctor's office). Nurses
and support workers can be devalued and ridiculed at this stage.

Progress is eventually made by facilitators being clear that the group is
not a vehicle for individual care planning and that defined spaces exist for
this function outside of the group. Second, there needs to be a subtle
deferment of responsibility for the content of the group from staff to the
older people themselves. A useful response to a ridiculing attack on an
untrained member of staff, for example, is to point out respectfully that at
least 90 per cent of the wisdom in the room resides in the older people
themselves. Teachers, soldiers, pilots, clergy, nurses, carers, patients . . .
all with a lifetime of experience. How audacious it would be to offer

advice before the group had heard from the many diverse voices that are so far disempowered and infantalised by the fear of becoming a 'psycho-geriatric patient'! Once a group begins to form, there is often a phase of sharing the common suspicion and contempt for the 'young of today', and many hours can be spent rehearsing reactionary arguments and myths around the universal destructiveness of 'progress' and the view that society is engaged in an inescapable death spiral that began a couple of decades ago. Minority groups represented in either the staff or clients in the group can be attacked and isolated in this process, and the facilitators may need to negotiate group rules around the discussion of contentious 'political' issues, such as racism, and lay ground rules against abuse or intimidation of individuals. It is only when this negative emotion is expressed that the group can begin to validate each other's personal experiences and genuinely use their own wisdom to support and heal each other; as Winnicott (1962) puts it: 'I'm seen or understood to exist by someone . . . I get back (as a face seen in the mirror) the evidence that I need that I have been recognised as a being.' Such an experience in a group for older people can be surprisingly moving and empowering. The biggest asset in any such group is always the wisdom contained within the older people themselves.

Tackling ageism in wider health and social care services can be a daunting task for any individual. Professionals working exclusively with older people are often assumed to be sub-standard, moving into these traditionally under-subscribed fields because they could not get a job elsewhere. The scale of ageism in general hospitals and casualty departments where older people are openly talked about as 'crumble', 'bed-blockers' and 'geris' can provide a hostile environment in which to change attitudes and cultures. Junior staff in medicine and nursing tend to rotate or change posts frequently, making it difficult to establish credibility and make positive relationships. As an old-age psychiatrist I am often looked upon with suspicion and anger when I venture from the sanctuary of my own service and into general medical settings. I am seen as either incompetent and lazy, and thus to be ignored and ridiculed, or as powerful and withholding – responsible for all the clinical and financial problems in the hospital by my failure to treat or remove the 'geriatrics' that are overburdening the wards. It is by the patient and meticulous cementing of alliances and friendships that respect is built up and ageism can be challenged in a way that is constructive and not threatening or blaming.

The main point to be conveyed is that older people are the same as everyone else and deserve the same quality of diagnosis, treatment and care, despite the complexity of their problems and disability. It is ageist to equate age with quality of life in a non-discriminating manner. Effort must be made to make the best decision for each individual patient, taking into account their wider identity in both the past and the present. Experiential workshops, where younger staff are encouraged to explore the nature of disability and sensory deficits, are an excellent way to begin to break down barriers. 'The geriatric obstacle course' (Fleisher *et al.* 1996) is an interesting way to simulate the older patient journey in a general hospital setting. Workshops mimicking physical and sensory disability (with the use of restrictive binding, earplugs, spectacles creating visual deficits and other imaginative techniques) can be a true eye-opener for staff and also help them to get over the projected humiliation they feel as part of an older person's service.

The integration of psychological therapy services for older people with services for adults of all ages is an important step in the breaking down of structural and institutional barriers that partly account for the lack of services for older people. This can be achieved by setting up a psychological therapies network (PTN) where supervision and assessment structures can cross organisational barriers and where practitioners working in the same type of therapy modality can share experience and training opportunities despite the age restrictions governing their other clinical roles. (For more information on this model of service provision refer to Hepple *et al.* 2002, ch. 7.) The structure of the PTN removes ageism from operational policy and, perhaps most importantly, allows groups of staff working with different age groups of patients to communicate, share their wisdom and reduce the ignorance and stigma around work with older people.

Closing thoughts

Writing this chapter has been an exploration for me of thoughts, feelings and intuitions assembled over a fifteen-year period of working predominantly with older people. It is difficult to separate ageing (an inevitable part of living) and ageism (an avoidable prejudice) in one's own mind and harder still to become aware of one's own response both to older people and to society's view of those working with older people. Many of the difficulties of working in this field can be usefully understood with reference to an ageism paradigm, and I hope these reflections will prove of interest to the reader and help in the promotion of older persons' services to a position of equity and respect that is long overdue.

References

Abraham, K. (1919) The applicability of psychoanalytic treatment to patients of an advanced age. In *Selected Papers on Psychoanalysis*. London: Hogarth Press.

Anouilh, J. (1976) *Ring Round the Moon*, adapted by C. Fry. London: Samuel French.

Arden, M., Garner, J., and Porter, R. (1998) Psychoanalytic understanding and old age psychiatry. *Psychoanalytic Psychotherapy* 12(1): 57–73.

Berezin, M. (1972) Psychodynamic considerations of ageing and the aged: an overview. *American Journal of Psychiatry* 128(12): 1483–91.

Butler, R. N. (1969) Ageism, another form of bigotry. *The Gerontologist* 9: 243–6.

Butler, R. N. (1975) The elderly: an overview. *American Journal of Psychiatry* 132: 893–900.

Camus, A. (1973) *A Happy Death*. Harmondsworth: Penguin.

Collins, E., Katona, C., and Orrell, M. W. (1997) Management of depression in the elderly by general practitioners: referral for psychological treatments. *British Journal of Clinical Psychology* 36: 445–8.

Erikson, E. (1963) Eight ages of man. In *Childhood and Society*, 2nd edn. New York: Norton.

Fleisher, I. F., White, L. J., McMullen, M. Jo., and Chambers R. (1996) The geriatric obstacle course: a training session designed to help pre-hospital personnel recognise geriatric stereotypes and misconceptions. *Journal of Emergency Medicine* 14(4): 439–44.

Freud, S. (1905) *On Psychotherapy*. Standard edition vol. 7. London: Hogarth Press.

Garner, J. (2002) Psychodynamic work with older adults. *Advances in Psychiatric Treatment* 8: 128–37.

Garner, J., and Arden, M. (1998) Reflections on old age. *Aging and Mental Health* 2(2): 92–3.

Gatz, M., and Pearson, C. G. (1988) Ageism revised and the provision of psychological services. *American Psychologist* 43: 184–8.

GeriNotes editorial (1996) Sub-species of ageists. *Gerinotes* 3 (3).

Hepple, J., Pearce, M. J., and Wilkinson, P. (eds) (2002) *Psychological Therapies with Older People: Developing Treatments for Effective Practice*. Hove, UK: Brunner-Routledge.

Hildebrand, P. (1982) Psychotherapy with older patients. *British Journal of Medical Psychology* 55: 19–28.

Hunter, A. J. G. (1989) Reflections on psychotherapy with ageing people, individually and in groups. *British Journal of Psychiatry* 154: 250–2.

Jacques, E. (1965) Death and the mid-life crisis. *International Journal of Psychoanalysis* 46: 502–14.

Jung, C. G. (1929) The aims of psychotherapy. In H. Read, M. Fordham and G. Adler. *Collected Works*, London: Routledge & Kegan Paul.

Miller, P. N., Miller, D. W., and McKibbin, E. M. (1999) Stereotypes of the elderly in magazine advertisements 1956–1996. *International Journal of Ageing and Human Development* 49(4): 319–37.

Murphy, S. (2000) Provision of psychotherapy services for older people. *Psychiatric Bulletin* 24: 184–7.

Ryle, A. (2000) What theory is CAT based on. Origins of CAT. ACAT online. http://www. acat.org.uk (accessed 5 October 2000).

Ryle, A., and Kerr, I. B. (2002) *Introducing Cognitive Analytic Therapy: Principles and Practice.* Chichester: John Wiley.

Segal, H. (1958) Fear of death: notes on the analysis of an old man. In *The Work of Hanna Segal.* London: Jason Aronson.

Traxler, A. J. (1980) *Let's Get Gerontologized: A Training Manual for Practitioners Working with the Aged.* Springfield, IL: Illinois Department of Aging.

Winnicott, D. (1962) Ego integration in child development. In *The Maturational Process and the Facilitating Environment.* London: Hogarth Press.

Chapter 3

Why do so few become elders?

Mark Dunn

Throughout most of human history the oldest members of the community have been in charge. Until the advent of reading and writing, the oldest were the most valuable because they had had the most experience and had accumulated the most knowledge of how to survive and live. The young, who often did not survive into adult life, were of much less value. Over the last three thousand years this changed slowly, with more power devolving to younger adults. In the last hundred years this shift has accelerated rapidly. Information storage systems developed slowly over time, from the scroll through to the book; only elders of church and state and their scribes had access to the knowledge they contained. Now in the computer age, as knowledge has been synthesised and stored in books and internet websites, anyone of any age has access to the world's knowledge store. The old no longer have a monopoly on knowledge and thereby power. In politics in the USA, the Senate where the *senex* (Latin for elder) meet to discuss and plan have for a long time been usurped by the thrusting youngers of the House of Representatives. This pattern is mirrored across society as grandparents lose power and devolve their traditional roles, becoming baby-sitters or home helps to the powerful careers of their children. When no longer needed for that, or when too demanding or time-consuming to be easily cared for, they are devolved further away from the heart of the family into 'ghettoes' known as old people's homes. What has been lost in these changes?

Considering the mirror of popular culture briefly the view of the elderly is split. On one hand we can see in the film *Star Wars* two examples of powerful elders, Obi Won the idealised mentor to the young hero Luke Skywalker as well as his powerful shadow-father Darth Vader, both of them strong, competent, capable and decisive fathers; on the other hand television offers us Victor Meldrew from *One Foot in the Grave*, struggling with retirement, depressed, anxious, a fatalistic curmudgeon. Further on from that lie the portrayals of senile alcoholics such as Father Jack in *Father Ted* and the Colonel in *Fawlty Towers*. It seems we crave strong elders we can trust while laughing anxiously at what we fear we will become.

The question arises; what are old people for these days? What can their function now be? Without role or function old people are increasingly perceived as a useless and costly burden. They can easily become isolated and are then vulnerable to mental illness and crime. Not all old people end up in that situation. Some live very different lives in old age at the centre of family or social groups and are highly valued as elders. What then is the difference between an elder and an old person?

This chapter will attempt to address these questions by first reviewing the traditional role of elders through the lens of indigenous communities where elders are still functioning, second offering a possible definition of modern-world elders, third looking at what has been gained and what lost by deposing elders and fourth commenting on why and how psychological development towards elderhood might be pursued. From this we can form a view of why elders may still be very valuable members of the community.

What is the function of an elder?

The era of automatic deference to age is almost dead, but the dying has happened only recently. Arguably this can be dated to the First World War (1914–18) and the widely held view that the aged Generals in Europe persisted in sacrificing the youth in the trenches. In many countries revolutions brought about the overthrowing of the old order and its elderly conservatives. However, it was not until the 1960s that youth culture became a powerful social force and had the resources to ignore the disapproval of elder members of society. The notion that elders knew what was right, knew how to get things done, could be relied on to be fair and reasonable and were the guardians of moral and cultural standards was really put into question by youth. Trust in elders finally evaporated.

From a family perspective, elders have always been responsible for survival, continuity and growth, all of which require an accumulation of knowledge and experience. That knowledge and experience has to be passed down the generations, so elders have to be teachers too. For example, before the advent of agricultural college and industrialised farming, any farming enterprise required an elder farmer who knew, because he had been taught by his father, all of the processes, timings and techniques of running a productive farm. Even now it is doubtful that farming can be learned from a book. Similarly, before the advent of medical schools and the NHS, childbirth was in the hands of female elders or midwives who had learned all that was required and had acquired plenty of experience through practice. By contrast childbirth is now often in the hands of young male surgeons performing caesareans. Historically the struggle for survival often necessitated the exercise of rigid, authoritarian control by family and community elders. With power goes responsibility, however, and elders provided containment and security to those under their care and accepted responsibility when things went wrong.

It is not difficult to imagine what could go wrong. Everything is threatened with collapse, disaster and even death for want of vital pieces of knowledge and a willingness to take responsibility. A recent television programme showed a group of modern people attempting to live in Iron Age conditions. They quickly came to grief without experienced elders to provide organisation and guidance. Another example is provided in William Golding's novel *Lord of the Flies*, where a group of pre-teens have to survive on their own without elders in extreme circumstances and end up killing one of their number.

Elders have traditionally played a major role in the organisation of hierarchical social structures such as churches and religions, councils and political groups, schools and colleges. History is littered with examples of young inexperienced inheritors of the crown being unable to cope, this resulting in civil war. These hierarchical power structures may be beneficent or malign depending on circumstances and the elders' personality, but without them society flattens out into anarchy and chaos. Benign elders are able to listen to and value all members of society; malign ones can perhaps be defined by only attending to a narrow group who are in support of their dictatorial aims. Finally towards the end of their lives, elders in retirement have usually had a role as containers or reservoirs of wisdom and have acted as consultants to those in power (in the Senate as within the family).

The function of elders in indigenous or native cultures

Their function in indigenous or native communities provides a more elaborated idea of the role of elder. Malidoma Patrice Somé, a medicine man and teacher from Burkina Faso in North West Africa, gives some helpful descriptions in his books on Dagara culture (Somé 1993, 1998). Martine Prechtel writes as a shaman and chief among the Tzutujil Maya of highland Guatemala in Central America (Prechtel 1998, 1999). Both write as fully functioning members of their cultures, not as Western anthropologists observing from outside. On the role of elders they broadly agree.

In these cultures, structurally pre-modern, people still live in closely knit communities. Physical survival depends upon tight community interdependence and adherence to the social and symbolic order. The community takes power over and responsibility for the psychological development of each individual member across life through a continuing cycle of initiations. To opt out of the culture is to leave the community. Enforcing initiation ensures the survival and transmission of the culture. The elders of these indigenous cultures are the enforcers of initiation. By contrast, in our modern world, we live in a culture of shared signs (for example the English language) and with a profusion of optional symbolic orders (the marketplace of modern religions and spiritualities).

In these cultures every child is seen as being born with an unknown gift to contribute to the continuation and well-being of the community. It is the role of mentors, who are not parents but other parent-aged adults, to encourage and lead these gifts into expression. When an individual's gift becomes apparent, the role of the elder is to foster the circumstances that maintain its sustenance and growth in the individual. Elders here are somewhat like psychotherapists, facilitating growth and development but fundamentally interested in the archetypes being expressed through the individual and the value of these to the community. In this sense ego strength is axiomatic, a product of the individual's acceptance and integration in the tightly knit community.

The processes of initiation of teenagers and the young pays particular attention to what we would call the psychology of early development. In indigenous language, it is the development of an individual's relationship to the sacred realm of gods, nature spirits and ancestors through ritual and myth. Initiatory processes enforced by male and female elders provide care, attention, valuing and acceptance as well as being demanding and challenging. Particular attention is paid to encouraging healthy narcissism and self-esteem through valuing beauty, fierceness and eloquence in service to the community. For example adolescent male testosterone-fuelled aggression is admired and channelled into the public service of protecting the community. Military service had this function in the Western world for a time, and the culture of team sport attempts to serve it now, but often it is demonised and punished. Indigenous initiation requires a willing submission to community, spiritual practice and discipline which serves to prevent the excesses of individualism and a driven ego. The elder's aim is to help the young move beyond heroic individualism (dangerous both to the individual and to the community) into ordinary good-enough living as a productive and creative member of the community.

Elders are also primarily responsible for justice, retribution and righting wrongs. Through the enforcement of boundaries and rules, they not only maintain order, but also aim to act as earthing rods for the negative feelings in the community. They gather negative transference in order to protect the community; they can allow themselves to be hated so that others don't end up hating themselves. To be able to do this requires a large group of elders working together and supporting each other. Somé speaks of the importance elders attach to providing guidance and correction without shaming those who have done wrong through criticism, judging and punishment. Shame is seen as a deadly force that collapses a person's psyche and alienates individuals from the community. Like grief or rage, it requires ritual activity in sacred space to reintegrate the individual back into the community. In the modern world these ideas can still make sense, particularly in therapeutic settings such as therapy groups, though in an unintegrated society generally, public shaming becomes one of the main tools of control. Female elders are particularly valued for conflict resolution and preventing force and violence as they are seen to be able to contain rather than react to the emotional energy of others.

Prechtel, now living and working in the USA as a writer, workshop leader and healer, describes Mayan elders and how they act in ways that provide inspiration and a wish to live to grow old in the young. Through active participation in ritual and social life into great age, and as storytellers and bearers of memory, they operate as a council of the wise, passively observing all that is going on in the community with a sense of inclusivity and tolerance. Through this council of elders wisdom is fed into the social system without the wielding of authoritarian command (rather like consultants to business). The elderly offer the wisdom of having lived through cycles of change and provide a living memory and a long-term perspective that youth and the middle-aged lack. Becoming an elder requires continuing initiation, from adolescent to young man, to middle-aged man, to elder. Each initiation is acknowledged by the community and is understood as akin to gaining another extending section of a telescope; it enables the person to see further and deeper into things and thereby become even more useful to the community. In effect the status of an elder cannot be achieved without a community to serve. Somé and Prechtel both describe youth as associated with 'wetness' and the ageing process as one of drying out, but the description lacks the negative associations the modern world attributes to it. This 'drying out' is like the seasoning of timber which stays straight, and doesn't bend or deviate. Elders do not drink heavily or get drunk as this would be seen as a regression back to a need for 'wetness'.

In the modern world we most often have difficulty defining ourselves as elders because our community is not so clearly structured and contained nor as imaginative in its requirements of groups and individuals. Often we belong to several overlapping communities at the same time – work, family, school, church, and so on. Our communities are also 'partial', such as one's therapy clients, or 'virtual', such as an author's readers. Somé helpfully defines an elder as: (1) someone whose words command respect and attention; (2) someone who has changed lives through teaching or writing; (3) someone who can listen and support others in difficult situations; (4) someone who can attend to another's grief without being overwhelmed; and finally (5) someone who can share their own experiences of difficulties without telling a person what to do (Somé 1998). Having lived extensively in the West he points out that all of these qualities can be actualised in individuals here. He sees a lack of these qualities in older people and a great hunger for them in the young.

The modern-world elder

While the modern world differs significantly from the indigenous world, with lateral thinking we can usefully define some characteristics of elderhood that might act as a template or target to aspire to and by which we might identify those who might be called elders.

1. *Experience and knowledge.* An elder is a person of vast and varied experience which has over time been reflected upon and incorporated into a body of knowledge. Such a person is most likely to be of advanced age. For example an elder surgeon who has carried out hundreds or even thousands of operations has a great deal to offer the community of junior and mainstream medics in terms of being able to foresee problems before they arise.

    A fundamental value of an elder is the ability to discriminate between information, knowledge and wisdom. This is discussed below.
2. *Listening and communicating.* An elder is able to listen. She is not so full of her own ideas that she has no room to listen to others. She is able to listen to all sides of an argument and make a wise judgement.

A high court judge would be a good example of this. Similarly in negotiation or conflict resolution an elder is able to listen to all sides and then make difficult decisions which will displease or anger some and be able to tolerate critical or hostile feelings directed at her without reacting oppressively. (Again a judge is a good example.)

An elder is able to be interested in and listen to young people, to see their potential and to encourage its expression and not exploit or abuse them. She also has perspective on the value of adolescence and the necessary freshness and challenge it brings to the community. Experienced educators may be excellent elders as mentors to both youth and also young teachers.

3. *Teaching and the facilitation of learning and growth in the community.* An elder has the ability to teach the knowledge and skills that they have acquired. Historically all apprenticeships were based upon a novice working to a master craftsman, whether a wood carver, jeweller, plumber or accountant. An elder is interested in passing on knowledge and skills rather than seeing them die out and will seek out apprentices.

Psychologically, an elder is able to hold psycho-social space within which she facilitates communication, clarity, inclusion, co-operation and conflict resolution. In the modern world this is the specialised function of all types of consultants. More usefully, these skills need to form part of the basic knowledge of every person in a management role.

Psychologically, an elder has the ability to value qualities in others that are deeper than the concerns of the person's ego and to encourage their expression. This is the domain of both the psychotherapist and the spiritual teacher who can look toward the person's purpose, meaning and functioning.

This is by no means a complete definition but is perhaps sufficient for the purposes of this argument. There are few accounts of life cycle development in the psychological literature. It is preoccupied with the traumas and tribulations of early development as explanations for adult maladaptation. While this is helpful, and in many cases the maladaptations continue unabated into old age, therapy is usually aimed at helping a person arrive at a reasonably functioning adult state. The transition to older ages is not much theorised.

Worth mentioning here are the writings of Robert Moore and Douglas Gillette, Jungian analytical thinkers (Moore and Gillette 1990). They describe a life cycle developmental path based on Jungian archetypes known as the Warrior, the Magician, the Lover and the King/Queen. These are seen as pathways for individuation based on the activation in the psyche of the energies of these archetypes at successive points in life. The authors provide a wealth of detail, setting the path in a historical, cultural and biological context. Briefly summarising the masculine path: the Warrior is the archetype of testosterone-driven teenage-hero energy that, if channelled successfully, leads a male adolescent into the Magician phase of young adult life. For the Magician, the tasks are about achieving a career, a home and a family and learning to solve problems within commitment. In middle age the Lover archetype is activated, which relates, in this account, not necessarily to sex or personal love but more to love of community, nature, beauty and generally a love of life. Beyond that in older adult life and on into old age the King archetype is activated, and that energy pushes a person to take up the challenges of being an elder as described above. This developmental life path is not like a snake shedding skins, but like the telescope already mentioned; each stage is lived, reflected on, understood and integrated. A person in King or Queen stage is able to consult knowledge attained in the previous stages in confronting any particular person or problem.

In this account the absence of elders to move individuals on in life leaves most people stranded as corporate Warriors or Magicians. Failure to reflect on and integrate each archetype leaves a person vulnerable to acting it out in a Shadow way as seen when an adolescent man exercises Warrior energy in gangsterism or when an elderly leader expresses King energy in a dictatorial tyranny. Moore argues that modern culture reflects a childish concern with toys and consumption, the teenage Warrior's idealistic anger and the Magician's attempts to solve the world's problems, examples being genetically modified foods and animals, medical gene therapy, Star Wars style missile defence systems and so forth.

Why elders can no longer be trusted

It can be confidently asserted that we are in an age that no longer trusts those in power and by extension that old people are no longer to be trusted. Whenever the leaders of the modern world meet, ostensibly to discuss the health and wealth of everyone, they are opposed by thousands of rioting youths who feel ignored and unheard and that those in power are endangering the planet. How can we understand this phenomenon?

The conflict is no longer about the traditional opposition of conservative elders who value stability, versus youth who value change, though this element exists. The conflict is more about growth at the expense of

destructive environmental change, the increase of wealth for the first
world at the expense of the wealth and health of the third world
(economic debts and HIV-Aids), and a sense that the elders of the first
world are, for their own benefit, excluding large numbers of people from
a satisfactory life. As an undercurrent to this I would add that many feel
that the elders are either asleep to the consequences of their actions or
actively and intentionally being abusive and oppressive of those who
should be under their care.

The perception that elders are incompetent and abusive has been
strengthened by the wealth of information that is now available through
the media and the internet. Priests, schoolteachers and carers who are
sexually or violently abusive to children in their care are now more often
exposed in the news and pursued through the courts as a result. The
ability to cover up these activities has decreased. Parents are less tolerant
of their children being bullied or shamed at school. Doctors and psychiatrists
who act like gods of life and death over their patients are now being
challenged to be more respectful and open. The scandal of hospital
doctors retaining the organs of dead children to be used for medical
research has significantly undermined public confidence in their probity.
In agriculture, farmers who have themselves suffered financially through
foot and mouth disease in their animals, are unable to find much sympathy.
There is a feeling that farmers no longer respect nature and are too easily
led by business and industry into unnatural farming practices that have
resulted in vCJD in the human population. In relation to the police force,
many people, and in particular ethnic minorities, perceive it as corrupt
and abusive from the top down, and society's confidence in their functioning
is undermined. In the management and financial arena there is a
general feeling that directors will always put shareholder profits ahead of
customer service or safety. This was seen clearly during the recent
Railtrack fiasco in which the chairman who presided over the most recent
fatal accidents received a huge payoff when he left. Finally one can say
little about politicians other than that confidence in their probity and
abilities is at an all-time low. The helpful result is that those in power are
now required to be much more ethical and publicly accountable.

In mitigation it is only fair to say that these abuses have probably
always existed. It is only now, when the spotlight and magnifying glass
of the media can bring things so swiftly to our attention, that our
confidence in those in power can be so easily undermined. One result is
that we develop greater expectations of those in power and are more
condemning when they prove to be fallible human beings. At the same
time we are less interested to be in power ourselves, feeling that power

corrupts and should therefore be avoided. It is as if we behave like teenagers, angry at those in power because they have not made an ideal world for us to live in. It is perhaps more accurate to say that those in power are suffering from a failure of personal psychological develop-ment. They have the trappings of power and their hands are on the levers, but they do not have the psychological development or inner authority to wield power ethically or empathically.

A further point in mitigation would be to accept a systems theory view of the modern world, for example that presented by Peter Senge and col-leagues (Senge 1999). He argues it is impossible for any one person or group of persons to understand the complexities of the modern world, let alone control them, without adopting a systemic perspective. The many groups involved have different aims and goals, as well as different values and belief systems, with the result that much of what doesn't work cannot easily be solved. The global system now clearly limits the power of any elected politician, with the result that electorates feel marginalised and demoralised but also anxious and angry. An honest politician would admit his limitations and be held accountable; politicians who won't admit their limitations are mistrusted and felt to be corrupt.

Psychologically our reactions to the world situation could be described in terms of a Kleinian paranoid-schizoid defence (Segal 1964). We seem generally unable to work things through to a realistic acceptance or depressive position but are stuck in the dilemma of either feeling paranoid about what those in power are up to or withdrawing into a schizoid 'head-in-the-sand' position, ignoring it all. Alternatively and increasingly people set up sub-cultures within their own definitions of right and wrong and good and bad. These definitions are almost always in some form of opposition to those in power and are usually the forerunners of revolutionary or counter-cultural movements. These movements run in cycles, as with the Bolshevik resistance to the despotic Czars which led eventually to *perestroika* and the collapse of the despotic soviets.

The loss of trust in those in power leads to a loss of respect and trust for old people generally, with the result that they are marginalised. This both causes and compounds the failure of old people to become elders. The elderly feel most often ignored, embittered, burdensome, useless and resentful. The result is that young people often find old people critical and disapproving without realising that that attitude stems from their feeling anxious and vulnerable. It is important to state clearly that the failure to become truly elder is not a personal or deliberate failure but should really be seen as a social systems failure resulting from the breakdown of the social order. What results is a vicious circle. If the elderly cannot be trusted, are not wanted or are not needed, why would anyone aspire to become an elder or undertake the difficult developmental work involved? Old age becomes something to dread and youth something to be stretched out as long as possible.

The sibling society

Robert Bly, poet, mythologist and writer on personal development, discusses many of the issues that trouble a society suffering from a lack of elders (Bly 1996). He describes the flattened structure that develops from the idea that everyone is equal psychologically and socially, which results in perceiving each other as symbolic siblings. This in turn has resulted from the rejection of authority and hierarchy in the social revolution of the 1960s. Part of this trend is the idea that all opinions are equally valid and that, in a post-modern sense, all values and beliefs are relative. The values and beliefs of the powerful or elderly are seen as having no more validity than those of the young. The idea of elders as a psycho-social phenomenon is rejected. There are only equal persons of different ages, young or old. Bly rejects this and takes a deliberate stance as an elder in favour of elders. He argues that calling traditional power structures into question is necessary to address abuses but that the baby of equal opportunity is in danger of being thrown out with the bath-water of injustice by flattened structures. What results is a psychological vacuum that is inadequately filled by social and psychological theorising and personal therapy. Young people move into powerful roles with no sense of how to behave and with no mentors or elders to guide them. The young become like sorcerers' apprentices, able to get things going but unable to sustain them or bring them to a safe or successful conclusion. Examples are easy to find: the internet dot.com genius who makes paper millions and employs hundreds of people who are then put out of work when it crashes; the entrepreneur who leverages a company to the point of being unsustainable and bankrupts a region.

The pursuit of psychological development towards elderhood is now an individual choice and an individual cost. It is a difficult process and if undertaken usually goes unacknowledged. It requires commitment to a community of some sort. It is different from the individual pursuit of therapy as the benefits to the self are aimed primarily at the community. There are no obvious rewards and one simply becomes qualified to handle greater levels of difficulty and conflict. Given that it is optional it is understandable that most people settle for a quiet and easy personal life.

In Cognitive Analytic Therapy Ryle proposes that the failure to expand a limited repertoire of roles and behaviours simply leads to the continuance of 'narrow-band' functioning (Ryle 1995). This can be described as a defensive position in relation to new experiences. The failure to reflect on experience with others leads to processing all experiences through a narrow range of roles with particular set perceptions, beliefs, moods, aims and action-planning. The monologue of the anxiously closed or depressed and uninterested mind results in a failure to develop new knowledge from new experiences and the endless elicitation and repetition of old experiences which serve to confirm the anxious and depressed orientation to life. CAT aims to broaden the repertoire of roles by taking control of unhelpful elicitation and reciprocation. This and other personal developmental experiences should hopefully result in an open and curious stance, a position of dialogue with others where new experience results in new knowledge, what one can call 'broad-band' functioning. In terms of a sibling society, there is a division between those who are caught up in the conflicts of the successful or unsuccessful elicitation of their reciprocal roles, a kind of sibling rivalry of competing monologues, and those whose acquired flexibility allows them to resist reciprocation and pursue negotiated mutuality through dialogue. This is one way into psychological elderhood.

Information, knowledge and wisdom

Traditionally elders have been seen as purveyors or containers of wisdom. There is an important question here as to what wisdom is, how it relates to information and knowledge and what happens if wisdom is lost or is no longer available.

Information or facts collected over time form the basic level and foundation of all knowledge. Knowledge structures are built up through reflecting on and testing out facts. Since the advent of formal science, scientific knowledge structures have grown in depth and complexity in extraordinary ways. In the arts and social sciences there has been a similar exponential growth but with a problem attached; the validity of artistic and social science conclusions is impossible to prove and what results is a multiplicity of competing opinions all drawn from an ocean of information too huge for anyone to encompass. This can be demonstrated by searching the internet on any particular topic. One encounters diametrically opposed facts (or rather opinions). What is needed is some access to wisdom, some standard by which its value may be measured. In formal science wisdom is certainly needed in understanding the ethical issues of applying new knowledge to everyday life. In the arts and social sciences a Tower of Babel tends to result from the competing monologues. This confusion may not be too important in the arts, but in the social sciences, which often inform governments' policies and spending, wisdom can be seen to be a crucial element.

Wisdom here might be defined as knowing what can and cannot be changed in a person or system. This includes a sense of knowing what must be suffered because it cannot be easily changed. Many things can only be changed by increasing suffering or by engaging in prohibitive costs. This bears on the relationship between the micro and the macro where most often the individual is made to suffer for the greater good. Examples of this would include decisions about medical treatment of illnesses or changes to interpersonal relating in a family system. This kind of wisdom can only be achieved by living through impossible or insoluble situations. If you have not lived through such situations the temptation is always to assume that with enough knowledge solutions will be inevitably found. In this sense an elder can be defined as someone who has knowledge but who also has the experience to know when it can be useful and when not.

It is tempting to assume that old people are being bypassed by modern information systems, but this is not true. They are proving perfectly capable of surfing the web and engaging with other technologies to their own benefit. The problem lies more with those in power who rely upon information systems and knowledge structures but fail to seek or accept the wisdom accumulated by elders. If modern systems are now so complex that they tend to defeat improvement, the risk is that without trust in elders' knowledge too much energy will be spent constantly reinventing the wheel. Knowledge gained from reinventing the wheel is seen as worth more than knowledge available within elders. The results in commerce and industry are repeated cycles of business failure, due to consequences which arguably might have been foreseen, and overly linear thinking. In the personal arena it similarly results in repeated cycles of relationship breakdown due to inescapably narrow roles and unidentified and unchanged transference.

Senge, originally a family therapist, describes helpfully the parable of the 'boiled frog' (Senge 1992, pp. 22–3): a frog put in a pan of boiling water immediately jumps out, but when placed in warm water the frog gets comfortable, and as the heat increases becomes too addled to get out and eventually boils to death. A business example would be a company that believes it has cornered the market in its product, complacently fails to invest in research and development and then finds itself losing out to the competition. A relationship example would be the happy marriage where one of the couple settles into lazy or irritating habits, believing everything is fine because the other does not complain, and is then surprised when the other runs off with someone else. Only an elder who has been through, or been close to, the experience and has evaluated and understood it can wisely describe what is happening. The foolish young frog believes that everything is fine – and please don't interfere. Senge also points out that statistically most companies or marriages only last about five years. A small amount go on to about 40 years. Most people are incapable of seeing over the horizon. Elders can because they have been there; they are able to speak from a place beyond the horizon.

In a similar way indigenous communities have been sustaining their equilibrium (cycles of growth and decay) for long periods of time, in many cases hundreds of years, and this requires the memory and accumulated wisdom of elders. Modern corporations (lasting 5–40 years) tend to destroy indigenous communities because corporations operate to a cycle of continuous linear growth (a conquest agenda), which such communities and their agricultural land cannot sustain. For example cash-crop coffee in Guatemala and Nicaragua was imposed by these countries' governments under military and economic pressure from the USA. Growing only coffee made the people dependent on government coffee-cash for everything that they used to make or grow for themselves and at the same time ruined the fragile fertility of the thin soil, thereby reinforcing their addict-like dependency on the government. Of course the governments were happy to have the peasants become more dependent on them because it made them easier to control. To ensure this, most of the tribal elders, shamans and community leaders of those countries were 'disappeared'.

The example of cash-crop coffee illustrates the problem of short-cycle economics but also reflects the values of modern culture and industry. It is the economics of obsolescence, focused on producing goods for possession, consumption and disposability. Large amounts of information and knowledge (and the world's dwindling resources) are applied to creating the vast array of these goods, but with little wise reflection on their necessity or their ultimate cost to renewable resources. Much of what is produced is made by the young, marketed to the young, owned, used and disposed of by the young. Someone interested in personal growth and elderhood soon develops less of an interest in consumer culture because their values change (for example recycling of resources and sustaining community become important). The guiding principle for an elder is not about what harms or benefits the individual but what harms or benefits the community, particularly in the long term. Information and knowledge may be seen as value-neutral and free-floating, but wisdom always exists in relation to the community it serves and the elders who contain and apply it.

Finally it may be helpful to reflect briefly on the values applied to learning. Today, emphasis is very much on knowledge and skills-based competence acquired through rigorous training programmes rewarded with qualifications. This type of goal-oriented, activity-based learning should result in an efficient and effective workforce who are able to *do* things correctly. It is important to contrast this with the more traditional values of education where intelligence moves forward through curiosity, openness and exploration with the aim of producing individuals who can think for themselves and eventually reflect on life with a certain degree of wisdom and *being-ness*. Of course both styles of learning are valuable and it is very helpful to be able to move between them depending on the learning task. It is however probably fair to say that the demands of the modern economy put great emphasis on knowledge-based doing and devalue being-based wisdom.

Conclusion

This chapter aimed to give an outline understanding of the concept of elderhood, the characteristics of elders in the indigenous and modern world and the differences between being chronologically old and psycho-logically and socially elder. It then looked at some of the consequences of the withering or erosion of the archetype of the elder for society, how trust has been lost in them and the vicious circle of not developing because it's difficult and not wanted or valued. Following that, I have attempted to make a case for the necessity of wisdom, which one can see as being a key characteristic of elders. I will conclude with a brief look at some of the hidden costs closer to home of the absence of elders.

In the first world there has been a shift in the function and roles that children fulfil for their parents. In the past having children was an economic and practical necessity in terms of running the family business, looking after the elderly and earning extra money. In the third world this is still the case. In the first world, however, children are no longer needed to do these things so the choice to have them is a sentimental or emotional one; they are love objects. The consequence of this is that they are accept-able so long as they remain lovable; if they are difficult or stressful they can be attacked or abandoned and become hate objects. Their upbringing is therefore focused on being loving and loveable rather than facilitating optimum survival and value to the community (J. Low, personal communication). The same argument can be used in relation to the elderly, and grandparents in particular. In the third world the elderly have many functions including looking after the young children. They are hardly ever abandoned. In the modern world relations with elderly grandparents are sustained if they remain lovable and useful (for example in terms of baby-sitting or giving money) but if they become difficult or stressful they can be neglected or abandoned into the paid care of strangers. Grandparents excluded from any elder role towards their children or grandchildren other than as functional servants often withdraw and neglect or abandon their own children and grandchildren. The breaking apart of families mirrors the breaking apart of society. The loss of elders is part of the breakdown.

The emotional currency of this social fragmentation is seen every day in NHS psychiatry and psychotherapy clinics. A key theme is loss of trust, both in others to provide containment (security, safety, acceptance and facilitation) as well as a loss of trust that others will contain themselves (not attack, seduce or abuse). Loss of reciprocal trust results in defences of cynicism, paranoia and selfishness. If others cannot be trusted to behave as contained adults, let alone elders, why should anyone try to behave that way themselves? Commitment, discipline and personal development become foolish or unnecessary choices, as does public service. In the absence of trust, betrayal ceases to be betrayal; in a marriage or a job, it simply becomes a choice to move on. The collapse of marriages often leads to single or multiple parenting, and the increased possibility of abuse, neglect and abandonment. In mental health we see the steady increase of borderline disorders and their associated problems of drink and drug abuse and suicide. For youth the physical absence of fathers and lack of trust in male elders leads to increasing gang violence, drug use and crime.

Psychotherapy itself shrinks in a fragmented society and restricts itself to the strengthening of the ego rather than the development of deeper self-structures and more complex interpersonal relatedness that are required for continued personal development through a whole life and into old age. It is as if without a community-built raft steered by elders on which to float we are all condemned each to our own little rowing boat and forever threatened by stormy seas.

References

Bly, R. (1996) *The Sibling Society*. New York: Addison-Wesley.

Moore, R., and Gillette, D. (1990) *Warrior, Magician, Lover, King: Rediscovering the Archetypes of the Mature Masculine*. San Francisco: HarperCollins.

Prechtel, M. (1998) *Secrets of the Talking Jaguar*. New York: Tarcher-Putnam.

Prechtel, M. (1999) *Long Life, Honey in the Heart*. New York: Tarcher-Putnam.

Ryle, A. (1995) *Cognitive Analytic Therapy: Developments in Theory and Practice*. Chichester: John Wiley.

Segal, H. (1964) *Introduction to the Work of Melanie Klein*. London: Hogarth Press.

Senge, P. M. (1992) *The Fifth Discipline: The Art and Practice of the Learning Organisation*. London: Century Business.

Senge, P. M. (1999) *The Dance of Change*. London: Nicholas Brealey.

Somé, M. P. (1993) *Ritual, Power, Healing and Community*. Portland, OR: Swan-Raven.

Somé, M. P. (1998) *The Healing Wisdom of Africa*. New York: Tarcher-Putnam.

Chapter 4

Individual CAT with older people

Clinical examples

Madeleine Loates

As a psychologist working with older people, I often carry out psycho-therapy assessments and make decisions over the most appropriate interventions. For some clients, a straightforward approach using cognitive behavioural methods to cope with current issues may be the therapeutic choice, but for others there is a necessity to understand the meaning of symptoms and to acknowledge the roots of the problem that may emerge decades later, sometimes in response to other changes in a person's life. For example two referrals for treatment of anxiety may reveal completely different reasons behind the overt symptoms. In the first instance a woman became anxious in response to physical symptoms arising from stress that led her to believe she was having a heart attack. In that situation education and stress management was the most helpful intervention. A man in his sixties presented with extreme anxiety, such that his wife would not leave him on his own for more than ten minutes for fear that 'something would happen to him'. Anxiety management had been attempted but had made no impact on his symptoms. Assessment revealed that this man's mother had been unable to cope with her fear of separation from her youngest son and in consequence he had stayed home from school on the slightest pretext. While he had coped during his adult life, ageing and health problems had resulted in the re-emergence of the anxiety of abandonment and it was with the psychodynamic understanding of CAT that we were together able to make sense of the meaning of his symptoms, and this allowed other changes to come about.

Therefore in this chapter I hope to illustrate the type of older clients I have worked with using the CAT model. CAT is quite able to reformulate the problems of milder depression, bereavement and anxiety-based disorders, but it is most suitable for more complex or indirect presentation of distress with antecedents in early life experience. In these cases I have found the approach to be a collaborative, engaging and human way of helping people with the problems they encounter in later life.

Selection of clients for individual CAT

Particular features would tend to preclude clients from individual CAT – these include those in acute crisis including acute in-patients, acute psychosis or delirium, or those with significant cognitive impairment, particularly short-term memory deficits. Some clients may be helped by systemic CAT, and for a more detailed discussion over the selection of such clients, see Hepple (2002). Certain themes have emerged in clients offered this approach, and are reflected in the following case studies.

Clients with long histories of mental health problems, often with treatment-resistant depression – Mrs A

Many clients in services for older people have had long histories of mental health problems mostly treated with medication or physical interventions such as ECT, but it has been very rare to find any who have been offered therapy in the past. Mrs A, a woman in her seventies, presented with obsessional thoughts and ruminations with an underlying depression, and significant social anxiety. She had been treated with an anti-depressant for a year with no improvement before being referred for therapy. She had suffered a breakdown some 20 years before and had experienced recurrent bouts with similar symptoms as at the time of referral, each time treated with medication. She was very anxious about being referred for therapy and seemed overwhelmed by being offered more than three sessions.

Her history revealed her to be the only surviving child of elderly parents. She had heard through people in her village that her mother had lost twin baby boys but it was never discussed with her. Mrs A remembered the relationship as close, but her mother had suffered anxiety and depression most of her life and Mrs A had to care for her throughout her teenage years. Mrs A told me that her mother had stopped her from playing as a child. When Mrs A expressed her anger, her mother would get angry back and Mrs A would always be the first to anxiously apologise. Mrs A's mother had refused to allow her to attend music college and was both envious and critical of any achievements. In consequence Mrs A's belief in her own ability was low and she was critical of her own performance. She also found it almost impossible to accept gifts or compliments, believing that she did not deserve them.

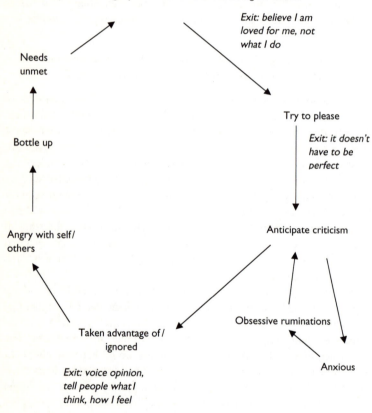
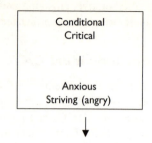

Figure 4.1 Mrs A's placation trap

As we started to meet for therapy, Mrs A's overt problems of obsessional thoughts and ruminations dissipated with little direct intervention, but it became apparent that her self-beliefs, low self-esteem and anxiety influenced her everyday life and were causing her immense distress.

When she was offered a sixteen-session CAT Mrs A was anxious and almost overwhelmed. She felt she did not deserve the time, that others would have greater need, and worried that her problems would be overwhelming for me as the therapist. But she was able to accept the reformulation letter and to acknowledge how difficult she had found her mother's envious and depriving nature. One of Mrs A's target problem procedures read: 'Believing yourself to be unlovable unless attending to other people's needs, you try to get it right and agree with anyone's request. You put your own needs aside and therefore remain unheard. This leads to other people ignoring or taking advantage of you. You become angry with others and yourself but then feel guilty. This confirms your belief that you are unlovable and must not express your own needs.'

Figure 4.1 demonstrates the placation trap worked out with Mrs A, together with the exits – the points for therapeutic intervention. A second SDR (Figure 4.2) is related to Mrs A's snag – her belief that she did not deserve anything good. We found that this was crucial to the change that came about during therapy, and had a direct impact in her relationship with her husband. Mrs A made significant changes over the weeks that we met, taking the courage to express her feelings and put her own needs first, and in consequence this enabled her husband to do the same. She allowed herself to receive as well as to give and learnt to ride a bicycle for the first time in her life. At our last session Mrs A was able to look forward to the future, and to the life that she and her husband were choosing to partake in, rather than feeling driven to look after others. In her goodbye letter I talked about the search for meaning around her mother's anxious overprotection, wondering whether this was influenced by her having lost children prior to Mrs A's birth, but also acknowledged the critical and depriving side of her nature which had left Mrs A with a belief that she was not good enough to deserve nice things. Mrs A shed tears at the ending of our relationship, expressing apprehension about 'having to do it on her own', but in her own goodbye letter was able to talk about the changes she had made, commenting 'your sessions have been a great help to me and also to Mr A. We now communicate more openly – even if we have a tiff and then a laugh – much healthier. We are now thinking more of our own needs and not always of others, and recognize the fact that we deserve things in life as well.'

At follow-up at three months Mrs A told me that for the first month

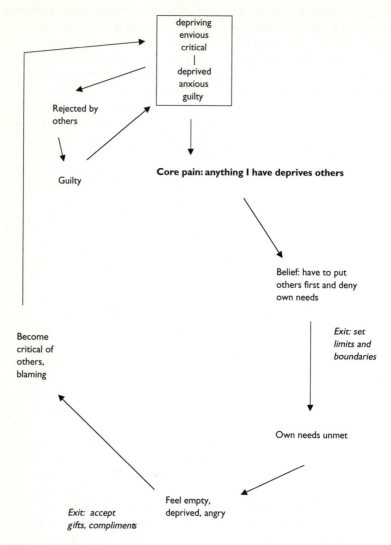

depriving
envious
critical
|
deprived
anxious
guilty

Rejected by
others

Guilty

Core pain: anything I have deprives others

Belief: have to put
others first and deny
own needs

*Exit: set
limits and
boundaries*

Become
critical of
others,
blaming

Own needs unmet

*Exit: accept
gifts, compliments*

Feel empty,
deprived, angry

Figure 4.2 Mrs A's snag

after our sessions she had felt bereaved, and she had been surprised by the strength of her feelings of loss and anger. Gradually her mood had lifted and she felt normal again. She had managed to maintain the changes she had made, being able to express her needs and make decisions for herself with her husband.

Clients with personality traits labelled as 'difficult' and 'manipulative' – Mrs B

There are some clients who present to mental health services later in life and are quickly identified as 'difficult to help'. They have often coped throughout their middle years by their immersion in energy-consuming defensive procedures that, temporarily, concealed their core pain (for example, attempting to be an ideal carer to an abusive partner, a successful business career or being a selfless perfect parent to a large family). Late life brings losses and changes, which both disrupt the defensive procedures and uncover borderline personality traits that have their origins in early life experience. In Chapter 8 of this book, Jason Hepple discusses the nature and treatment of these 'resurgent borderline traits' in older people. These people are often labelled as 'manipulative', 'abusive' or 'behavioural' due to the indirect presentation of their distress and the expression of despair and anger by passive aggressive strategies. Sometimes these changes in someone's ability to cope rock the whole family structure, and it is only at this point that knowledge emerges of significant traumatic or abusive events in a person's early life. For such clients a straightforward approach such as bereavement counselling for the death of a spouse may not successfully deal with the emotional consequences because the root of the distress lies in early family relationships.

Mrs B, a woman in her seventies who was in poor health, lost her husband two years previously, and was re-referred to the mental health service because of depression and difficulty in coping. She had a long history of depression and anxiety and had been described as 'hard to help'. Anti-depressants prescribed at this time made no difference; she rejected all other help offered and was angry and dismissive of the services, while still complaining of being depressed.

Assessment for CAT revealed the following information: Mrs B had grown up in a family where her mother was violent, withholding of any affection and contemptuous of perceived weakness. She described her father as weak, a clever but insecure man who used to cover for his insecurity by boasting. As a child Mrs B had been physically abused, her mother contemptuous of her daughter's physical looks and intellectual ability. Mrs B had coped by burying herself in books, her self-esteem integrally related to her mental abilities, and she sought no close emotional relationships. She married a man, attracted to him by his appearance of psychological strength and coolness that she thought would protect her, but he too was physically abusive and became an alcoholic. She contemptuously described his perceived strength as a cover for an inability to feel or empathise. They had three children, and despite their turbulent relationship they survived forty years of marriage, Mrs B coping by being the intelligent strong woman who could outwit her husband and would then belittle him to her children. In later years his physical frailty and poor health gave rise to a period of relative peace in their relationship, and Mrs B cared for him until his death. With his death it seemed as if her vulnerability and neediness were exposed. She sought support from her children who responded with exasperation and contempt to what they saw as her unnecessary demands and complaints, accusing her of 'crying wolf' in response to complaints about her health.

Mrs B attended regularly and, while often appearing bright and chatting anecdotally, gradually gave me the history outlined above and began to express sadness at her own history and apprehension when recalling the relationship with her mother. She admitted to bottling up her feelings, claiming that no-one would understand if she talked about how she felt, and that she worried about what other people would think of her. However, she also admitted to being unreasonably angry, sarcastic and hurtful to her sons at times. It was at times difficult to empathise with Mrs B's situation – she talked about her family members and others, including colleagues, in contemptuous and abusive tones. The history of her own family experience was interspersed with critical anecdotes about others. In the early part of the therapy she frequently commented that she did not see the point of attending as talking could change nothing. Supervision helped me to identify the extent to which Mrs B attempted to escape from the core pain of feeling contemptible and abused, either by seeking a relationship in which she could be cared for or admired (for being stronger, brighter), or by fending off her feelings by her contempt for others.

Her reformulation letter read:

It seems as if in response to the circumstances of your early life you were faced with a dilemma – whether to be on the side of strength or weakness. To be strong was to push away any emotional needs. But to be weak was to show your vulnerability and neediness, to want protection and emotional closeness with other people. It seems as if you had to learn early on that in order to survive in your family you had to choose to be strong, and in meeting your husband you were faced with the same dilemma. If you had not been strong perhaps he too would have hit you more than once. In order to make sure you and your children survived you had to deny what you may have perceived as the 'weak' side of yourself. You became the powerful protector of your children, rejecting of help but also contemptuous of others who were weaker than you.

Despite your difficult situation you loved your husband and there was a closeness which you have missed terribly since his death. You described it as if the equilibrium in your life has shifted. The position you were forced to take when he was alive acted as a protection for you – you knew where you stood – but it is no longer there and your hope and expectation is for emotional closeness from your children, although you are aware that this is not the relationship you had with them when they were younger. It seems as though they may have been faced with the same dilemma as yourself and are unable to give you the emotional support you need and want. Whilst you have been able to show me the sad side of yourself, it may be that your sons have never seen that side and cannot believe it exists. Maintaining the image of 'strong B' may always keep your sons at a distance but allowing them to see your other side may allow them to respond to their mum in a different way.

She was moved by the letter and elaborated further on the hurt she had experienced within her family of origin.

We began to construct a diagram with the core reciprocal roles existing in two dissociated self-states (Figure 4.3), she and her husband mirroring the Admiring-Admired state, and Mrs B as the Ideal Carer to her husband. It seemed that while Mr B was alive, Mrs B had felt largely sustained within the fantasy of these two states. With his death the fantasy of these states was exposed and the disillusion and anger sent Mrs B crashing into the core pain of the lower roles. At these times Mrs B experienced the pain of humiliation, contempt and abuse by her children, while fending off the pain by contemptuous rejection of any help offered as 'not enough and not good enough' and by verbal abuse.

As therapy progressed Mrs B was able to accept the time offered and attended regularly. She talked with genuine sadness about her own upbringing but also the impact on her children of Mr B's alcoholism and her failure to protect them from the consequences of that. To an extent Mrs B was able to accept and own her contemptuous and sarcastic nature. We developed exits focusing on her acceptance of the help that could be offered either from her children or from others and on the consequences of Mrs B being able to share her feelings in a way that would not invite contempt. Mrs B found these exits very hard to follow consistently. From our discussions and knowledge of her family it was clear that they had been influenced in turn by their parenting, and despite

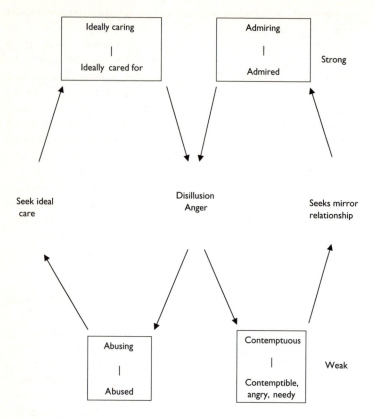

Figure 4.3 Mrs B's self-states

Mrs B trying to follow different ways of doing things, her children often responded with contempt and verbal abuse. However, Mrs B was able to acknowledge the limitations and constraints of their lives and the problems she had brought about by 'crying wolf' in the past, now at a time when her own health was poor in reality.

As we approached the end of therapy Mrs B talked more about her husband's death, and shed tears not only for his death, but grief for herself and her life. She felt at that point that she might not survive the winter. At our last meeting she was able to acknowledge the help that therapy had been but her sadness at the ending of our meetings together. However, some three years later she continues to live in her own home, has not been referred back to the psychiatric service and is a less frequent attender at the GP surgery.

Somatisation syndromes resistant to CBT – Mrs C and Mrs J

Some clients have presented with physical or mental symptoms for which no cause is found. Mrs C came from a physically and emotionally depriving family and her way of coping had been to give everything of herself. Her belief was that to have anything for her would deprive others. She worked outside the home, cleaned, cooked, ironed for her family but would reject any offer of help until they stopped offering. For years she swallowed her resentment, developing digestive problems and ulcers for which she took constant medication. As she reached her late sixties, the effort to keep up defeated her and her GP recognised the extent of her depression and referred her for therapy. Mrs C had carried unexpressed anger and resentment for over 60 years. Within the CAT structure she found the opportunity to tell her life story and the validation of the reformulation allowed her to grieve for the relationship that she had wanted from her parents.

Part of her reformulation letter read:

> You were the eldest child of three but the overwhelming feeling was that you were born to work for your parents. Your father was a bully who thought women were fit only for the kitchen or for bed and he was both emotionally and physically abusive to you. Your mother was an ill, unhappy woman, you described her as the most unhappy woman you have ever met. You have no memories of being cared for by your parents – you learnt early on that you had to care for your own worries and anxieties and that you had to care for your parents physically and emotionally, always trying to make your mother happy, spending your pocket money on her, not on your-self.
>
> You were a bright intelligent girl but your father seemed resentful, jealous of your achievements and denigrating of any success. Not only did your parents fail to give you care but they took from you as well – your childhood, parts of your education, your own possessions. Hating your body and all the parts of you which you recognise as coming from your parents you have tried all your life to be utterly and absolutely opposite to all that they represented, and this has meant cutting out parts of you, not allowing yourself or others to see or experience the normal human feelings of irritation and annoyance.
>
> You escaped from this life by marrying in your early twenties but felt trapped by your marriage, pregnancy and your husband's illness. Part of the reason for choosing your husband was the difference

between him and your father but despite many years of marriage you have always hated the sexual side of your marriage, but I wonder if this has also left you feeling resentful of your parents with a sense of 'what might have been' but also guilty because your husband has so steadfastly loved you all these years.

You have coped with your feelings by frenetic activity, driving yourself so you wouldn't have to think or feel but you have suffered the consequences in terms of your physical and mental health. As you have reached retirement age you have found it impossible to cope in the same way.

With the process of therapy her physical symptoms abated and her good-bye letter summarises some of the themes of therapy:

During therapy we have been able to make the link to understand why, when demands were made of you, or you disagreed with what was said or asked, you found it impossible to voice your opinion. Time after time over the years you have swallowed your feelings, gritted your teeth and said nothing in order to avoid disagreements or quarrels because to experience or even observe a quarrel would leave you feeling abused in the same way as your parents abused you over the years.

You have struggled with the reality that you are your parents' daughter. Perhaps part of our work together has been to accept those 'darker' aspects of yourself – that there will be times when you are angry or hurt but that to show the more vulnerable aspects of your-self does not mean that others stop loving or liking you and does not make you into the bully that your father was.

We have also talked about your relationship with your husband and the feeling over the years of 'what might have been'. You have had to settle for the reality of ordinary marriage with the difficulties and demands that that has involved but it seems as if your affection for your husband has deepened over these last months. I wondered whether by giving yourself more time and not feeling his sexual approaches as yet another demand to be made upon you and over which you had no control, that you have allowed yourself to relax and receive affection and comfort in a way that was not possible in the past.

Mrs C began to be able to set limits on others' demands, learning to say no. She was able to stop knitting compulsively for her grandchildren, spend time and money on herself and accept love and care from her husband.

For several women there has been a pattern of caring for others at the expense of themselves, but with the physical changes associated with getting older, what has been a coping strategy for perhaps seventy years can no longer carry on. For example, a woman in her mid-seventies was referred by her GP because of her great anxiety that she was developing Alzheimer's disease. She was unable to concentrate and could not remember what she had done, or what she was meant to be doing next. Formal assessment of her memory showed a pattern of normal learning and recall, but it became apparent that Mrs J had difficulty concentrating and on enquiry it seemed that she was thinking of all the things to be done after the appointment and it seemed that she had always been a woman who had worked to look after others but was no longer able to keep up the punishing schedule that she set herself.

Mrs J was always on time for her appointments, and would arrive apologising. She appeared younger than her years. She talked rapidly, as if she had to cram the words in the time, and would become anxious towards the end of the hour, saying that she was aware that I had other people to see and apologising for keeping me late. Mrs J had been brought up in a loving but large family. Her father had been injured during the First World War and was left with a significant disability. Mrs J became sensitive to his needs early in her life but would anxiously protect others from her concerns about him. Being the eldest girl she had to help look after her younger brothers and sisters. If she expressed anxiety or tiredness her mother would get angry with her, so she quickly learnt to say nothing. She became a mother to her sisters, particularly her youngest sister, born when her mother was in her forties and when J was in her early teens. She ended up working to support her family, and continued this role both physically and emotionally all her life. Ultimately she married a man who had similar medical problems to her father, and devoted herself to the cause of keeping him alive. Even in her mid-seventies her younger sisters lived near her and depended on her.

Part of her reformulation letter reads,

> In certain respects you learnt to look after yourself but perhaps you never learnt to recognise or acknowledge your own emotional needs. Whilst your experience of growing up gave you the discipline to accomplish much more than most, the downside is that people have come to expect you to be there, demand of you and become angry when you cannot meet all their needs. And perhaps because you learnt very early on to look after others and that you would not be looked after in the same way, it has meant that you find it almost

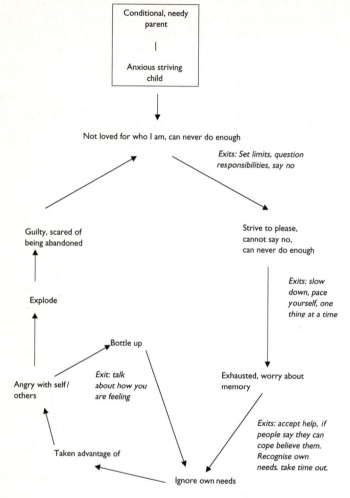

Figure 4.4 Mrs J's SDR

impossible to accept help from others or accept that others can do more for themselves.

In trying to understand why your situation has become so difficult, I have wondered whether your deepest underlying belief is that you cannot be loved for who you are (with all your angry, hurt feelings and basic human need for love and affection), and that people will only love you or stay around if you look after their every need.

We worked towards an SDR (Figure 4.4), acknowledging the inner child who, when faced with anxiety because of the fear of criticism, or the fear of loss (by death, or loss of control), coped by trying harder and harder with no acknowledgement of her own needs. Exits were hard to negotiate, as her fear of change was very great, partly because of the length of time that she had been behaving in this way, and as a consequence, others expected her to stay the same and resisted any perceived change. During therapy we related her fear of losing her memory not only to her fear of loss of control and sense of agency, but also to the punishing schedule she had set herself, thinking ahead three steps and therefore not concentrating on what she was doing at the time. Over time she was gradually able to say no a little more easily and to stop taking responsibility for everything that occurred by no longer constantly saying 'sorry', but in her goodbye letter wrote, 'When I can't remember things I get so afraid, I think where did this woman go, who could sort out everything, took charge of the sick, remember everything, be worried yes but not unhappy. . . . O.K. I'm older now, but I must remember I am still ME.'

At follow-up six months later she talked about her fear of being abandoned, and how that drove her to care for others in order to try and keep them alive. Sadly she had not maintained any changes and was compulsively attending to everyone's needs but her own, while continuing to worry that she was developing Alzheimer's disease. This remained the position four years later, although assessment of her memory showed no change.

Summary

This is clearly not an exhaustive review of those clients for whom individual CAT would appear to be a good therapeutic choice, but suggests some of those features in a client's presentation that may lead you to consider this kind of approach. There are also elements within the therapy that seem well suited to work with older people.

Unfortunately many services view older people from an almost entirely biological and ageing perspective, treating distress or difficult behaviour as if it existed separately from the person's life, their history and relationships, with no search for understanding of the meaning behind the symptoms or the roots of their distress. CAT explicitly avoids an illness model, being based in interpersonal understanding, and therefore can help search for meaning behind symptoms, when the meanings may be unique to that individual.

Reminiscence and life review are two well-established ways of working with older people. CAT takes a life story perspective but through the reformulation is able to offer a narrative reconstruction of the client's story. The experience of being listened to, and to bring new understanding to a story that may have been held for seventy or eighty years, can be a powerful tool, strengthening the working alliance but also challenging societal views about the older person being 'past it', or 'not worth bothering about'. The fact of having written reformulations and diagrams is helpful to all ages, but especially so for older people.

More recent theoretical developments with CAT also address cultural and cohort differences – an area of great importance when working with older people where the norms and values of gender or behaviour may have significantly changed, for example the expectation that the youngest girl in a large family would stay living at home to look after her parents in their old age, or where people have lived through events which had great significance such as the evacuation of very young children during the Second World War.

The collaborative nature of CAT and search for understanding also helps counter intergenerational negative transference that can be encountered when working with older people, who can feel patronised or misunderstood by younger 'experts'. Older people will often find that they have time to think or work between sessions, and for many there is the sense that the therapy work undertaken is in time for them to think again about their lives and make changes, or perhaps reparation with others – as Laura Sutton (1997) wrote, 'as a supervisor, herself retired, said to me once, it is not that it has come too late – it has come just in time'.

References

Hepple, J. (2002) Cognitive Analytic Therapy. In J. Hepple, J. Pearce and P. Wilkinson (eds), *Psychological Therapies with Older People: Developing Treatments for Effective Practice*. Hove, East Sussex: Brunner-Routledge.

Sutton, L. (1997) Out of the silence: when people can't talk about it. In L. Hunt, M. Marshall and C. Rowlings (eds), *Past Trauma in Late Life: European Perspective on Therapeutic Work with Older People*. London: Jessica Kingsley.

Part II

The developmental conditions of later life from a CAT perspective

Introduction

Jason Hepple (with the Narcissus myth as abridged by Mark Dunn)

In the previous section of this book we hope to have laid the ground for a move away from a purely biological view of ageing. While it is undoubtedly true that older age brings with it biological changes that can affect physical and mental abilities, to overemphasise these at the expense of a more developmental psychological approach is ageist and likely to provide a formulation of an individual's problems that is ultimately limited. While adolescents are expected to suffer from 'identity crisis', emotionality and challenging behaviours, similar difficulties in older people struggling to adapt to the changes and challenges of later life are often described in biological rather than psychological terms. Cognitive impairment, cerebro-vascular disease, dementia and 'reactive' depression can provide blanket 'organic' labels that encourage no further exploration of possible underlying psychological issues. It is rarely all 'organic' or all 'psychological'. The key to greater understanding comes through an empathic description of the interaction between the life events and losses confronting an individual and the personality and coping structures that have got the person to this point in their life.

In fact, the interaction between organic and psychological factors is often cyclical and can require considerable untangling if progress is to be made. For example, a person with mild memory problems due to Alzheimer's disease may present with depression, irritability and loss of confidence. The disability has awakened deep feelings of inadequacy or 'stupidity' that were laid down in the person's early life by critical parents and unfavourable comparisons with an idealised sibling. A treatment approach aimed at both recognising and utilising existing cognitive strengths, and an opportunity to process the issues around self-esteem that the new disability has awakened, is likely to be more effective than either approach alone. Another older individual, with a more secure self-esteem, but with exactly the same memory problems, may laugh about their disability and rise to the challenge of adapting and explaining to others the change in their abilities. The difference between these two individuals is clearly psychological rather than organic. Even in severe dementia, a person's distress and agitation is so often described as being a behavioural manifestation of the degenerative process that is going on in the brain rather than as the interaction between personality and disability. It is perhaps challenging to many to keep this dual perspective in mind. To acknowledge the persistence of the personality is to identify more closely with the psychological distress and threatens the ageism defence where the 'victim of dementia' is in a different human category to that of the observer.

In this section we will describe two broad areas where the interaction between personality and the developmental challenges of later life create distress and mental health problems. The roots of this developmental approach are described in Erikson's last two dichotomies (see Chapter 2): Generativity versus Stagnation and Ego Integrity versus Despair. The theoretical extension made here is to adapt the model of developmental hurdles (or milestones) to differing individuals. How a person reacts to a life event or loss providing a chilling glimpse into the fantasy of these dichotomies, depends so much on who they are, their reciprocal role repertoires, their life experience and their capacity for self-reflection. In order to frame some general observations learned from working with older people tackling some of these issues, we have suggested two general categories: (1) Narcissism, and (2) Trauma, borderline personality traits and involution (which includes severe depressive states as well as true dementia). The cases described in the individual chapters are all informed by the CAT model, which is, of course, highly customised to the individual. Categorisation is based on similarities in reciprocal role patterns and procedures, something many readers will be familiar with if they have used the CAT model with younger people. We hope that these descriptions will begin to fill a gaping hole in the developmental psychopathology of later life and help professionals, carers and older people grasp an essentially new approach to the challenges of ageing.

Narcissism

We devote two chapters to the discussion of narcissism and its presentation and treatment in later life from a CAT perspective. The original source of the term is the Roman writer Ovid's mythological stories from his hugely imaginative and archetypal series called *Metamorphoses* (see

Ovid, in Hughes 1997). The following is an abridgement of the myth as retold by Ted Hughes, written by Mark Dunn.

Once long ago in ancient Greece, before the beginnings of recorded history, a young water nymph was seduced by a river spirit and became pregnant. When the baby was born everyone admired his astonishing beauty. She named the boy Narcissus. Concerned for his future the nymph consulted the prophetic vision of blind old Tiresias saying 'Can the boy live long with such perfect beauty?' The seer replied 'Yes, unless he learns to know himself.' The nymph took this riddle literally, keeping mirrors away from him. The boy grew up strong and beautiful but somewhat haughty and proud of his looks so that others did not get too familiar with him. Those that tried were often rebuffed.

One day when out hunting with his teenage companions Narcissus found himself lost in the woods where Echo caught sight of him and instantly fell in love. Echo was a pretty but lonely nymph who had been banished and cursed by Juno to only be able to repeat the last words anyone said (Juno had been in pursuit of philandering Jupiter and had been distracted on several occasions by Echo's idle chatter). She followed him through the woods desperate to speak to him and as he called to his friends she repeated his words – 'Where are you? I'm here!' 'I'm here, I'm here, I'm here.' Narcissus shouted again 'Come and meet me!' Echo replied 'Come and meet me, come and meet me . . .' and revealed herself reaching towards him. Narcissus turned and flew from her saying 'I'd rather be dead than let you touch me!' Echo, rejected and heartbroken, uttered a curse: 'Let Narcissus love and suffer as he has made me love and suffer!' Nemesis the Corrector granted her wish. From that day on Echo kept to herself in the woods and approached no-one, pining and wasting away until only her voice was left echoing faintly in the hills.

Tired and hot, Narcissus came across a pool of clear cool water and lay down to drink. He saw the beautiful face of a stranger in the water and fell instantly in love. He wanted to touch and kiss this stranger but every time he tried the face dissolved in ripples. He did not recognise himself; neither could he tear himself away from the beautiful vision. In agony and ecstasy he lay staring into the pool. For many days or years he lay there unmoving and unloved until too late and close to death he realised that the reflection was actually his own self. He wept tears of grief and turning from the water, lay down and faded from this world. Where his body had been grew a tall white and yellow flower, the Narcissus.

All the elements of a modern understanding of narcissism are here. Narcissus begins life as special and admired by all, but there are hints that his mother's seduction by a river spirit may have provoked original feelings of shame and defilement with perhaps an initial contempt or rejection of the child. The establishment of the grandiose, beautiful boy may have served the defensive needs of both shamed mother and con- temptible child. The warning of Tiresias touches on the fragility of their grandiose creation – self-awareness leads to a collapse of the grandiose self, leading to despair and emptiness. Echo, in contrast to Narcissus, has a need to relate to another to become whole (symbolically needing the words of the other to communicate). Narcissus' contemptuous rejection of her (with the projection of his contemptible self) leads to her psycho- logical death through isolation. Her vengeful curse predicts the vulnera- bility of the grandiose Narcissus as he faces himself in the reflection of the forest pool. Initially he believes that the reflected image can fulfil all his needs and cannot draw himself away from his own image (the mirror relationship). Inevitably, self-awareness strikes and the grandiose self is irreparably deflated, revealing the underlying emptiness and despair at the heart of narcissistic personality structure.

Since Ovid, the concept of narcissism has long presented the student of psychological thought with a series of confusing and sometimes contradictory theoretical positions that take in object relations theory (Rosenfeld 1971), self-psychology (Kohut 1971; Kernberg 1975), recent developments in schema-focused cognitive theory (Young 1990) as well as attempting to describe a cluster of personality traits representing the Narcissistic Personality Disorder of *DSM IV* (American Psychiatric Association 1994). Core features common to all these theoretical perspectives can be summarised as follows: (1) Narcissism is a defensive strategy developed in order to protect a vulnerable and devalued self. (2) The defence involves the creation of a grandiose and over-valued self, the denial of emotional needs and an avoidance of dependency on others for fear of the exposure these bring. (3) This idealised self is itself vulnerable to disillusion and criticism leading to feelings of rage and despair that are difficult to own. (4) Repressed despair can lead to the contemptuous devaluing of others in an effort to protect the exposed, vulnerable self.

CAT provides an understandable interpersonal framework for the understanding of narcissistic personality structure. From a CAT perspec- tive, the self is split into at least two dissociated self-states named typi- cally as: 'admiring relating to admired' and 'contemptuous relating to contemptible'. Early experience of highly critical, conditional care with an avoidance of the expression of strong emotions (particularly neediness and anger) can lead to an introspection and the creation of an escape fantasy where the self will be shown to be effortlessly successful and admired and where there is no vulnerability deriving from dependency on others. As Ryle and Kerr (2002) summarise:

> 'Purer' examples of NPD (Narcissistic Personality Disorder) show a predominant preoccupation with issues of surface, appearance, success and status; their search is not for care and love so much as for admiration. The preferred reciprocal role relationship for a person with NPD is to feel admired by an admirable other. Where this is unachievable, the concern is with the relative status of self and other and hence with occupying the more powerful contemptuous role in the reciprocal role pattern contemptuous in relation to contemptible. Because emotional neediness is closely identified with the contempt-ible role, therapy, as an admission of need is hard to seek or persist with.
>
> (Ryle and Kerr 2002, p. 185)

It is not uncommon for the defensive grandiose self to be maintained into later life. Through talent and achievement, power or omnipotent caregiving, an individual may preserve the position of 'splendid isola-tion', by exhaustive striving or through a series of 'special' and only superficially intimate relationships with others. The challenges and losses of later life, however, may suddenly wreck the person's ability to sustain the grandiose self, leading to 'narcissistic collapse' and a sense of over-whelming emptiness, despair and unfocused rage. Individuals whose grandiose selves depend on looks, intellect, ability to seduce another or the maintenance of an exhausting pace of life, for example, may find get-ting older incompatible with the preservation of this stable sense of self. This can lead to isolation, rejection of others and, in more severe cases, in dissociation or pseudodementia with high dependency needs (see Chapters 8 and 9).

Sally-Anne Ennis in her 'King Lear: the mirror cracked' (Chapter 5), takes perhaps the archetypal example of fragile narcissism in old age, Shakespeare's King Lear, and analyses the text and characterisation from a CAT perspective, uncovering the core reciprocal roles and procedures that bring together the plot and characters in this great tragedy. In this 'narcissistic tyrant' one glimpses the power and destructiveness of the long-repressed rage and despair as the losses and disabilities of older age impinge on the fantasy of the grandiose self and the fear of dependency and exposure of the long-guarded vulnerable self seems unthinkable and terrifying.

In Chapter 6, Madeleine Loates describes the case of Michael – an older man with a narcissistic personality structure who is struggling to maintain his sense of self (and specialness) in his older age. Madeleine eloquently describes the challenges and rewards of working with this group of clients, and the case, I think, will illuminate the day-to-day experiences of many professionals working with older people. She draws on the concept of a 'good enough' therapy and the importance of supervision to identify re-enactment of narcissistic role-play in the therapy relationship.

Trauma, borderline traits and involution

In the final chapters of this book we offer case material to illuminate a theoretical understanding of the severer manifestations of the developmental psychopathology of later life. In Chapter 7, Ian Robbins and Laura Sutton review the advances made in the identification and treatment of post-traumatic syndromes that manifest themselves in later life. Individuals who have had direct experience of the Second World War, the Holocaust and later wars and oppressive regimes may use dissociative defences for many decades, fearing that the trauma must remain 'unspeakable', in order to protect against overwhelming emotional states that may engulf both client and potential therapist. Ageing may evoke similar feelings of powerlessness and entrapment as a recent experience, leading to the presentation of post-traumatic illness in later life. Moving from Cognitive Behavioural Therapy (CBT) towards CAT, the therapeutic relationship is seen as the key opportunity to offer both the 'possibility of the caring response' (thus breaking the generational 'conspiracy of silence') and the containment and 'non-collusion' needed to allow 'debriefing' of the traumatic experience and the possibility of mourning and eventual reconnection. The tools of CAT, particularly the SDR, assist in naming the dissociation and split-off states and creating shared meaning between therapist and client.

The chronically endured trauma of abusive childhood experience can also have life-long effects. In Chapter 8, Jason Hepple examines the evidence for the existence of borderline personality traits in later life as part of the literature describing the field of 'personality disorder in the elderly'. A little objective data and a large amount of clinical experience suggest the notion of the 'unmasking' of regressive and destructive coping strategies and reciprocal role states when faced with the losses of old age. Far from 'burning out', people with abusive and depriving backgrounds may successfully supplement, repress or compensate for their underlying low self-esteem, anger and sense of helplessness for many years. Illness, disability or loss of a significant other later in life can lead to a resurgence of the *DSM IV* borderline traits, which need to be understood in a developmental context. Jason suggests similarities and differences between the presentation of these traits between younger and older people; less overt self-harm, more somatisation and abuse of prescribed medications and a tendency to prolonged dissociative states with dependency needs (conversion pseudodementia). He uses case material to illustrate therapeutic interventions derived from the CAT model aimed at both the individual, by a couple therapy approach, and the wider system of care surrounding a patient.

Finally, in Chapter 9, Laura Sutton discusses case material that illustrates the way that CAT-derived insights can help to understand older people with chronic depressive illness and true dementia. The concept of 'involution' can be useful in these cases, where the individual is 'left behind' by younger carers and therapists who, unwittingly, play out the roles 'outpacing to unbearably pressured'. The only place to go is into the self, the 'cocoon'. In the case of Brian, where relation to others is avoided and feared, Laura draws on the Vygotskian ideas of the 'Zone of Proximal Development' (ZPD) to retune, through supervision, the therapist's expectations to meet with the needs and potentiality of the client. In true dementia, involution may occur in response to an environment that is, due to memory loss, constantly beyond understanding and where relating becomes progressively more difficult (after the patient is considered to have 'settled in' rather than retreated into themselves). Using Tom Kitwood's 'Malignant Social Psychology' of dementia care as a basis for a CAT understanding of harmful role play in dementia care, Laura shows how, in the case of Geoffrey, 'difficult behaviours' can be understood as a means of individual survival using tried and tested aspects of his social or adaptive self that is so under threat in the hostile ward environment Geoffrey finds himself in. Applying those ideas in the field of dementia care is potentially challenging as it can easily upset the 'equilibrium' of the biological model and the distancing ('as if' ideally caring defences) of those working with people with dementia. Close supervision and a team approach can begin to bring therapeutic and developmental perspective into this neglected area.

To conclude this introductory section, we hope that the theoretical ideas and clinical examples discussed in the second half of this book may at least resonate with many working with older people in the NHS and other institutions and may, for some, offer a new way of seeing their patients and the role of self in their work with older people.

References

American Psychiatric Association (1994) *Diagnostic and Statistical Manual of Mental Disorders,* 4th edn. Washington, DC: American Psychiatric Association.

Hughes, T. (1997) *Tales from Ovid.* London: Faber and Faber.

Kernberg, P. (1975) *Borderline Conditions and Pathological Narcissism.* New York: Jason Aronson.

Kohut, H. (1971) *The Analysis of the Self.* New York: International University Press.

Rosenfeld, H. (1971) A clinical approach to the psychoanalytic theory of the life and death instincts: an investigation into the aggressive aspects of narcissism. *International Journal of Psychoanalysis* 52: 169–78.

Ryle, A., and Kerr, I. B. (2002) *Introducing Cognitive Analytic Therapy.* Chilchester: John Wiley.

Young, J. (1990) *Cognitive Therapy for Personality Disorders.* Sarasota, FL: Professional Resource Exchange.

Chapter 5

King Lear

The mirror cracked

Sally-Anne Ennis

Slowly, stealthily but surely, it was creeping up: the effect of ageing in the consulting room. Increasingly the therapist was witnessing either the presence of shocked family members or the provocateur of their emotion: the retiring father or husband. The latter was also shocked at his behaviour and feelings, but defensive and raging at his family's perceived betrayal and intolerance. The star, out of kilter, had disoriented the revolving planets into a spin revealing their shadow sides too, plunging the universe into chaos. Where was the literature with bite on this subject to help me? Upon what rack could I stretch CAT to see if it could withstand and illuminate the process?

Cox, the man who had the inspiration to take Shakespeare to Broadmoor, reminds us that:

> Shakespeare's plays are distinguished by the intensity of the investment in the family and its continuity across generations. His writings, therefore, are exemplary for those who wish to study object relations.
>
> (Cox and Theilgaard 1994, p. 263)

Consequently, with CAT's emphasis on reciprocal roles, it should have something to offer:

> The reciprocal role procedures evolved in early interactions are the foundation upon which later role procedures are built; they are also the source of the inner dialogue on which self-management is based and from which inner conflict stems.
>
> (Ryle 1994, p. 109)

In '*King Lear* and some anxieties of old age' Noel Hess (1987) considers if the dread of being abandoned to a state of utter helplessness is defended against by narcissistic tyranny. There is still some reluctance to understand later ageing in terms other than biological. Furthermore, the narcissistic patient is also considered extremely challenging as he shines upon us his scornful glare.

In 'Narcissism: the term and concept' Pulver wrote: 'In the voluminous literature on narcissism there are probably only two facts upon which everyone agrees: first that the concept of narcissism is one of the most important contributions of psychoanalysis; second, that it is one of the most confusing' (1970, p. 320). The concept, while having experienced metamorphosis through Freud, tells a mythical story and has relevance to the understanding of *King Lear*.

The seer Tiresias, when asked whether Narcissus will have a long life, replies: '*Si se non noverit*': 'Yes, if he does not come to know himself' (Jacoby 1990, p. 9). This has interesting connotations when one considers how the narcissistic person maintains functioning in the precarious reciprocal roles of admired–admiring, and yet, if he glimpses a flaw the mirror cracks, and it is then the narcissist may present for help.

Lear's 'madness' may be exacerbated by a glance of self-knowledge behind the image from which he vigorously turns away and dissociates: rejecting himself as he has been rejected. It may also bear reflection of the relationship between narcissism, envy and old age.

Many people have experienced elderly relatives becoming more unpleasant and spiteful as, perhaps with terror, they lose their power. In contemporary society the elderly are often treated as a nuisance, parasites on the wealth and time of the young, and targets of bullying. They draw on the narcissism of the young, and are seen not only as a burden, but a picture of the future. Oscar Wilde's Dorian Gray gives up his soul so that his portrait will grow older instead of his body. The portrait mercilessly records the traces of his excessive lifestyle, until he can no longer bear the sight of his 'mirror, mirror on the wall', and slashes it with a knife, and thus destroys himself. It is as if between youth and the elderly are the reciprocal roles of envied–envying and spontaneously powerful–powerfully weak.

Although Lear's professed intent is to retire, it soon becomes apparent he has no real wish to relinquish control but intends to function imperiously. It is as if the ageing process is an unreasonable and non-negotiable demand which brings a choice of responses, for example: (1) to gloomily submit, (2) rebelliously to take risks, or (3) to swap roles and make unreasonable and uncompromising or critical demands on the young.

Both Kohut (1972) and Kernberg (1984), while different, see narcissism as serving a defensive purpose against acknowledging the vulnerable, weak, dependent and devalued aspects of the self. Kernberg would see pathological narcissism as a sub-category of the Borderline Personality Organisation: the essential difference being that the narcissistic personality is characterised by an integrated, although highly pathological, grandiose self.

The borderline is seen, among other things, as displaying greater capacity for affect, which is certainly something we can relate to Lear as the play progresses. The four critical features of this personality structure according to Kernberg are:

1. Non-specific manifestations of ego-weakness;
2. A propensity to shift toward irrational dream-like thinking patterns in the context of generally intact reality testing;
3. Predominance of developmentally less mature psychological defences such as splitting, projection and projective identification and identity diffusion;
4. The related specific pathology of internal object relations, such that mental representations of important others are fragmented and strongly charged as either good or bad.

(Higgit and Fonagy 1992, p. 24)

In 'The borderline-narcissistic personality disorder continuum' Adler (1981) draws a developmental line with 'borderline aloneness' at one end, characterised by feelings of emptiness, hopelessness and despair, and at the other end 'a mature aloneness'. Borderline aloneness is different from loneliness in which a person longs to regain a lost object or experience. Instead there is an emptiness, possibly accompanied by rage and panic, and hence the difficulty for people with borderline personalities in coping with endings.

Empty feelings can escalate to intense, disintegrative anger, and empathic failures can become justifications for unbearable fury. This breakdown can progress to include fears and feelings of annihilation and disintegration. Decompensation can proceed to psychosis, but this is usually transient. If narcissism is a compensation then when that fails, borderline-like decompensation may occur. Does the narcissist, whose compensatory shell is cracked open, retain narcissistic traits but also shift states to a more borderline one?

Lear's reverberations split other characters so severely that there is a transference to his audience. This leads to an almost pantomime enlistment of the readers to take sides with the goodies and the baddies.

Bradley clearly confirms this when he writes how he feels haunted by the feeling in *King Lear* 'that we are witnessing something universal – a conflict not so much of particular person as of the powers of good and evil in the world' (Bradley 1910, p. 262).

From the start we are warned of the narcissistic use of children by ageing parents and the wielding of inheritance as power: Gloucester struggles with which son he favours most and whether to own the bastard Edmund. Then Lear manipulates his daughters thus:

> Meantime we shall express our darker purpose.
> Give me the map there. – Know that we have divided
> In three our Kingdom: and 'tis our fast intent
> To shake all cares and business from our age;
> Conferring them on younger strengths, while we
> Unburthen'd crawl toward death.
>
> (*King Lear*, 1.1.34)

We are warned that despite the reasons given we should be prepared for a 'darker purpose', the shadow side of the king contaminating his avowed aim. This play begins with endings, the process of which will explode a thunderbolt of light onto the reciprocal roles within the royal family, and there is strong symbolism in the splitting of the land.

We are introduced to Goneril, Regan and Cordelia as they are subjected to a ritual public humiliation whereby, in order to gain their inheritance, they must openly compete with each other for their father's love and state their devotion to him. Goneril confirms the task:

> Sir, I
> Do love you more than words can wield the matter;
> Dearer than eyesight, space and liberty . . .
>
> (*King Lear*, 1.1.54)

While Goneril can see the need to bend to her father's demand one senses she has paid the price of lack of power and liberty all her life. Sadly, as she later tries to change this she loses all. It is as if Goneril moves from a place of being powerlessly controlled by the insensitively controlling parent to a role of ruthlessly controlling others, almost being gnarled by power and freedom in her own ageing.

Cordelia introduces herself after this speech with an aside. This is an interesting, nay telling, way to introduce a character whom so very many critics, be they literary or psychoanalytic, see as so open and pure. She expresses part of her dilemma: 'What shall Cordelia do? Love, and be silent' (*King Lear*, 1.1.61). Does she mean true love or showpiece love?

Regan begins her speech in equally telling fashion:

> I am made of that self metal as my sister,
> And prize me at her worth. In my true heart
> I find she names my very deed of love
> Only she comes too short
> (*King Lear*, 1.1.68)

Regan refers to her alliance with Goneril, which by implication suggests she is not of that 'self metal' as Cordelia. Later Goneril is to remark how Lear always 'loved our sister most'. Unable to gain the same attention or love, Goneril and Regan grab power and land instead.

After Regan has spoken, there is another aside from Cordelia:

> Then, poor Cordelia!
> Any yet not so; since I am sure my love's
> More richer than my tongue.
> (*King Lear*, 1.1.75)

Note the initial seduction into feeling sorry for Cordelia followed by her assumption of superiority. We can consider the traditional view, that she is unwilling to betray her love in such a way, that she holds truth. Yet is that so? Is it only the ageing parent whose shadow side is being revealed? Lear then demands, 'what can you say, to draw / A third more opulent than your sisters? Speak' (*King Lear*, 1.1.81).

Rather than an opulent, flowery response Cordelia delivers the opposite: 'Nothing my Lord' (*King Lear*, 1.1.86). Lear can hardly believe his ears. He asks her to 'mend' her speech, but she continues:

> Good my lord
> You have begot me, bred me, loved me: I
> Return those duties back as are right fit,
> Obey you, love you, and most honour you.
> Why have my sisters husbands, if they say
> They love you all? Haply when I wed,
> That lord, whose hand must take my plight, shall carry
> Half my love with him, half my care and duty:
> Sure, I shall never marry like my sisters,
> To love my father all.
> (*King Lear*, 1.1.95)

Again we have the seduction of the dutiful daughter followed by contempt towards her sisters masked as logic. While clearly all her love could not rest with her father, surely it is a different kind of love? And yet is it? She uses the traditional marriage vows to describe how she has related to him. Of course, this could feed the incest theories that abound regarding Cordelia and Lear, which are also considered as explanation for her rejection of him. This could be dangerous speculation and equally, one could speculate the opposite: Goneril and Regan, abused and thrown to one side, while Cordelia is pure and unobtainable. Just.

More generally this rejection is viewed as Cordelia as heroine, standing firm, loving her father but unwilling to be manipulated. Hanly defends Cordelia:

> Lear's rage, which causes him to unleash the series of events leading to the final scene of destruction, is a reaction to Cordelia's perfectly healthy, decent and honest refusal of Lear's demand for an avowal that she love only him.
>
> (Hanly 1986, p. 214)

Cordelia's response to Lear would be perceived by Kohut as a flaw in a narcissistically perceived reality. In 'Thoughts on narcissism and narcissistic rage' Kohut describes aggression as it arises from the matrix of narcissistic imbalance. He points out that human aggression is most dangerous when it is attached to the 'two great absolute psychological constellations: the grandiose self and the archaic omnipotent object' (Kohut 1972, p. 378). Cordelia is a recalcitrant part of an expanded self over which Lear expects to exercise full control and whose mere independence or other-ness is an offence. There is no rest for those who have suffered a narcissistic injury.

With the help of Cordelia's prompting, Lear feels he has received 'nothing'. The focus is very much on Lear's response as he lashes out in rage: 'Here I disclaim all paternal care', and later, when Kent tries to intervene:

> Come not between the dragon and his wrath.
> I loved her most, and thought to set my rest
> On her kind nursery.
>
> (*King Lear*, 1.1.112)

In 'The absent mother in King Lear' Kahn (1986) considers Lear's 'darker purpose' to be both his frustrated incestuous desire on the one hand, and Lear seeing Cordelia as the rejecting mother in the above speech on the other.

Adelman (1992) in *Suffocating Mothers* sees Lear simultaneously as the father who abdicates and the son who must suffer the consequences of this abdication. While writers offer an explanation for Lear's appalling response does this necessarily mean Cordelia is fundamentally innocent in all this? Cordelia speaks hardly more than one hundred lines and yet has a huge impact on the play. Her allegiance to right obscures not only her truth, being a misunderstanding of love to father or husband as mentioned previously, but also rose-tints her severe response to the audience in an adulation of youth and beauty.

Bradley states, 'the reader refuses to admit into it any idea of imperfection, and is outraged when any share in her father's sufferings is attributed to the part she plays in the opening scene' (Bradley 1910, p. 317). Yet, who is publicly humiliating whom? Perhaps the answer is both: the reciprocal roles of rejecting–rejected. To paraphrase Ryle (1993) it follows that to 'understand' a relationship satisfactorily we need to understand two role procedures.

Cordelia's rejection of Lear is clearly shocking, particularly in Lear's assumptive world. His narcissistic crown is split asunder. In the rarefied air of his grandiosity he may well feel he has provided ideal care, particularly to Cordelia, and the script suggests this. We know, in the aforementioned 'dragon and his wrath' speech, Lear had set his heart on receiving ideal care from Cordelia in his twilight years. It is as if this slips out as Lear rapidly shifts states from admiring–admired to contemptuous –contemptible, and, in further uncontrolled reaction, ricochets into desperately seeking a haven in the ideal care state from which he is madly torn by the state of abuse until the end of the play. He is never to return to his original state. Ryle reminds us that those with personality disorders 'will operate with polarised judgements, the angels have the habit of falling to join the predominant demons populating their world and they know no middle ground' (Ryle 1993, p. 101). It is the disordering of personalities which gives the play such pace, the source of the real battle scenes.

If Cordelia is so good why put him through this? Questioning herself in asides, standing her ground is certainly not naive impulse. This is not Cordelia simply rebelling, this is Lear's cherished 'best object' annihilating him in public. She is bound to know this; indeed, she has longer to prepare her response than her sisters. How much would the favoured daughter find such public displays in competition with her sisters an affront to her position? Indeed, she may resent sharing at all, let alone being bandied as a prize for foreign kings.

Narcissism is deeply antagonistic to self-knowledge. Symington points out that one of the ways in which a person powerfully dominated by narcissistic currents destroys self-knowledge is to project the unwanted aspects of their character, 'jealousy, envy, sadism . . .' (Symington 1993, p. 11).

How much of Cordelia's baggage do we allow her sisters to carry? Perhaps, of course, she does not recognise Lear's narcissism, and consequently the risk of her own rejection, because she refuses to acknowledge her own narcissism. Whichever way we look at it we keep arriving back to narcissistic reciprocal roles. Favoured above all others and invested with narcissistic expectations, the little princess rears up and spits upon her father. They usurp each other from their thrones of admiring–admired, and if we understand this it explains how so many critics have been left clinging on to admiration and avoiding the fact that it is Cordelia's rejection which is the ultimate swerve setting the tragic course of the play. The mother is absent, generally long-deceased and thus missing to the ageing person as they step towards what terrifies them. Cordelia offers no comforting breast and highlights Lear's aloneness. Lear begins to decompensate at this colossal public exposure and the shattering of his image of Cordelia. All following rejections add salt to the gaping narcissistic wound.

It is as if, at this point, the maternal presence splits in two; the benign and nurturant mother, with whom Lear would merge, generates her opposite in his eyes, and she becomes the annihilating mother who seeks his death. She reiterates the threat of death itself: 'Nothing'. This having been set in motion it is Goneril and Regan who are seen to be the real annihilating mothers as Cordelia successfully splits off that part of herself, still seducing our admiration.

Cordelia tries to convince us of her piety:

> If for I want that glib and oily art
> To speak and purpose not; since what I well intend,
> I'll do before I speak.
>
> (*King Lear*, 1.1.223)

This shows how carefully she thinks before she speaks. Lear has perhaps picked up on this inadvertently, when earlier in the scene he says, 'Let pride, which she calls plainness marry her' (*King Lear*, 1.1.128). Cordelia is further inflating herself with superiority disguised as virtue in response to Lear's inflation of rage, triggered by his deflation by Cordelia. She continues this stance to the end of the scene when, with

Lear out of earshot, she addresses her sisters. Note it is Cordelia who uses her tongue scathingly in this exchange:

> I know what you are;
> And, like a sister, am most loath to call
> Your faults as they are named
> . . . stood I within his grace
> I would prefer him to a better place.
>
> (*King Lear*, 1.1.267)

Again the good–bad split which one finds in so many readings of this play. Even the feminist writers, such as Kahn, have not been able to struggle out of this crevasse: 'Cordelia's goodness is as absolute and inexplicable as her sisters' reprovable badness' (Kahn 1986, p. 46). The skin of the family splits and falls away like dead cells.

If one uses reciprocal roles to help reformulate Scene One one can see not only how Cordelia inherited the narcissistic crown of procedures from Lear but also how Goneril and Regan must have suffered: how their father treated them as less than, and now rejected, becomes dependent on them. No wonder they reflect on this scene with trepidation. As they discuss what has occurred they consider that Lear will now be staying with each of them alternately, which implies it will be harder to stand up to him separately. Goneril attributes age to Lear's outburst and change of heart and is clearly perturbed: 'he always loved our sister most, and with what poor judgement he hath now cast her off, appears too grossly . . .' (*King Lear*, 1.1.287). While Regan agrees that age is playing its part, she reminds Goneril, 'yet he hath ever but slenderly known himself' (*King Lear*, 1.1.290). Goneril agrees but feels age will only serve to make things worse.

> The best and soundest of his time hath been but rash; then must we look to receive from his age not alone, the imperfections of long-engrafted condition, but therewithal, the unruly waywardness that infirm and choleric years bring with them.
>
> (*King Lear*, 1.1.292)

Long-suffering, they fear more 'unconstant starts'. Shaken by his treatment of Cordelia, they fear what will rain down on them: 'We must do something, and i' the heat' (*King Lear*, 1.1.304).

They do well to fear the future as well as grasp opportunity. In the absence of a balancing mother the Oedipal conflict is careering out of control. So far Cordelia has been closer to the parent Lear, at the expense not of her mother but of her sisters. Thus Cordelia has replaced the mother as envied object to be slain. But Lear has strangely put her out of harm's way, for now. The Oedipal conflict has to set its sights elsewhere and in the meeting of Narcissus and Oedipus it fragments as the older sisters wish Lear dead, and turn on each other. As they struggle to cope with Lear they also struggle with a change in their position.

Edmund offers a replacement home for Goneril's and Regan's original repertoire of reciprocal roles now contaminated by being in different, more powerful positions: not least because of Lear's unexpected change of heart regarding Cordelia and his consequent dependence upon the two older daughters. Paradoxically this increases their fear of him. The unleashing of Lear's rage includes envy of his daughters' comparative youth, creative potential and sexuality. This explodes as if ageing were both narcissistic injury and castration. He cries:

> Into her womb convey sterility
> Dry up in her the organs of increase,
> And from her derogate body never spring
> A babe to honour her.
> (*King Lear*, 1.4.79)

Pearl King (1980, p. 153) writes of the pressures which seem to operate as sources of anxiety and concern during the second half of life, including the fear of loss of sexual potency. The idea of retiring suggests a loss of sense of identity, children having left home, awareness of ageing and probable dependency on others and the inevitability of death. In narcissism the ego can become parasitical on one's role. If there is no adequate image, apart from the role, it can be a consequence that there is no appropriate sense of ontological security. The fear of loss of sexual potency may bring on a version of castration anxiety, and indeed, Kohut's old-fashioned notion of organ inferiority.

For Goneril and Regan as sexual adults, Edmund particularly offers a reciprocation for their learnt sado-masochism, as well as his own urge to be free of the bondage of bastardy and to penetrate to the power of others in the process. Already, Goneril and Regan are seemingly dominatrix in their marriages and Edmund offers the sadistically seductive reciprocation of dominator. This is further tantalised by the sisters' competition with each other in a fairy tale of 'who is the fairest?'. Their internal demons become like the wicked magician in *The Snow Queen* and make this 'mirror, mirror on the wall' not only one which rids the play of hope, by having the power to cause everything good and beautiful reflected in it to shrink up almost to nothing; but also ugly and useless things were made to appear ten times larger and worse than they were. Like ageing.

The quickening tempo of the dance of death begun by Lear is not only between Edmund and Goneril or Edmund and Regan. As Edmund engages in dominatrix–dominatee with Goneril, Regan is dominated by this exclusive pairing which in the true sado-masochistic stimulation excites her appetite further as she responds by seeking to dominate her sister in order to receive domination from Edmund. Ultimately the interplay of these reciprocating roles escalates into a bloody lust slaying the flesh with the perfect sado-masochistic reciprocating climax of murder and suicide.

Goneril and Regan also identify with Edmund as outcasts: he also suffered deprivation and rejection, he in favour of 'legitimate Edgar', they in favour of Snow White Cordelia:

> Why brand they us
> With base? With base-ness? Bastardy? Base, Base?
> *(King Lear*, 1.2.9)

Edmund uses being the outcast as his reason to let the id run amok:

> Thou nature art my goddess; to thy law
> My services are bound.
> *(King Lear*, 1.2.1)

Edmund's war cry 'Now God stand up for bastards' reminds us that his problem is simply one of legitimacy: Gloucester is mentally whole. Goneril and Regan though are struggling with Lear's disintegration. In the first scene Lear hints towards the urge to regress and the want for ideal care. The frustration of his fusion fantasy contributes to the borderlining of the state.

Ryle states, 'In both conditions [borderline personality, narcissistic personality] abuse or contempt of the self may take place. In Borderline Personality (BP) organisation the breakthrough of unintegrated extreme feeling states may occur, but the narcissistic individual is characteristically out of touch with deep feeling' (Ryle 1993, p. 106). By the middle of the first scene Lear is beside himself and certainly in touch with deep feeling; Cordelia maintains her stance despite the verbal assault. Much as Lear tries to compensate with Goneril and Regan, there is a desperation which suggests he knows that not only has he lost Cordelia but there is no ideal care to be had elsewhere.

Lear seems to become almost delinquent if we believe Goneril and Regan's description of his behaviour as he carouses with his men. Perhaps the shaking off of all responsibilities, perhaps the acting out of rage towards death, is part of this:

> every hour
> He flashes into one gross crime or other,
> That sets us all at odds.
>
> (*King Lear*, 1.3.4)

The rattling to a borderline state continues as Lear lurches from one pole of his dilemma to the other: narcissistic tyrant to aggrieved victim. Is it so monstrous that Goneril wishes to avoid Lear? Or, does it put us in mind of many who buck-pass with difficult elderly relatives? Remember, she is frightened of this man and it is not surprising when she gets the opportunity for power over him that she seizes it. How long had she reciprocated with cloying submissiveness? The Fool tries to warn Lear, as usual to no avail:

> The hedge-sparrow fed the cuckoo so long,
> That it had its head bit off by its young
> So, out went the candle, and we were left darkling.
>
> (*King Lear*, 1.4.216)

Goneril may well be guilty of malicious exaggeration as she drives Lear away with criticism and rejection of his behaviour. Lear's response is from a violently conflicted state and it is clear she is expected to pay for him being her father:

> Ingratitude! Thou marble-hearted fiend,
> More hideous, when thou shew'st thee in a child
> Than the sea monster.
>
> (*King Lear*, 1.4.260)

He then grieves the perfect reflection he lost:

> O most small fault,
> How ugly didst thou in Cordelia shew!
>
> (*King Lear*, 1.4.267)

Cordelia still haunts them both. Lear is unable to see beyond this as he cries:

O Lear, Lear, Lear!
Beat at this gate that let thy folly in
And thy dear judgement out!
(*King Lear*, 1.4.271)

But folly and judgement pass each other by.

Lear, already badly shaken by Goneril's rejection, tries to cling on to the last delusion that Regan will offer him comfort. This includes the only reference to their mother, one of contempt when he states that if Regan had not been glad to see him he would divorce himself 'from thy mother's tomb, / Sepulchring an adult'ress' (*King Lear*, 2.4.127). He fawns over Regan while denigrating Goneril:

You nimble lightnings, dart your blinding flames
Into her scornful eyes! Infect her beauty,
You fen-sucked fogs, drawn by the powerful sun,
To fall and blast her pride.
(*King Lear*, 2.4.161)

Regan astutely protests that it will soon be her turn, but Lear is blind to the obvious: 'No Regan thou shalt never have my curse' (*King Lear*, 2.4.166). There follows an auction as Goneril and Regan bargain with Lear to reduce his train and Regan compounds his humiliation by advising him to apologise to Goneril. Lear is tossed backwards and forwards as he begs for a home, bewildered by Regan's stand. It is too painful for him to see.

Lear seeks two mutually exclusive things at once: to have absolute control over those closest to him and to be absolutely dependent upon them. When Cordelia does not feed him with love he thinks angrily of eating her:

The barbarous Scythian,
Or he that makes his generation messes
To gorge his appetite, shall to my bosom
Be as well neighbour'd, pitied and relieved
As thou my sometime daughter.
(*King Lear*, 1.1.115)

In the child's pre-Oedipal experience of himself and his mother as an undifferentiated dual unity, she and the breast are part of him, at his command. Freud refers to this ironically as 'his majesty, the baby' (1912, p. 72): a second childhood?

Adelman asks us to consider how Lear might be glimpsing another truth. As he recognises his terrifying dependence on female forces outside himself he is equally terrified with how this puts him in touch with the femaleness within himself:

> That thou hast power to shake my manhood thus:
> That these hot tears which break from me . . .
> > . . . Old fond eyes,
> Beweep this cause again, I'll pluck you out.
> > (*King Lear*, 1.4.299–305)

and later:

> O, how this mother swells up toward my heart!
> Hysterica passio, – down, though climbing sorrow.
> > (*King Lear*, 2.4.54)

Lear is not only trapped in his assumptive belief of his place in the world as King and Father, but also as a man. I wonder if as his need for the mother increases with age and loss of power he feels his loss of manhood as physical strength and sexual libido withers and softens, imagining the penis becoming the labia to which he is drawn with contempt, loathing and fear. No wonder he curses Goneril, 'Dry up in her the organs of increase' (*King Lear*, 1.4.280). By the end of Act One Lear is battling against losing his mind, seemingly aware of how toxic his anger can be:

> O let me not be mad, not mad, sweet heaven!
> Keep me in temper; I would not be mad.
> > (*King Lear*, 1.5.3)

Cox and Theilgaard refers to Lear's madness in the storm as due to 'senile dementia and dissociative phenomena' (1994, p. 392). Despite his rantings Lear shows no signs of short-term memory failure. Are the mental difficulties of the elderly too often termed senile dementia?

Kernberg's text *Severe Personality Disorders* is one of the few that acknowledges personality disorders in old age. Narcissistic personalities experience throughout the years a deterioration of their world of internalised object relations, including the unconscious devaluation of both their own past (in order not to feel envy of the past) and of what others have (in order not to envy others). Hence these people do not have at their disposal the normal gratification that comes from memories of past experiences and of others they love. Lear's fantasy has been torn out. Kernberg states that 'in many cases the vicious circle of devaluation and emptiness becomes insurmountable' (1984, p. 72). Couple this with the falling away of support, death of peers, and failing health, and it suggests old age may well exacerbate known personality disorders or latent ones. For Lear it brings his target problem harshly in front of his face: 'I do not know how to cope with any disturbance to my omnipotent reflection.'

By the time Lear reaches the heath the rejection he has experienced is staggering. In *Shakespeare Comes to Broadmoor* actor Brian Cox finds 'Lear as a part, monstrous; a real monster of a part. It is partly because it is all to do with rejection' (quoted by Murray Cox 1992, p. 51). Certainly Lear has plenty to dissociate from.

Davies (1992) points out that Lear goes mad after a series of disasters. Presumably as the body becomes weaker so does the mind, so healthy defence against mental difficulties becomes harder and recovery less complete. Bradley writes: 'What are those sufferings of a strong man like Othello to those of hapless age?' (1910, p. 274).

Borderline patients and psychotics have great difficulty dealing with the boundaries of self and other. Either the size of the boundary is exaggerated or the wall is so frail that it fails to separate self and other, so that identity confusion, diffusion or even dispersal can result. Such boundary issues influence the mode of psychological defence that defends most effectively. Thus projection necessitates a line of division, a wall over which feelings and attitudes can be thrown. Cox and Theilgaard (1994, p. 353) point out that at the psychotic extremity, projection becomes nigh on impossible because there are no self–other boundaries. He has in mind such processes as encroachment or engulfment when self–other boundaries operate more in the nature of an amoeba, as described by Kernberg (1984).

Lear's last clear attempt to despatch his pain is upon meeting Poor Tom (Edgar disguised as a lunatic). Completely caught up in what he feels is persecution by Goneril and Regan, he projects that Poor Tom is in a similar state: 'What have his daughters brought him to this pass?' (*King Lear*, 3.4.62), and, despite Kent's interventions continues unabated:

> Death, traitor! nothing could have subdued nature
> To such a lowness, but his unkind daughters.
>
> (*King Lear*, 3.4.69)

Lear seems to tip over the edge at this stage as if seeing Edgar's feigned madness as a true reflection of himself. Edgar meanwhile is in his plight due to his father's blindness, the parallel process of the sub-plot. One wonders how sane he really remains, confronted with mad father Lear ranting about betrayal. Furthermore, Gloucester, unwitting in Edgar's company, cries:

> I am almost mad myself: I had a son
> Now outlaw'd from my blood; he sought my life,
> But lately, very late: I loved him friend, –
> No father his son dearer.
>
> (*King Lear*, 3.4.166)

Meanwhile Goneril and Regan act out their fears of annihilation on Gloucester. Their cruelty is hideously out of control as Goneril demands, 'Pluck out his eyes' (*King Lear*, 3.7.5). Their way of trying to hide their bullying state is not only to punish Gloucester but to rid themselves of the observing eyes. One has a sense of mocked–mocking in this scene. After Gloucester has one eye gouged out Regan remarks: 'One side will mock another; the other too' (*King Lear*, 3.7.70). One wonders how often Regan has felt mocked by her father, who only had eyes for Cordelia, by Goneril, and now by anyone whom she might suspect of truly seeing her. It is she who disabuses Gloucester of the idea that Edmund might help him:

> Thou call'st on him that hates thee: it was he
> That made the overture of thy treason to us.
>
> (*King Lear*, 3.7.87)

Kohut notes that 'the ability to perform an act of gross self-mutilation depends, in some instances at least, on the fact that the organ which the psychotic removes has lost its narcissistic libidinal cathexis i.e. it is not any more part of the self and can therefore be discarded as a foreign body' (Kohut 1972, p. 376). It is as if Goneril and Regan have projected their masochistic loathing of self-reflection onto Goucester, twisting the biblical command, 'If thine eye offends thee pluck it out' (Matthew 18.9). It is so utterly awful that it almost elicits the hysterical response of laughter, as Regan mocks Gloucester some more: 'Go thrust him out at gates, and let him smell / His way to Dover' (*King Lear*, 3.7.92). It is difficult to hang onto Goneril and Regan as damaged children at such a point.

This brings me to the penultimate part of the play, and to what could be considered Gloucester's reformulation. The bloody plucking results in blind Gloucester, with weeping sockets, finally gaining some insight. It prepares the possibility for the still disguised Edgar not only saving Gloucester from killing himself (his response to being blinded by the truth) but also to turning this to advantage and giving some weight to his precarious self, lost and bruised by colluding with Edmund's manipulation. As Gloucester stands at the cliff edge he has to rely on Edgar's description of life below, no longer having eyes to lower to look down from an exalted place:

> and you tall anchoring bark
> Diminish'd to her cock; her cock a buoy
> Almost too small for sight.
> (*King Lear*, 4.6.18)

When Gloucester jumps but a few feet, Edgar convinces him it is a miracle, the implication being Gloucester deserves to live. I cannot help but wonder if Gloucester was not humouring Edgar, for indeed this brings Edgar back from the brink too. Certainly as a suicide reformulation exit, it works.

What becomes of The Fool? For many it is an incomplete ending. A Fool of such significant speech is simply mentioned no more. Many assume his plight is referred to in Lear's final speech: 'And my poor Fool is hang'd' (*King Lear*, 5.3.305). However, I believe this refers to Cordelia. Davies points out that 'The Fool disappears as soon as the king in his madness takes over the role of expressing the unpopular truths about the harsh realities of an unjust world' (Davies 1992, p. 46) where old is expendable and death is inevitable.

While I consider the use of The Fool as observing eye later, I consider him as damaging eye now. The Fool points out harsh realities, but as Therapist he is like the psychoanalyst holding up a terrifying mirror for the borderline to face everything he has tried to keep at bay. It will not go away and The Fool will not be quiet. As Therapist The Fool exposes too much too soon and Lear fragments in the face of truth and goes mad. It warns us of the danger for any therapist making omnipotent observations and interpretations ahead of the patient's process. Lear loses sight of the therapist but also destroys him.

Unlike Bradley I do not believe Lear was healed by his long sleep and sojourn into madness. It is as if Bradley had in mind the biblical reformulation where, cast out, one finds one's true self and thence, returning from the wilderness, all is well. The snag is, this leads to expectations of perfect endings. At the end of the play Lear is still seeking his paradise.

There are some changes in Lear. The psychosis has abated. He has been able to tell Gloucester that he, Lear, 'smells of mortality' (*King Lear*, 4.6.133), which has a sense of major developmental achievement. The rage has subsided as he moves forward from his dilemma of either aggrieved victim or narcissistic tyrant. Or does he?

Hanly (1986) clearly feels that Lear's narcissistic blindness persists to the end. The insights that took his mind by storm concern the reality of the human condition when the narcissistic supports and stays of office, privilege, wealth and power have been stripped away.

> Poor naked wretches, whereso'er you are
> That bide the pelting of this pitiless storm,
> How shall your houseless heads, and unfed sides,
> Your loop'd and window'd raggedness, defend you
> From season such as these? O, I have ta'en
> Too little care of this! Take physic, pomp;
> Expose thyself to feel what wretches feel.
>   (*King Lear*, 3.4.28)

Quite rightly, Hanly turns to Lear's relationship with Cordelia to assess where Lear has moved to in the final scene and suggests that Lear remains 'as blind as ever to Cordelia's needs, to her separate existence' (Hanly 1986, p. 217). As at the beginning, the heart of the matter lies in Lear's relationship to his daughters and to himself.

Kahn (1986) is more forgiving and feels Lear has realised what his original childish demands on his daughters led to. She cites his literal awakening as evidence, his tears those of ashamed self-knowledge:

> Do not laugh at me;
> For, as I am a man, I think this lady
> To be my child Cordelia.
>   (*King Lear*, 4.7.68)

He can stop imagining her as the maternal woman that he yearned for and accept his separateness from her. Yet he also calls her his child, acknowledging the bond of paternity that he denied in the first act.

Unconvinced, I wonder if Lear, rather than moving forward from his dilemma has not in actuality reversed out of it, still caught up in a fantasy. I think the following speech is essential to understanding where Lear is at the end of the play: as they face prison, Lear says to Cordelia:

> Come, lets away to prison:
> We two alone will sing like birds i'the cage;

> When thou dost ask me blessing, I'll kneel down
> And ask of thee forgiveness. So we'll live,
> And pray, and sing, and tell old tales, and laugh
> At gilded butterflies, and hear poor rogues
> Talk of court news.
>
> (*King Lear*, 5.3.8)

Kahn reflects on this that 'parent and child are equal, the gestures of deference that ordinarily denote patriarchal authority now transformed into signs of reciprocal love' (Kahn 1986, p. 48).

Again, as at the beginning, we need to refer to Cordelia. Lear shows no signs of considering his daughters' feelings, nor that they may well be executed. Lear's speech above is a response to Cordelia's response to being arrested:

> We are not the first,
> Who, with best meaning, have incurr'd the worst.
> For thee, oppressed king, am I cast down;
> Myself could else out-frown false fortune's frown.
>
> (*King Lear*, 5.3.4)

This speech sums up the beginning of the play for Cordelia as much as the end. She is telling us that the predicament she now finds herself in is due to her trying to do her best, just as she maintained she was in the first scene. Whatever remorse prompted her to try and help Lear, once again she executes it with lofty thinking without considering the consequences. Those, such as Albany, who would not have fought against Cordelia or Lear have been forced into that position in a defence of their country against the French army. Again, Cordelia has acted in a way that is a magnet for public attention, and again Lear is impervious to all but what he wants. I can almost imagine the prison bars as those of a cot as Lear copes the only way he can.

Weighed down by his procedures, it must be a struggle for Lear not to regress to Cordelia as mother, particularly as he now truly faces nothing. In Cordelia's death is his own. We now experience Lear with a dignity sorely missing from many of our encounters and perhaps he needs to be forgiven at the end. For Hanly this is impossible, and he views Lear with contempt while telling us that 'Cordelia is nature's martyr' (Hanly 1986, p. 217). While others do not share his harsh view of Lear, by this stage the sanctifying of Cordelia is almost unanimous.

Adelman sees Cordelia transformed from loving but stubbornly self-righteous daughter to 'holy mother surrounded by the nimbus of redemption' (Adelman 1992, p. 120). As the script comments, when

Cordelia originally hears of Lear's plight, 'there she shook / The holy water from her heavenly eyes' (*King Lear*, 4.3.30). Adelman suggests Cordelia's return seems to give Lear everything he wanted (everything he had been punished for): a renewed fantasy of fusion. But surely Lear is punished again by Cordelia's death?

Kahn eulogises Cordelia in the same vein: 'Like the Virgin Mary, she intercedes magically' (1986, p. 47). While Bradley points out that the devotion Cordelia inspires almost inevitably obscures her part in the tragedy, he still refers to her as 'enskyed' and 'sainted' (1910, p. 317). What Bradley and the psychoanalysts fail to point out is the connection between Cordelia and the Virgin Mary's son: martyrdom in death.

Cordelia's stage exit, in taking us to the borderline of idealisation, is perhaps the perfect narcissistic death. When the rest of us become nothing the martyr becomes someone, held aloft, memory only serving to paint a more perfectly pure picture, vehemently guarded by time. The long rope back to her original childhood script has finally choked her words to death.

Momentarily fused, Lear carries her like a new bride across the threshold. Is Shakespeare trying to help us reflect on the true relationship when he gives Lear a mirror to hold over Cordelia to see if she still breathes: an ironic touch in a tale of lack of self-reflection and eyes blinded by procedures.

In true bodily reciprocation Lear's throat begins to constrict: 'Pray you, undo this button' (*King Lear*, 5.3.309) and as the living do for the newly dead, vainly hopes for signs of life. It takes until his last blink for him finally to see, what?

> Do you see this? look on her, – look, – her lips, –
> Look there, look there! (*He dies*).
>
>   (*King Lear*, 5.3.310)

Lear leaves us as he began, unable to face an ending.

Due to its insistence the patient and therapist agree to the timing of the conclusion in advance; the time-limited model of CAT turns us to face endings in the therapeutic arena. This can also cause us to experience the reverberations from endings in the past. We cannot turn away as Lear does or scornfully minimise the deaths of Goneril and Regan as Albany does.

> Produce their bodies, be they alive or dead! –
> This judgement of the heavens, that makes us tremble
> Touches us not with pity.
>
>   (*King Lear*, 5.3.228)

It is in the meeting of Edmund's dying words with Goneril and Regan's bodies that so much tragedy is gathered as words in a teardrop. It was not always so – typically Edmund's attitude to the overtures of Goneril and Regan has been one of supreme callousness.

> To both of these sisters have I sworn my love;
> . . . Neither can be enjoy'd
> If both remain alive.
>
> (*King Lear*, 5.1.55–8)

His dilemma is solved when Goneril poisons Regan and later kills herself. But, as he lies dying and sees their bodies, Edmund is stirred to grieve for all the unwanted children: understanding that nothing equals love.

> Yet Edmund was beloved
> The one the other poisoned for my sake,
> And after slew herself.
>
> (*King Lear*, 5.3.238)

Nothing but abuse.

It has been essential to witness their pain, just as it was essential to recognise Cordelia's reciprocal role. She is not a million miles from her sisters. Kernberg (1984) has referred explicitly to the psychopath as a severe variant of the narcissistic personality disorder. Meloy reminds us that the weight of clinical research supports this. Perhaps, in an explanation of Goneril's and Regan's object relations, he states: 'In the case of the psychopathic character, the result would be a primary identification with the aggressor and a renunciation of weaker, more benign, and perhaps more nurturing object representations' (Meloy 1988, p. 19).

What damns Goneril and Regan and their ilk further is men's demand that they be ideal carers, and women's collusion with that: the universal rule that bad women are more evil than bad men! The feminist psychoanalyst subjugates her politics by seeing Cordelia as martyr, the ideal and antidote to her sisters. It is the integration of women that is the exit.

What of Lear? Where is his exit? The integration of The Fool may give Lear insight, but I cannot agree with Miller who states, after The Fool disappears, 'everything Lear says afterwards is sane and wise' (1993, p. 36). We need the integration of The Fool as observing eye so that Lear is supported in a growing sense of the relation between cause and effect. CAT, through its concept of the Procedural Sequence Model, focuses on the linking of aim, plan, action, result and evaluation. As Bradley points out, the behaviour and thinking of Lear shows 'a strict connection between act and consequence' (1910, p. 284). Perhaps Lear needs to lose his senses in order to restore his sanity. Shakespeare uses Lear's madness as, among other things, a device for stripping away the narcissistic illusory aspects of royalty in order to try and lay bare what is essential to the human condition, including ageing. Hanly reminds us that 'it is this very narcissistic illusion which Shakespeare was concerned to penetrate, that many critics have found necessary to preserve their idealisation of Lear' (1986, p. 211).

With his penetrative wit The Fool punctures the straitjacket of 'Look at Me!' – 'What will People think?' He trips up shame and ruffles the stately hair. His aim seems to be to induce Lear to 'resume' his power and he acts as the king's pricking conscience. It is a perilous position and we know how easily the observing eye can become 'a vile jelly', bloodshot with the stare of the cruelly powerful therapist.

In the infancy of this play CAT shows how Lear and all his daughters turned away from each other and from self-reflection while initially professing to do the opposite. In identifying the target problem CAT shows how dreadfully Lear compounds this through the procedures, and the CAT focus of reciprocal roles and the impact of endings helps show the first and last scenes in their true expanse. We are able to hear their stories as they speak:

> The description of a person's reciprocal role repertoire, constructed on the basis of the early history, patterns of relationships, evident self-management procedures . . . offers a valuable, high level understanding of intrapsychic and interpersonal processes and of their relation to each other.
>
> (Ryle 1994, p. 109)

In summary for the King himself:

Target Problem:

I do not know how to cope with any disturbance to my omnipotent reflection. (I do not know how to cope with ageing.)

Target Problem Procedures:

Trap:

'Nothing begets nothing.'

Dilemma:
> Either narcissistic tyrant or aggrieved victim.

Snag:
> 'Lest his ungovern'd rage dissolve the life that wants the means to lead it.'

The lesson of flawed procedures:
> To try and give up responsibility but to try and retain power throws everything and everyone out of balance. The unbalanced characters fragment and go mad or move toward psychopathic activities.

Lear has not learnt the lesson of suffering by the end of the play. Hildebrand (1982) states that with ageing comes a considerable change in object relations and suggests that brief therapy is of more use to older people, as time is clearly limited. Personal Construct Therapists emphasise the need for the elderly to have their stories heard.

> By holding up a mirror to nature, Shakespeare's portrayal of men and women, fathers and mothers, sons and daughters gives an ontological status to object relations. This has not been surpassed by modern methods of coding information and collecting data.
>
> (Cox and Theilgaard 1994, p. 263)

Shakespeare, as teacher of the life cycle, shows us the changing dynamics of ageing in which the elderly are deemed a burden and treated with contempt. *King Lear* illuminates this contemporary position that affects us all. The psychotherapist had better be prepared.

> but I am bound
> Upon a wheel of fire, that mine own tears
> Do scald like molten lead.
> (*King Lear*, 4.7.46)

References

Adelman, J. (1992) *Suffocating Mothers: Fantasies of Maternal Origin in Shakespeare's Plays*. London: Routledge.

Adler, G. (1981) The borderline-narcissistic personality disorder continuum. *American Journal of Psychiatry* 138(1): 46–50.

Bradley, A. C. (1910) *Shakespearean Tragedy*. London: Macmillan.

Cox, Murray (ed.) (1992) *Shakespeare Comes to Broadmoor*. London: Jessica Kingsley.

Cox, Murray, and Theilgaard, A. (1994) *Shakespeare as Prompter*. London: Jessica Kingsley.

Davies, D. R. (1992) *Scenes of Madness: A Psychiatrist at the Theatre*. London: Routledge.

Freud, S. (1912) A note on the unconscious in psychoanalysis. In *General Psychological Theory* (1963). New York: Collier Books.

Hanly, C. (1986) Lear and his daughters. *International Review of Psycho-Analysis* 13: 211–20.

Hess, N. (1987) *King Lear* and some anxieties of old age. *British Journal of Medical Psychology* 60: 205–9.

Higgit, A., and Fonagy, P. (1992) Psychotherapy in Borderline and Narcissistic Personality Disorder. *British Journal of Psychiatry* 161: 23–43.

Hildebrand, H. P. (1982) Psychotherapy with older patients. *British Journal of Medical Psychology* 55: 19–28.

Jacoby, M. (1990) *Individuation and Narcissism*. London: Routledge.

Kahn, C. (1986) The absent mother in *King Lear*. In M. Fergusson, M. Quilligan, and N. J. Vickers (eds), *Rewriting the Renaissance: The Discoveries of Sexual Difference in Early Modern Europe*. Chicago: University of Chicago Press.

Kernberg, O. (1984) *Severe Personality Disorders*. New Haven and London: Yale University Press.

King, P. (1980) The life cycle as indicated by the nature of the transference in the psychoanalysis of the middle-aged and elderly. *International Journal of the Psychoanalytic Association* 61: 153.

Kohut, H. (1972) Thoughts on narcissism and narcissistic rage. *The Psychoanalytic Study of the Child* 27: 360–400.

Meloy, J. R. (1988) *The Psychopathic Mind: Origins, Dynamics and Treatment*. Northvale, NJ: Aronson.

Miller, J. (1993) *King Lear* in rehearsal: a talk. In B. J. Sokol (ed.), *The Undiscover'd Country: New Essays on Psychoanalysis and Shakespeare*. London: Free Association Books.

Pulver, S. E. (1970) Narcissism: the term and concept. *Journal of the American Psychoanalytic Association* 18: 319–41.

Ryle, A. (1993) *Cognitive-Analytic Therapy: Active Participation in Change*. London: John Wiley.

Ryle, A. (1994) Projective identification: a particular form of reciprocal role procedure. *British Journal of Medical Psychology* 67: 104–14.

Shakespeare, William (1994) *King Lear*. Ware: Wordsworth Classics.

Symington, Neville (1993) *Narcissism: A New Theory*. London: Karnac.

Chapter 6

The case of Michael
(Therapist Madeleine Loates)

Madeleine Loates

The following case is that of a 70-year-old man, referred for therapy by a psychiatrist who had been treating him for depression. He has given consent to material from our sessions together to be used in this case study. All names have been changed to preserve anonymity.

Michael was a 70-year-old man, married to a woman in her early forties, with whom he had had two children, now teenagers. He was referred for therapy by a psychiatrist who had been treating him for depression. He had found anti-depressant medication of no help, and the psychiatrist felt unable to help him further, having felt exasperated by his attitude to her. Michael in turn remarked at our first meeting that he felt the psychiatrist was not intelligent enough to help him.

Assessment

Michael was the eldest of three boys from a town in the north. His parents were a professional couple and he described the family setting as 'formal'. His father was an intelligent and thoughtful man but a little distant from his children. Michael's mother was domineering and controlling of her husband, imposing her sense of how she felt he should live his life. She was intensely ambitious for her children, feeling that nothing was good enough for them. Michael remarked that she taught her children contempt of others, that to be 'normal' or 'average' was terrible, a view of oneself therefore as contemptible if one did not shine. Michael's recollection of early family life was of happiness – he was allowed enormous freedom to follow his creative instincts from an early age, but as he grew up he became aware of tension between his parents, and by the time he reached teenage years began to feel constrained by his mother's need to live through her children, and her desire for their affection and company. He was aware that his mother would act the martyr – responding with tears and a sense of recrimination if Michael would not spend time with her. Michael found a way of coping by entertaining and thus diverting his parents in order to diffuse difficult situations. He went to university locally but after a year felt he had to leave the stifling atmosphere of home and 'escaped' abroad. However, he described the event as being 'unfaithful' to his mother, giving some sense of the intensity of the relationship. He described finding a series of people in his life that had 'rescued' him from difficult situations.

Over his adult life Michael had significant creative and financial success. He had three long-term relationships, with adult children from his first marriage and teenage children from his present marriage. However, he felt that his current difficulties had been developing over the last ten to fifteen years – a major creative project had not developed as expected, leaving him with significant financial problems, and he now felt that others would perceive him as too old to be employed. In addition, his marriage was under strain – his wife had 'grown up' during their time together, and had become independent of him. In recent months his teenage sons had become rude and demanding, playing their parents off between each other, with Michael giving in to them. Michael's wife Isabelle blamed him for their behaviour, accusing him of spoiling them when they were young.

Michael named his problems as depression and procrastination and said that he wished to regain his verve, but it was difficult beyond that to explore what he felt might be different as a result of therapy, as much of the focus at that time was the failure of a business venture. During the assessment Michael would frequently go off at a tangent, quoting books he was reading, including books by other therapists. He talked about well-known people with whom he had been involved in business, telling stories about exploits which while entertaining seemed to purposefully demonstrate his many successes in earlier life. I found myself struggling to find a way to get him back onto talking about his current difficulties, and this style of relating featured throughout the whole of therapy.

Michael was asked to complete the Psychotherapy File, but he came to the next session angry and dismissive of it, feeling that it categorised and limited him, and wondered how anyone could react in such a black-and-white way. However, part of the form was completed in discussion and he identified the following:

Traps: 'fear of hurting others'.

Dilemmas: 'keeping feelings bottled up' (only in relation to his wife

Isabelle); 'if I must then I won't'; 'either I look down on other people, or I feel they look down on me'.

Difficult and unstable states of mind: 'sometimes the only way to cope with some feelings (being unreasonably angry) is to blank them off and feel emotionally distant from others'.

Different states: 'cut off from own feelings, cut off from others, disconnected'; 'vulnerable, needy, passively helpless, waiting for rescue'; 'resentfully submitting to demands'.

During these early sessions certain patterns and themes emerged.

Michael's early pattern of relationships was based on his being special and different from others, and that to be 'ordinary' was to be beneath contempt. An intelligent man, he had been successful in both creative and financial terms, and this had sustained him during adult life. However, having reached older age several things had changed – others no longer recognised or rewarded his creative skill and he was highly contemptuous of those who he felt had treated him badly. He was unsure of his employability because of his age. His wife and children whom he had 'created' were growing up and away from him and were treating him with bullying contempt.

Michael had never had a need for others but had always 'lived in his head'. He recognised that he had admired skills in others and had used them. As his relationship was deteriorating he found himself unable to talk to his wife and children about what was happening.

From the history and my experience during the assessment sessions, several reciprocal roles suggested themselves. There was a strong sense of *Admiring–Admired*; it felt as if Michael wanted me to know the circles he had moved in, and there was a seductive battle to draw me into discussion of his reading and thinking about topics that had nothing to do with therapy. *Contemptuous–Contemptible/humiliated (angry)*: At the same time I was conscious of his contemptuous manner towards others in the past, particularly within his creative world but also currently with those who failed to recognise his ability and genius. There was a strong sense of *Controlling–Controlled/suffocated or rebellious,* both from the early family history but also within current relationships, and this was strongly evident within the therapeutic relationship. *Critical bully/rejecting–Criticised/crushed/rejected* was also suggested in the same way.

Reformulation

The purpose of the reformulation letter is to summarise key events from the past and try to understand how the negative patterns learnt from early experiences are being repeated or how alternative patterns developed in order to avoid these early ones have themselves become restrictive or damaging. Michael's reformulation was shared on the sixth meeting, and extracts from it are shown below:

Dear Michael,
You have come into therapy because you have lost your zest for life, feeling that your creativity has been stifled, and that your response has been procrastination to the point that you have found it difficult to even open an envelope. You have also been experiencing diffi-culties in relationships with your family – it seems as if they are all growing up and growing away from you. You have found it hard to make sense of your situation and your stuckness, and in coming into therapy perhaps have hoped for rescue, from someone who will open up opportunities and allow a way forward as has happened in the past.

[A retelling of his personal history as previously outlined in the assessment was included.]

In telling me your story there has been a sense of split in your life – it is as if there is the successful 'free spirited' creative Michael who lives in his head, and does not need close adult relationships, but needs the recognition by others of his talents. Perhaps this is the part of you that is able to create an intense fantasy world with your children, has taken on the role of 'creating' Isabelle and the part of you that is able to perform. But for a variety of reasons the circum-stances have changed – Isabelle is 'growing up' and demanding her independence, no longer an adoring wife, your children no longer want to share in your fantasy world and you feel your creativity has been stifled by others, your talents unrecognised.

But instead of being able to address the difficulties directly with Isabelle, it seems as if you have felt victimised, powerless and abused by others. Perhaps this mirrors your father's situation and like him your response has been procrastination and withdrawal, but with a sense of suppressed anger. You also described a sense of being emotionally cut-off and there have been times when I have had the sense that you have no knowledge of what your feelings are, or that you have no words for them. As in earlier times, your response seems to be to desire escape (back into 'free-spirit' mode) rather than confront the situation, but I would suggest that this will be an unsatisfactory long-term solution as it fails to address the issue about sustainable adult relationships.

Perhaps part of the problem is to do with issues of independence and dependency – it is as if dependency came to represent feeling overwhelmed and suffocated, a sense of being controlled; independence was freedom, creativity, and no need for others. But as humans we have emotional needs and the dilemma arises as to how your needs for dependency and independence are negotiated within an adult relationship. By coming into therapy at this point in your life, the focus of the work may be about understanding your part within relationships and learning to cope with your feelings and needs rather than either cutting off emotionally or escape into needing no-one. I wonder whether in the process you may find a different and rewarding source of creativity by being in touch with those other aspects of yourself which up to now it seems only lead to procrastination and cut-offness.

Your current difficulties may be described in terms of three procedures:

1. *Need to be special.* You learnt that being average was to be 'beneath contempt'. Only special success in your work and relationships seems enough to maintain your self-esteem. However, if things do not turn out to be perfect or you are criticised you feel angry and become contemptuous and critical of others. They then reject or avoid you which confirms your feelings of inadequacy.

2. *Expressing your feelings.* It is as if expressing your feelings makes you weak, contemptible or needy. You therefore bottle feelings up (particularly anger) which makes you critical and resentful of others and depressed, as unexpressed anger is turned against yourself.

3. *Procrastination.* Feeling let down and angry it is as if your resistance to others' demands proves your self-worth – 'if I must then I won't'. You put things off to the point when others criticise you and things get into a mess. You then feel out of control and humiliated which confirms your low self-esteem.

Relationships and events within the therapeutic relationship often face similar difficulties to those in life, and perhaps this has already occurred – you became angry when I asked you to fill in the Psychotherapy File, you gave me the impression that you felt I was trying to pigeonhole you, that you were different from the others whom I might see. As you know, I also felt cautious about writing this letter, perhaps afraid of your response – might you be contemptuous and dismissive of it, or might you feel criticised and bullied? The point is to recognise when such events and emotions occur and use them as a way of understanding and learning rather than be drawn into re-enacting the situations.

It may be that you find the end of therapy difficult to cope with – and your instinct may be to take control by leaving early and escaping. Endings are important and I hope you will be able to discuss your feelings rather than react as you have done before. I look forward to working with you over the succeeding weeks.

Michael's response to the reformulation was one of quiet acceptance and a deepening of rapport illustrated by his elaboration of situations in his past and current relationship with his wife and children. He acknowledged feeling humiliated and contemptible in response to others and although his reaction was of angry feelings he would avoid acknowledging them for fear of being 'out of control'.

Active therapy: sessions 7–14

Unfortunately, at the same time as the reformulation was given, Isabelle told Michael that their marriage was over and he started to make arrangements to move north, finding accommodation close to his son from his first marriage.

This slightly shortened the therapy but also shifted the focus onto how Michael was coping with the end of his marriage. However, during this time we worked towards a diagram (see Figure 6.1) that demonstrated the generation of problem procedures from the reciprocal role repertoire. Almost inevitably, loss became a major theme during our sessions although Michael commented on being unable to bear thinking about it. It seemed as if the losses from the past were recalled in resonance to the issues arising for Michael at the time we were meeting. He started by telling me about his middle brother who had committed suicide in his early twenties – this had never been discussed in the family for fear of emotional collapse, similarly the death of his parents was something to be

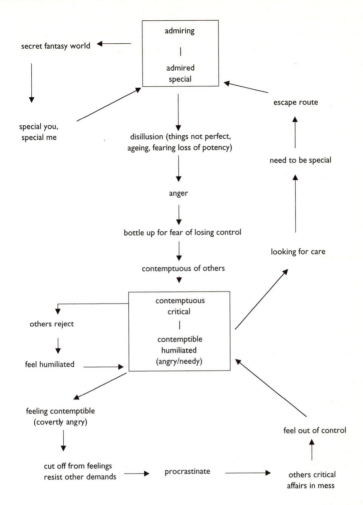

Figure 6.1 Michael's SDR

coped with by a stiff upper lip. He commented on the similarities in the way he had brought up children in his two marriages – in both instances he had created an intense fantasy world with his children to the exclusion of their mothers. His teenage children had moved from a position of being in a very close relationship to him to one in which they had become contemptuous and critical of him. Michael experienced the situation as one in which he felt himself humiliated and bullied but felt unable to talk about his feelings of sadness and loss at their changing relationship. He recalled his sadness at the way his relationship with his own father had changed, made more poignant by his absence from his father's funeral.

Underlying this were the losses associated with ageing, including the loss of sexual power and generativity associated with getting older, and this was reflected in a dream of physical weakness when Michael was unable to hoist himself over a wall. He commented that previously he had coped with depression by escape to new sexual partners who had given him new creative energy, but this time there was no relationship to escape to, and he was very conscious of taking his history and problems with him, writing 'Can I ever hope to change the habit of misery, or is it going to follow me wherever I go. Behind the horseman sits black care.' In spite of all that was happening he experienced great difficulty in communicating his feelings, writing, 'How do I feel? Do I know? Can I feel? Am I switched off from feeling? I am far from being happy. Tears are never far away, but too dry to see.'

Michael commented on recognising aspects of himself in the lower half of the diagram, in particular his ability to be contemptuous, controlling and critical, and wondered whether this recognition would contribute to his creativity, but I am unsure whether Michael or I recognised the extent of his sadness and vulnerability.

The 'symptom' of procrastination became worse over the time we were meeting, and while Michael recognised that this was making his situation worse (for example failure to complete tax returns), and that others became more critical and contemptuous of him in response, he seemed unable to counter this state to any degree. In his past he had had assistants (or partners) to do the routine things of life for him. As life had changed such expected help had disappeared and he found himself exposed but unable or unwilling to ask for help, and his inability to do such tasks seemed to invite further critical and contemptuous responses.

Endings

As we reached the end of therapy, so Michael was endeavouring to organise himself to move out – it brought back memories of the endings of previous relationships and recollections of how his children from his first marriage had coped compared to the present situation and he expressed great concern for their future. During therapy Michael did not keep a regular diary as requested, perhaps predictable from his response 'if I must, then I won't', but made occasional notes, including some for our last session. He listened to my letter quietly but made no comment. My goodbye letter read as follows:

Dear Michael,

We have reached the end of your therapy – a slightly premature ending given that your move is imminent, but I want to use this letter as the opportunity to reflect on some of the themes and issues that we have discussed over the last few months.

The reason you came into therapy was because of 'depression' characterised by procrastination and 'can'tness' – but against whom was this directed? Was it against Isabelle and the children? Or was it against the world for not recognising you as special, no longer giving you the recognition you felt you deserved? Was it ultimately directed against yourself – not even able to fill in tax returns or patent registrations, even though this ultimately could militate against you?

The reason I ask this is because of our conversations about your upbringing – you told me that your mother's attitude towards her children was that you were all special, different from others. The corollary of that was that to be normal or ordinary was to be beneath contempt. From our conversations it sounds as though you have passed this on to your children in turn. But I am struck by what a two-edged sword this 'gift' is. For a person to believe they are special may enable them to build a sense of achievement and self-esteem when things go well, but what if life does not go the way it is planned. To what does the child or adult attribute failure – do they blame themselves and feel that they personally are failures? Or do they blame everyone else for being stupid because others cannot see their obvious talents? If that is the nature of the problem, does it mean that you are dependent on success, whether it is by the way of projects or relationships in order to feel okay?

And if that is the case, how do you feel you will cope after moving? To some extent I think you see this move as your salvation but I am also struck by your comments about 'black care' (see comments above) that suggests that you are well aware that your problems may not be left behind but are an integral part of you. If the situation is such that you are either 'special' and okay, or normal (i.e. 'beneath contempt') and depressed, what is the solution? Can you conceive of accepting part of yourself as normal, i.e. succeeding in some things, failing in others?

Another theme during our time together has been talking about feeling in or out of control, and you commented on not wanting to lose your temper or cause upset. While I appreciate that Isabelle is also someone who doesn't easily talk about feelings, I have been surprised at the extent to which you have avoided talking about the situation (does this mirror previous break-ups and hard times?).

While this enables you to 'stay in control' it seems to have meant that you have had few conversations with your children about the impact of your leaving the family home. Perhaps they may need permission to be upset or angry directly with you before you leave in order to know that you do still love them. You have given the impression that somehow the situation with Isabelle and the children will resolve itself without any real effort on either of your parts, but I do know how concerned you are about the boys and how much you love them.

What of the course of therapy and our relationship? It has sometimes felt like a battle between us – attempts by me to keep control and stick to what I saw as relevant and appropriate content while it sometimes felt that you wanted to use the time to entertain me and engage me in stories about other people. It sometimes felt that you have tried to seduce me with words or stories or by making me laugh – is that because you have wanted to avoid talking about difficult things or have you seen them as irrelevant or wanted to take control? Perhaps this therapeutic relationship has demonstrated that another kind of relationship is possible – a non-sexual relationship but one in which feelings can be discussed. But at the same time you seem more comfortable reading and intellectualising about emotions than being able to confront and deal with them.

Unsurprisingly perhaps, as we have come towards the ending of therapy, so we have faced other endings – of your marriage to Isabelle, the death of your aunt, facing your older age and how you would like the end of your life to be in your control. I am still unsure about how you (and your family) cope with endings – a mixture of stiff upper lip, or escape into other situations? Except for the death of your cat when you, Isabelle and one of the boys allowed yourselves to howl. As I said before, perhaps you have to show your own sadness and loss in order to give permission to your children to show their feelings. This brings me back to our conversation last week about your relationship with your father and your evident sadness at not taking the opportunity for a relationship with him when you had the opportunity – I hope that you will take the risk of doing more to maintain your relationship with them than was possible for you.

The north of the country may not be the salvation you seek for a variety of reasons, but I sincerely hope that you find peace, fulfilment and creativity there, and that relationships with your children and others develop and flourish with the years. But don't forget that it may require both a recognition and acknowledgement of feelings on your part.

His notes read:

> After reading the chapter in Susie Orbach's new book, *Towards Emotional Literacy*, I am convinced that my circumstantial problems, – creative frustration with major projects in the hands of incompetents, desperate lack of money, domestic strife, highly critical teenage sons, a fledgling wife half my age who is stretching independent and ambitious wings and has withdrawn her love from me and isolation from like-minded friends – have led to my present state of what others might dub laziness.
>
> I can see how over the last 10–12 years, I have been ground down in self [?] esteem, how my responses to those nearest me have become critical, angry, alienating. The social changes that have destroyed the good inter-familial relationships I used to have and try in vain to maintain, have aggravated my plight.
>
> When I first came to you, my complaint was Procrastination, Can'tness. I could not bring myself to open letters, help in the house, and fill in forms. You asked me what I hoped your therapy might do for me. My answer was 'Give me back my verve!'
>
> I think we may have gone astray in believing that my main difficulty was with adult relationships as a possible consequence of my mother's character. I have always been an idealist, a perfectionist, highly creative, curious about everything, questing and questioning, impatient of fools and mediocrity. I still believe in my superior self, the essentially valuable nugget within me, but it will be a long time before I can recover from the traumas of the last decade. However, I am determined to make the effort. Once I have modest security, insulation from strife, the peace of my eyrie I hope I shall re-find myself and become enthusiastic and full of energy again . . . To paraphrase Montherlant, 'I shall cling to the wing of solitude and bid her lift me from the failures and frustrations of recent years.'
>
> This may be a vain hope: Black care sits behind the fleeing horseman. I love my boys and am anxious for their future. There will be an internal battle to justify my selfish rights, even although it is my wife who is throwing me out.
>
> However, there are seeds of new thoughts waiting to germinate when conditions are more propitious. This therapy, together with extensive and relevant reading, Orbach, Montherlant etc. have helped me towards a new era of reflection and conclusion. It is now for me to see what literary casseroles I can concoct – Procrastination permitting. Thanks for all your help.

As we parted there were tears in his eyes and I felt a real sadness at the ending of therapy.

Follow-up

No formal follow-up was arranged in view of the distance Michael had moved, but in requesting permission to use some of our case material, he wrote and let me know that his elder son with whom he had had such a turbulent time had insisted on moving up to live with him and attend school locally. He continued to have the hope of a creative project dangled invitingly and he remarked 'I desperately need the money, but can I really be bothered any more! Helping my son is perhaps more imperative.'

Transference and countertransference

Michael's opening remarks giving his view of the psychiatrist set the scene for the transference during the therapy. It seemed to act as bait to the reciprocal roles of Admiring–Admired, and initially I found myself striving to be the therapist who was good enough to understand and help him. Michael had previously looked for care by escape to new sexual partners, and part of the dynamic was the feeling of being seduced by his language. However, perhaps because of my resistance to being drawn into this reciprocal role, Michael became more dismissive of the therapy, referring to others that he felt had greater insight into the nature of his problems. This had the effect of leaving me feeling deskilled, critical and contemptuous of him while at the same time feeling empathy for the changes he was facing at this point in his life.

Overview

In reviewing this therapy there are different themes to consider. In particular, there is the impact of ageing on those people whose 'predominant preoccupation is with issues of success and status' (Ryle and Kerr 2002, p. 185). Michael had been sustained through life by the success of his creative ventures and the status arising from them. As he had reached his mid-fifties such success had begun to elude him and he found earlier established ways of coping to be unsuccessful. Added to that were the other issues of ageing which had a direct impact on his perception of himself, such as the loss of libido made worse by anti-depressants. He was also deeply conscious of the changing attitudes of his teenage children to their older father. Societal attitudes and behaviour towards older people in general also contributed negative and ageist views, reinforcing the humiliated and contemptible reciprocal role from which he cut off.

A second theme was that in Michael's family of origin there appears to have been no experience of acknowledging or talking about difficult feelings – they were dealt with by escape or bottling up. It would seem that in turn Michael's current family also felt unable to talk about their distress. His elder son in particular responded at times with anger, violence and absconding, but this behaviour in context also indicated the strength of loving bond between father and son.

For those people with a narcissistic personality structure 'their search is not for care and love so much as for admiration . . . Because emotional neediness is closely identified with the contemptible role, therapy is hard to seek and persist with . . . The key task is to make it tolerable for the person to be sad and vulnerable' (Ryle and Kerr 2002, pp. 185–6). I learned a great deal from Michael, but in retrospect, feel that I did not recognise or facilitate those feelings sufficiently, and although supervision helped me cope with feeling deskilled, it is with hindsight that it became apparent that the goodbye letter was couched in objective impersonal language perhaps as an attempt to distance myself from Michael's criticism. Despite all that was going on at the time, Michael attended regularly and it is possible that if he had not been at the point of leaving other change may have been possible. Overall I feel that the CAT was a good-enough experience for us both, and Michael's recent letter sounded positive and hopeful for his future.

Reference

Ryle, A., and Kerr, I. (2002) *Introducing Cognitive Analytic Therapy: Principles and Practice*. Chichester: John Wiley.

Chapter 7

A coming together of CBT and CAT

Sequential diagrammatic reformulation of the long-term effects of complex and distant trauma

Ian Robbins and Laura Sutton

The origins of this work were in the fruitful collaboration of the first author, whose origins were in Cognitive Behavioural Therapy (CBT), with a Cognitive Analytic Therapist working on the treatment of the psychological consequences of extreme trauma. As the collaboration advanced it was clear that there were many parallels but that there was also much that CAT had to offer in terms of the treatment of complex or very distant traumatic events. This lies in its attention to the nature of safety within a therapeutic relationship, defined as non-collusion (below), and in the clarity of its model to guide this for the therapist and client alike. This is particularly important in the case of severe traumata, in being confronted with the intensity of emotions involved, where the therapist is at risk of being either overwhelmed or numbed in the face of such harrowing experiences. In CAT this therapeutic 'containment' arises within the process of 'sequential diagrammatic reformulation': the 'SDR'.

Specifically, we are finding that the SDR forms a foundation for integration, or 'scaffolding', for the exposure-based and narrative aspects of behavioural and cognitive work developed in the CBT treatment of trauma, particularly in the case of complex or compounded traumata. Ryle, writing from the perspective of the effects of early abuses and deprivation on the development of the self, suggests that patients' ability to benefit from the SDR indicates that it is not the intensity of the affects or their defences that has prevented them from progressing, but the absence of an integrating commentary (including for the practitioner) such as the SDR represents (Ryle 1991). In this chapter we aim to develop this understanding further. We start by examining the impact of trauma from a CBT perspective, the current research with today's older adults, and current approaches to treatment of post-traumatic sequelae generally and in old age. Through this, we will draw out those aspects that have been developed within CAT, to show how the process of sequential diagrammatic reformulation arises and how it works, with two case examples. We finish with a consideration of the implications for the treatment of complex and distant trauma in later life and old age.

The impact of trauma: emotional and information-processing models

From a cognitive-behavioural point of view, traumatic events may have a profound impact because the experience cannot be reconciled with existing constructs or schema. Trauma may be any event which falls outside the normal range of human experiences and which threatens the life or well-being of the individual or those around them. Associated with the event are intense feelings of fear, horror or helplessness (APA 1994). Terr (1991) has suggested that it is useful to distinguish between short-term unexpected events (Type 1) such as accidents and assaults, and events which are sustained over a long time or repeated (Type 2) such as war, captivity or sexual abuse. It is also useful to distinguish at which developmental stage the trauma occurs, with severe trauma in childhood having more impact on development of personality and self-concept.

Bisson and Shepherd (1995) suggest that most people exposed to traumatic events experience acute effects. These include recurrent re-experiencing the event in the form of thoughts, images or nightmares, emotional numbing and avoidance of places, people and things associated with the event and intense arousal in the form of sleep disturbance, anger, irritability and jumpiness. This arousal is intensified by exposure to reminders. For the majority these symptoms dissipate spontaneously, but where they persist for longer than a month they form the basis of Post-Traumatic Stress Disorder (PTSD) as classically understood.

Horowitz (1986) proposes an emotional processing model of trauma. He suggests that individuals use mental constructs or schema of the world to process incoming information. He notes that it is an inherent trait to make mental models coherent with current information. For an event to be processed, pre-existing schema have to be adapted to integrate information which is derived from new experiences. Where trauma is extreme it becomes impossible to integrate them to existing schema. Horowitz describes a two-stage process of adjustment to traumatic events. The first stage involves trying to assimilate events and their meanings in the context of existing schema. Following this these schema are altered to incorporate information from the traumatic event. He suggests that the processes of assimilation and adaptation are characterised by alternating phases of intrusion and avoidance. Intrusion is accompanied by high arousal, intrusive thoughts and images, behavioural re-enactments and rumination, while avoidance is characterised by behavioural restriction and cognitive and emotional numbing. This is seen as a defence mechanism which prevents the individual being overwhelmed in the intrusion phase.

Horowitz sees successful adjustment as a state of equilibrium, which is achieved following this oscillation between intrusion and avoidance. Post-traumatic syndromes are seen as occurring when there is either a deficit or over-activity in the inhibitory defence mechanisms which protect the individual from being subject to overwhelming arousal. This approach has much in common with the work of Brewin, Dalgleish and Joseph (1996) in their information-processing model. They describe how normal processes of adjustment may become pathological and can lead to premature inhibition of processing or a state of chronic processing rather than achieving a successful conclusion.

Janoff-Bulman (1989, 1992) suggests that traumatic events violate a number of basic assumptions around which individuals lead their lives. Normally these assumptions are implicit and unchallenged. These beliefs provide the basic sense of security and safety that allow the individual to engage with the world without experiencing a constant state of threat. Once these assumptions are violated the individual is threatened with 'the terror of meaninglessness' (Janoff-Bulman and Frantz 1997). Janoff-Bulman (1992) groups the basic assumptions into three main categories. She sees the primary assumption being about the benevolence of the world. Within this category are assumptions about the extent to which the world is seen as basically a good or evil place and the extent to which people are kind and caring. The next category is about the meaningfulness of the world. This is concerned with natural justice where people get what they deserve. Included in this category is the extent to which precautions can be taken against bad events and the extent to which events are seen as predictable or random. The third category of assumptions is about the worthiness of the self. This is about self-worth and the extent to which others perceive people as good and worthy. It is also concerned with the extent to which individuals perceive themselves to be in control of themselves and the extent to which luck is seen as being protective.

Ehlers and Clark (2000) suggest that the impact of trauma is likely to persist when individuals process the trauma in such a way that leads to the perception of threat currently as being very high. They suggest that this is excessively negative psychologically, and leads to a disturbance in autobiographical memory characterised by poor elaboration and lack of contextualisation accompanied by strong associative memory and perceptual priming effects. The process of integration is more than simply abreaction. It needs confrontation both of the appraisal of the trauma or its consequences and of the disturbance of autobiographical memory that results in the increased sense of current threat. They suggest that there are a number of treatment implications from their model. The trauma memories have to be incorporated into the preceding and subsequent aspects of experience in order to minimise the intrusive re-experiencing. Appraisals of the trauma which are particularly problematic need to be addressed and challenged in order to reduce the level of current threat appraisal. In addition dysfunctional behavioural and cognitive strategies which impede memory elaboration, increase symptoms or stop the reassessment of appraisals need to be eliminated.

All of these models have in common a belief that successful adjustment to traumatic events involves some kind of cognitive-emotional processing of the event. They also highlight the importance of existing schema, beliefs and assumptions in adjustment. A significant part of the adjustment process is the reconciliation of these schema and beliefs with the information from the traumatic experience. The symptoms of traumatic stress syndromes represent a continued state of processing where the gap between information and schema is unresolved.

From a cognitive analytic point of view, in severe trauma, a person can experience an extreme shift in their lives, from a state in which the self, others and the world are benign enough, to one in which the self really is insecure and vulnerable to others who are indeed malign in a hostile environment. If this is an extreme shift, it would challenge the person's healthy narcissism: from a 'good enough' reflection of self from others/ world, this is shattered or potentially shattered, with potential for 'splitting', that is, yearning for a lost simpler ideal world, while fearing a malign one. The threat to a sense of continuity of self which our healthy narcissism sustains is great, and the person needs some way of dealing with that (Ryle 1978). This is perhaps what is disturbing autobiographical memory.

Putting this example of an existential dilemma into words, it is as if the person now experiences a dichotomy: *either* once reasonably in control and invulnerable (reasonably powerful) *or* now out of control and extremely vulnerable (utterly powerless). This can set up an anxious striving whenever a feeling of being 'out of control' is glimpsed, such as a distressing memory, or a reminder, or even potential reminder, perhaps a newspaper article, a dark cloud and so on. This re-triggers their hyperarousal, and in response to the new state of fear, the person may dissociate, that is they may numb in the face of what they fear as poten-tially overwhelming affect or consequence. In response to that numbed panic they may now feel compelled to keep things (beliefs, feelings, self, others) in perfect order ('meaningful', pseudointegration), lest a terrible mess ('meaninglessness', disintegration) be unleashed. As for Horowitz, this is seen in CAT as a survival procedure in order to be able to go on living (the term 'procedure' in CAT is used for theoretical reasons to distinguish it from the concept of 'internal object relations' in psycho-analysis and from 'schemas' in cognitive-behavioural psychology, cf. Chapter 1).

In CAT, the person's survival procedure is seen in this way as histori-cally justified but as perhaps no longer helpful. It can become pathologi-cal: for instance, such anxious striving maintains the hyperarousal, leading to ever-narrowed attention to threat-related appraisals or stimuli. Feelings, thoughts, actions can become over-restricted. In response to over-restriction the person may then either comply, and continue to keep things (feelings, thoughts, memories, behaviour, others) inhibited (in the extreme, inhibiting life itself in the form of impulse to suicide) or rebel against it, potentially feeding their feelings of being out of control, or turn to ever more extreme forms of numbing, such as alcohol or drugs, which then run the risk of reinforcing their feelings of worthlessness and alienation. It is in this way that the person is seen as in a state of chronic (narrow) processing, unable to find a resolution to their existential dilemma.

The aim is then together to 'name' – to *reformulate* – the *sequence* to their lived dilemma, showing it as a *diagram*. Hence, 'sequential dia-grammatic reformulation'. This is the beginning of 'confrontation' of their trauma and its effects, to begin to be able to bear this with their therapist. In time, 'exits' are developed together. This can be specifically to recognise the point at which their 'state shift' occurs (for example, from feeling all is well, suddenly to feeling threatened; that is, the moment at which thinking was overwhelmed). The person learns to see what is happening, and revise their response as a result, so that rather than following their usual unreflected procedure of numbing, they may instead practice the breath to manage the panic attack, in order to regain their capacity to feel and to think so that they are enabled gradually to 'bear to witness' their plight, so that reappraisal becomes possible. This named recognition at the level of a state shift represents an integrating commen-tary: the SDR represents the shared voice of the therapist and client at this level.

The long-term impact of trauma

The consequences of trauma may persist over a considerable time period. While childhood sexual abuse or chronic domestic violence may have a long-term impact, there is little systematic study. Specific studies of the long-term impact of trauma do exist, but they have largely been carried out with military veterans or Holocaust survivors. While this section as a result focuses on this, it in no way implies that other traumas are less important: rather it simply points to the lack of systematic study.

Many of today's older adults have experienced the impact of wars as either civilians or combatants. Despite the magnitude of the Second World War there was little research as to its impact. Even when the continuing impact of trauma has been identified it, is often ignored. Archibald and Tuddenham (1965) in a twenty-year follow-up of Second World War and Korean War veterans found significant effects of combat stress reactions. They also found an increasing number of new patients who were seeking treatment for war-related neuroses. They suggested that these presentations were the result of traumatic stress, the effects of which had remained latent until reactivated by the process of ageing. They concluded that:

> The impact of the war has not been fully realised two decades after its termination. The combat fatigue syndrome which was expected to vanish with time has proved to be chronic if not irreversible.
>
> (p. 475)

There was an almost total lack of interest or follow-up of Second World War veterans until the late 1980s when the majority of them would have recently retired from full-time employment. Similar issues have occurred with Holocaust survivors. This gives an impression of a collective process of denial involving both veterans and survivors themselves and the wider society which may ultimately increase the sense of isolation for those experiencing problems.

A number of studies have looked at the continuing impact of traumatic experiences among survivors of concentration camps during the Holocaust (Eitinger 1961; Chodoff 1963), where high levels of chronic psychiatric symptoms were reported. More recently Kuch and Cox (1992) reported that 52 per cent of concentration camp survivors and 65 per cent of a sub-group who had been in Auschwitz met the criteria for a current diagnosis of PTSD. They point to the clear role of severity of the traumatic experience in continued psychopathology. Mazor *et al.* (1990), in a study involving Holocaust survivors, suggest that while the majority of those interviewed have got on with their lives and had a similar range of achievements to those who did not experience the Holocaust, they have had to deal with their past in terms of intrusive memories and emotions on a continual basis. For many it was only as they entered their fifties that they started to open up to their experiences and try to give some meaning to their lives.

Since the late 1980s there have been a number of studies of veterans which have pointed to persistent problems associated with war experiences. Hamilton *et al.* (1987) looked at 32 Second World War veterans who had seen heavy combat. They found that 16 per cent of these subjects met the criteria for a diagnosis of PTSD. PTSD symptoms are more frequent in Vietnam veterans than Korean or Second World War veterans, with 46.2 per cent of the Vietnam group scored within the PTSD range as compared to 30 per cent of the Korean group and 18.5 per cent of the Second World War veterans. When the rates of problems were examined for veterans who had been prisoners of war (POWs) they found no significant differences in PTSD rates between the three groups, which were around the 50 per cent level (Blake *et al.* 1990). There have been numerous studies examining the long-term impact of being a prisoner of war (Zeiss and Dickman 1989; Sutker *et al.* 1990; Speed *et al.* 1989), all of which have found high lifetime rates of PTSD as well as higher rates of current psychopathology compared to non-prisoner veterans. The strongest predictors of PTSD were proportion of body weight lost and the experience of torture during captivity. They suggested that the persistence of symptoms for so many years is a reflection of the severity of the trauma.

Few studies however have looked at how veterans cope with traumatic memories and subsequent life events. An exception to this is the work of Fairbank *et al.* (1991), who compared former POWs of the Second World War with chronic PTSD with those without PTSD and a non-POW veterans group on measures of general psychological functioning, appraisal and coping. Appraisal and coping were assessed under two stressor conditions: memories of war and captivity experiences and recent negative life events. They found that ex-POWs with PTSD had poorer general psychological functioning, significantly less control over intrusive memories and more frequent use of self-isolation, wishful thinking, self-blame and social support in order to cope with the memories than did the other two groups. Differences were not so marked for coping with recent negative life events.

Hunt and Robbins (2001a, 2001b) examined the long-term impact of the Second World War on elderly veterans. In a large-scale study they found evidence of high levels of trauma-related distress in 19 per cent of their sample. Lower rank, captivity experience and retirement were all factors in the development of psychopathology. In a smaller sub-sample they also looked at coping strategies used in dealing with traumatic re-collections. Social support was used in very different ways. Comradeship was vital during the war itself, and even fifty years on comrades were a valuable resource for discussing war experiences and dealing with the content of traumatic recollections. While veterans relied on their families for help with the physical and practical aspects of coping they tended not to discuss their traumatic memories at all. Robbins (2001) looked at the reasons which veterans gave for non-disclosure to their families. He found that many of the reasons given revolved around the notion of shame and were similar to findings of Macdonald and Morley (2001), who looked at female attendees for psychotherapy, many of whom had experienced early sexual abuse.

It is perhaps useful to think about why older adults may be hesitant about seeking help in dealing with the current impact of distant trauma. In many cases this may be simply a belief that as so much time has elapsed nothing can be done. Robbins (1997) discusses a number of issues that emerged as important during the course of a therapy group of Second World War veterans. The fear of disintegration was an issue common to all. The clients seen felt that they had been holding themselves together, partly through refusing to talk about their experiences at all. There was a general reluctance to approach treatment because of a belief that if they started talking about their experiences they would fall apart completely and be unable to regain control again. The fear of disintegration was partly fuelled by the feeling that the memories were so damaging that talking about them would not only damage the client but would also affect the therapist. Throughout the treatment process there was concern expressed about the therapist having to listen to the things being talked about. The memories were perceived as having a corrosive quality which could eat through attempts to block them out, and it was this feeling which had eventually driven clients to seek help. There was also a qualitative difference in the nature of the traumatic memories. These are distinguished by the fact that they do not change but instead return in primary format each time and do not fade with the passing of time.

Most of the clients had been unable to talk with their immediate family about their war experience. On the few occasions they did attempt to, the result was usually in terms of platitudes rather than real discussion. Danieli (1985) has observed similar problems in Holocaust survivors being able to talk about their experiences with their own families. She also points to 'conspiracies of silence' between survivors and their therapist to avoid talking specifically about the trauma. Many described a sense of guilt about survival and the things done in the course of survival. There was also intense guilt about the gratuitous killing and other actions which in the heat of battle seemed normal or were exciting but which in retrospect were seen to be immoral or criminal. Elder and Clipp (1988) have also observed this problem in the context of Second World War veterans, and Danieli (1988) with Holocaust survivors.

The impact of ageing and loss of status, which had often led to a sense of helplessness, was reinforced by increasing infirmity. For many who had been POWs or concentration camp inmates this had reawakened emotions associated with their captivity experience. There is often intense anger associated with events of the past, and in particular behaviour of the enemy. For many, however, the anger has become attached to the way in which the government has responded both to their needs and to the countries that they were previously at war with. Increasing age and frailty have evoked similar feelings brought about by war experience. For some, the war contained many of their best experiences as well as the worst; it was the best of times and the worst of times of their lives. They found that thinking about one brought to mind the other. This gave a sense that the traumatic memories were contaminating both the memories of the past as well as their present existence.

In sum, the literature is finding that even when the continuing impact of trauma is recognised, it is often ignored, linked to collective processes of denial that may increase the person's isolation. In other words, recognising traumatic memories often leads not to a caring response ('caring-to-need') but to a response shift to 'ignoring-to-excluded'. This may be repeated at the individual, family or collective levels. This links in CAT theory to the integration of Activity Theory which so far has itself been excluded from therapy discourse (Chapter 1). The focus in CAT is on what mediates these relational sociocultural activities, principally language. The belief that 'so much time has elapsed nothing can be done', for instance, could be an internalisation of the ageist snag, mediated linguistically (Hepple, Chapter 2), as part of what mediates the sociocultural collusion of silence.

The interest is then on what mediates veterans' coping strategies. For instance, in the study by Fairbank et al. (1991) those who showed poorer psychological functioning, with less control over intrusive memories, made more use of self-isolation, wishful thinking, self-blame and social support. In CAT, 'poorer psychological functioning' would be an overall index, 'lack of control over intrusive memories' could be a 'target problem' for therapy. 'Target problem procedures' (TPP) are those procedures which in part maintain the target problem. Here, the sequential diagrammatic reformulation might involve a self-state in which the person is preoccupied with self-blame and self-isolation: this implies that one part of them is blaming and isolating another part. Hence, 'self-blame' and 'self isolation', although they appear as actions of an individual, are inherently dialogic and relational in structure.

This would form the basis of a 'reciprocal role': 'blaming and isolating-to-guilty and excluded' (Figure 7.1, solid line). The question is then how the person reacts to this. One response might be to accede by withdrawing themselves from company (either their own or other people's). This may bring relief for a time, but they are now alone. The wish to be a part of relationship and community inevitably arises and they may be moved to seek social support. It is not clear what they may be wishing for: social support is used in different ways. Perhaps, in order to be able to be with others, they do tend to talk in platitudes (as a response to an overwhelming shaming internal dialogue), finding it difficult to express what their needs are. The wished-for greater intimacy (less isolation) may continue to elude them, from which they may feel they are inadequate and unworthy of care, vulnerable to thinking this because deep down they believe they are guilty and shameful, and they remain isolated and inconsolable.

'Exit' points in the diagram would then be developed, for instance to learn to put their need as clearly as they can into words. This then gives the other person a chance to respond in a different way. This sets up the potential for a new 'reciprocity' (reciprocal role) (the 'zone of proximal personality development' in CAT). This connects to the issue of safety, because it opens up the possibility of a caring response, that is to experience the humanising of someone (themselves) they may believe to be unworthy. This makes dialogue, therefore debriefing, more possible. This could include, for instance, the fear that memories would be so damaging to the other that they must be blocked off. This sets up another 'TPP' in which the person may begin to learn to recognise what they do in response to any memory that surfaces, for example to immediately block it or ignore it (Figure 7.1, dotted line). In other words, the person is isolating their memories as well as their selves, preventing the much-needed elaboration and integration, and helping to keep them vulnerable to the intrusion of what they are trying to keep isolated. (The fear of the 'damaging to corroded' re-enactment, symbolised by the memories, is a relational issue, and potentially belongs in the 'blaming, isolating,

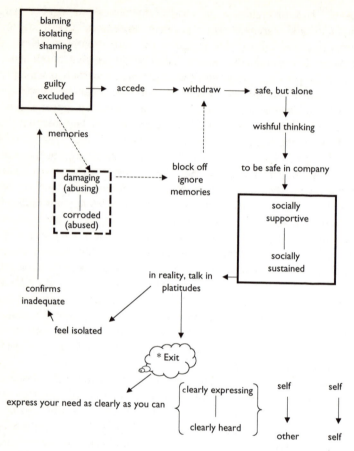

Figure 7.1 An hypothetical SDR surrounding distant trauma. See text for explanation

shaming to guilty and excluded' reciprocal role, indicated in Figure 7.1 via the use of dotted lines.)

Approaches to treatment

There have been two elements at the heart of most approaches to the treatment of trauma. The first is the exposure to the traumatic experiences. The second aspect involves the modification of maladaptive beliefs about events, behaviours or symptoms.

Ochberg (1995) suggests that treatment is never complete if the client has not disclosed the details of their trauma. He suggests that people who suffer 'victimisation' or PTSD are still captured by their trauma histories and that they are unable to recollect without fear of overwhelming emotions. They also recollect when they are unprepared to do so. The purpose of recounting the trauma in therapy is 'to revisit the scene of the terror and horror and, in doing so remove the grip of the terror and horror'. Ochberg emphasises the importance of the presence of the therapist which transforms the process from merely being cathartic to a partnership in survival. It is this partnership which enables the painful nature of the process to be endured.

Chung (1993) has suggested that the primary requirement of a treatment programme is the integration of one's understanding of the meaning of a trauma with current symptoms and life events. This can be achieved in a number of ways. Krell (1985) used tape recordings of disclosure of traumatic experiences to do this in sessions to help child survivors of the Holocaust integrate their experiences into a whole. Those who were unable to relate their stories often continued to suffer psychologically. This process of integration is more than simply abreaction. To integrate needs confrontation of the experience, in itself a painful process, and requires reprocessing of the emotions associated with it to allow reconstruction of a continuous narrative life story. This process of reconstruction has to continue until the client can withstand the experience.

An example of this process has been described by Mollica (1987), who discusses the central role of the 'trauma story' in treatment of PTSD among refugees from the war in Indochina. He suggests that once the patient is willing to tell the trauma story it opens up the possibility of changing previous interpretations of events. Previous feelings of helplessness and hopelessness can be reduced and a new story that is less rigid and fixed may be constructed. This allows the possibility of connecting survivorship in the present with having overcome the events of the past. Bleich *et al.* (1986) have also discussed recounting of events as a corrective experience. They point to its dramatic impact but recognise that the process may be extremely distressing. Patients may feel that they are about to be overwhelmed by the experience, but in talking they realise that they can undergo the experience without falling apart.

A number of authors such as Cienfuegos and Monelli (1983) and Agger and Jensen (1990) discuss the role of testimony in the treatment of political detainees and torture survivors. In addition to recounting the trauma story their method allows for the channelling of rage and anger into some form of indictment. As a consequence of this they feel that their client develops a better understanding of what has happened to them through integration of fragmentary experiences into their life history.

They also suggest that because the experience of suffering has been symbolised in a different form, in this case a written statement, whose importance was recognised by the therapist, the need to express the suffering through somatisation disappears. Similar approaches have been used with Holocaust survivors.

With respect to older adults, Orner and Loos (1998) describe the treatment of a Second World War veteran. The aims of treatment were to link present symptoms to past experiences and to develop a new repertoire of coping responses. Central to this was the use of the client's narrative. They point to the narrative as lacking in detail, and they saw increased articulation and detail as important in making the logical links between events, persons and experiences. This led to recognising the formative nature of some of these experiences and their direct impact on the client's life. This resulted in the client having considerably more insight and a perception of increased emotional control.

Another model of treatment which initially looked at the effects of war trauma, but was subsequently applied to other distant trauma, has been described by Robbins (1997, 2000). Robbins emphasises the need for a clear model given that the extent of the distress and the nature of some of the traumatic memories have the power to be overwhelming for the therapist. It is possible to feel helpless in the face of such intensity of emotion. A simple model is needed to enable the therapist to cope with the level of emotion expressed by the client as well as their own responses. Without a framework within which to work it is difficult to keep a clear direction in working through some of the experiences. The model has as an overall aim the reduction of PTSD symptoms, especially intrusion, and the development of symbolic integration of the trauma experience into the overall life experience.

Central to the development of Robbins's model was the work of Herman (1993), who has suggested that treatment has a number of stages or phases of therapy. The first stage is concerned with developing a sense of emotional safety. This may happen relatively quickly with clients who have had secure early attachments and a single discrete trauma. Where however there is a history of insecure attachments, early abuse and violation of trust, then the process of developing a sense of safety may be protracted. Safety is also about the perceived dangers to the therapist, so also important is the extent to which the therapist has experience of listening to accounts of extreme trauma. To be able to listen to extremely distressing accounts without being overwhelmed or numb is not easy. Clients need to feel that their therapist is able to cope with whatever they need to say.

The next phase is described as remembrance and mourning. This corresponds in CBT models to the exposure and identification of cognitions and emotions. During this stage what may be implicit memories become more explicit and are turned into coherent narratives. A part of these emotions becomes more explicitly linked to specific memories.

The final stage is about reconnection. This may be in the form of being able to reconnect emotionally with others; it may involve resuming occupations, hobbies, and relationships but may also be a more symbolic reconnection to the world. An integral part of reconnection is the ability to begin to look towards the future with a longer time perspective and to make plans rather than getting by on a day-to-day basis. Within the context of any model it is important that goals are negotiated between therapist and client and that they are achievable.

Harvey (1996) has identified a number of aims for trauma-focused therapy:

- to gain authority over the remembering process
- to integrate memory with affective states
- to build up tolerance for affective states
- to develop mastery over symptoms, especially hyper-arousal
- to rebuild self-esteem and self-cohesion
- to give the trauma experience some meaning.

In acknowledging these, the Robbins (1997, 2000) model consists of five stages:

1. Assessment of the nature of the problems is made, and of the extent to which traumatic experience has been a salient factor in the development of the current problems. Also important is the extent of existing coping and social support. If an individual is extremely depressed and socially isolated it may well be inadvisable to commence treatment without treating the mood disturbance and developing a support system. Most individuals will experience an increase in symptoms prior to any improvement. As a consequence it is important that discussion of the treatment approach also addresses the emotional 'costs'. Full information is given before treatment outset to enable the client to make informed treatment choices and to retain a sense of control. It is also important to screen for the presence of severe organic impairment. Those suffering from dementia will undoubtedly need help to deal with traumatic memories but the current treatment model which relies on retaining and processing

information between sessions would not be appropriate and indeed would be more likely to increase distress.

2. Disclosure of events. This is the beginning of the construction of the trauma story and is carried out in great detail occurring in two phases. Initially going through events to gain an overall picture of what happened followed by a more detailed review of events clarifying any confusion and identifying dysfunctional cognitions, such as irrational self-blame, and the emotions associated with them. During this stage there may be a high level of cognitive disorganisation with thoughts being very chaotic. The therapist by providing a clear structure to the individual sessions, keeping to the task of constructing a clear coherent narrative and bringing clients back to this when they become overwhelmed, can help clients to restructure memories of events.

3. Exploration of cognitions and emotions associated with events. This is carried out initially following a process of negotiation to identify specific issues for the individual which were referred to as themes for ease of working. The link between past events and current thoughts and feelings and their impact on behaviour is established.

4. Change strategies. Cognitions and emotions, the behaviours arising from them, and coping mechanisms used, are examined, and the potential for change in these areas is explored and implemented. This can involve anything from opening up communication with close relatives to anxiety management methods. Issues surrounding analysis of behaviour with a view to the individual taking responsibility for this process in the future are central to regaining a sense of control.

5. Termination. This phase is only partly about the ending of treatment and also involves the client assuming responsibility for planning for the future. Issues in ending treatment including the sense of loss which this brings about are explored, and issues around future contact and follow-up are examined. A major part of this is the expectation that recovery is a dynamic process and that if events in the future mean that clients have to revisit the treatment process, this does not imply failure.

In the above approaches the quality of the therapeutic relationship is emphasised. This links in CAT theory to developmental theory, and to the role of the other in early development, including in relation to states of mind and self. Fisher (1999) explores the relational origins of the capacity to face the truth of one's emotional experience. Ryle articulated this further drawing on child developmental studies from Vygotsky, following Winnicott, to note that the presence of an integrating parent – one who can comment and link the range of affects for the child – is probably essential to the development of the capacity to reflect on one's changing states (see Chapter 1). Where this is absent or where the adult has provided a distorted or inaccurate commentary then the child grows up lacking the capacity for self and other-reflection, or develops an untrustworthy inner commentary (Ryle 1991). This is said to be why the person is unable to reflect upon their disturbance, because there is at this point no self-reflective place to be: these remain unreflected states. Inarticulated, they are 'unspeakable' and 'unthinkable'. 'Exposure' is then understood, not as repeating the harrowing details in an unreflected way (this would be to repeat the trauma), but as exposure through 'response prevention' in the form of non-collusion with the person's characteristic problematic procedures. Reliable, that is trustworthy, non-collusion with the person's problematic reciprocal role procedures, which includes a reliable commentary on what is happening within the therapeutic relationship, is important if the therapist is going to be able to stand by the person while the pain of change is faced.

Robbins makes the point that the extreme nature of the distress in severe trauma has the potential to overwhelm the therapist. The therapist needs a simple model to guide their responses in order to maintain the focus. The CAT model represents the presence of 'an integrating other' to the therapist – in the form of the SDR, and supervision – to offer an integrating eye to the therapy process. From a CAT perspective, the person's procedures are basic survival mechanisms. Potentially, hearing such extremes of human suffering could trigger a state shift in the therapist, and as a result elicit their survival procedures, such as numbing. They too need a different 'procedure' to help them. The therapist can use the SDR not only to map where the client is at any point, but also to keep an eye on where they are too. This is the basis of emotional safety in CAT. It enables dialogue to happen: the symbolic integration of the trauma experience into the life story is defined in CAT as a relational process of 'becoming in dialogue' again mediated by the cultural tools of joint reflection in CAT like the SDR. For some people, as a result of early deprivations and abuses, they may 'become in dialogue' for the first time: the SDR representing the 'eye from which an I can grow' (Ryle 1990). This makes thinking and remembering more tolerable, unresolved tasks of mourning become more possible, and through this, the development of a more coherent life story.

The SDR represents an explicitly integrating commentary. Following

Winnicott, it is a transitional object which requires the continued presence of the therapist at first – so is a joint *semiotic*, that is, symbolic device, symbolising the joint reflections of the client and therapist – but which gradually is internalised with more practised separations. Thus, following Vygotsky, what starts out as an external integrating shared voice – the outer dialogue in therapy – enables the person to develop a capacity for a different, more integrated way of 'talking to themselves' (analytically, effects a change in their 'internal *objects*'). What then may seem to be a property of the individual (increased integration of the self, symbolic re-orientation to the world) is implicitly *relational* in origin. Hence, CAT enacts a 'semiotic object relations theory' (Chapter 1).

We will now look at an example of treatment in Robbins's model, incorporating the SDR, and then consider the role of the SDR in more detail, with an example of supervision in relation to someone with distant trauma compounded by poor early attachment and suspected early cognitive impairment.

An example of treatment incorporating the SDR (therapist Ian Robbins)

Mr A is a 68-year-old man who was born in Iran to a wealthy family. He studied law in Iran and the UK before developing a successful practice in Iran. He married and had six children, most of whom now live in America. During the reign of the Shah he fell foul of the authorities and was imprisoned and tortured. This was carried out over several years. He was released following the overthrow of the Shah's regime and he returned to his home. It took him several years to recover and resume his life. In 1998 he again was arrested and imprisoned. During his imprisonment he was again tortured and he also witnessed the torture of others. His release was obtained by his relatives bribing prison guards. On leaving prison it was decided that his life would be at risk if he remained, so he came to the UK and was granted political asylum.

He presented for treatment because he was troubled by re-experiencing his torture every day and for long periods in the day. Much of this re-experiencing related to events which had occurred more than thirty years previously. He also suffered very disturbing nightmares during which he would hit out at his wife or would get out of bed and cower in the corner of the room. He was angry, irritable and hyper-responsive to noise. He felt a sense of detachment from others and as a consequence he avoided other people from the Iranian community in the UK. He was severely depressed, experienced suicidal ideation and felt a profound sense of guilt and low sense of self-worth. He was using high levels of benzodiazepines in order to sleep and to control arousal symptoms during the day.

Prior to commencing treatment Mr A was withdrawn from the benzodiazepines and was prescribed a Selective Serotonin Re-uptake Inhibitor (SSRI) anti-depressant. This was linked to the offer of psychological therapy. While there appears to be good clinical evidence that SSRI anti-depressants are compatible with psychological treatments, and may indeed act synergistically, tranquillisers are not compatible with trauma-focused psychological therapy. Initially he was extremely sceptical about the value of talking about his trauma. He felt that the notion of talking was counter-intuitive. Treatment was carried out over 24 weeks with follow-up for a further year. The outline of treatment was:

Session 1:	Assessment and introduction to the model.
Sessions 2–7:	Disclosure of events.
Session 8:	Diagrammatic reformulation and identification of dysfunctional cognitions and emotions.
Session 9:	Shame and degradation.
Session 10:	Survival guilt.
Session 11:	Injustice.
Session 12:	Self-worth and refugee status.
Session 13:	Contamination.
Session 14:	Nihilism.
Session15:	Identification of change strategies.
Session 16:	Talking with wife about his imprisonment and torture.
Session 17:	Meeting other torture survivors.
Session 18:	Meeting other Iranians.
Session 19:	Taking control.
Session 20:	Developing a sense of purpose.
Session 21:	Writing and working.
Session 22:	Future plans.
Sessions 23–24:	Termination.

Follow-up occurred at three-monthly intervals for a year.

At the beginning of treatment Mr A was troubled by symptoms of PTSD. In addition he was very depressed and had a very low sense of self-worth, limited social contacts and few purposeful activities. During the course of treatment he experienced very high levels of distress, especially during the process of elaborating his life narrative. In the phase of identifying dysfunctional cognitions and emotions the diagrammatic reformulation allowed identification of the factors maintaining the current sense of threat. Mr A's use of English was excellent, but the use of the diagrammatic reformulation allowed the rapid identification and communication of very complex processes.

In the course of treatment he gradually assumed more control over the sessions, his arousal decreased and his sense of humour emerged. At the same time his cognitive processes became more organised and purposeful. By the end of treatment he pointed to the change in the nature of his memories. They were still distressing but he had to recall them and the intensity of the distress was reduced. The memories were no longer in the forefront of his mind, his arousal was reduced and his mood was no longer depressed. He had also increased the range of activities which he participated in and this widened his social network considerably. He was able to regain a sense of purpose and worth by putting his legal skills to work on behalf of other refugees. He remained on the anti-depressants until the six-month follow-up point, after which they were gradually withdrawn without any serious alteration in mood. Subsequent follow-up revealed that his improvement had been maintained and that there had been further improvements as his re-engagement with the world increased.

An example of the use of the SDR in supervision (supervisor Laura Sutton)

Maria, now eighty-eight, was referred to the day hospital five years previously with behavioural problems. She was complaining of nausea; she was putting herself on the floor, and was described as 'histrionic', 'attention-seeking', and 'somatising'. Maria was from Spain, but had fought in the French Resistance, coming to London later in life. She was finding it difficult to speak in English now, possibly with early memory problems, but remained fluent in French. Sarah was allocated as her primary nurse because she spoke fluent French.

As a young woman in Spain, Maria had married and had a daughter, but during the Spanish Civil War her husband was imprisoned and she had fled to France with her daughter. Her activities within the Resistance meant she was often faced with risk to her own and to her daughters' life, and she was witness to atrocities. It was later that she learned that her husband had been executed. After the war Maria remarried. Her husband was English and they had a successful business, eventually moving to London on his retirement. He had died about fifteen years ago; her daughter phoned regularly from France and visited as often as she could.

Maria, however, was now preoccupied with her wartime experiences, which were extremely distressing for her. The person who told Maria of her husband's execution had witnessed it, and had described the moments of his death in detail. It was these moments which she was recounting to Sarah so vividly that it was as if she were hearing it for the first time each time, reliving it. It was difficult for Sarah to keep on hearing this, and she decided she would like supervision.

Sarah seemed overwhelmed by the harrowing nature of Maria's disclosures: she spoke of her exasperation and anger at Maria's constant retelling. I also noticed though that there was more than this. Sarah would shut off a little as she spoke of Maria here. Maria's mother apparently used to say to her that she had 'driven her mad'. To our contemporary ears it sounded like her mother had suffered post-natal depression; she went on to commit suicide. Maria's father had been sexually abusive towards her. Maria, still a young girl, went to live with her grandparents. They were wonderful, said Maria, 'spoiling her'. Sarah also spoke warmly of Maria and had commented to her once that she should have written a book about her life. Maria replied that would love to have written a book. So, it sounded like Maria would like to tell her story to Sarah, who, speaking French, was in a position to hear, but these painful transference-countertransference aspects were making this difficult.

We formulated Sarah's work with Maria as autobiographical, while the group would support her with the difficult relational aspects. Meanwhile, as supervisor, I was reflecting on what might be happening between Sarah and Maria (Figure 7.2). I was concerned that Sarah was suffering secondary trauma from hearing Maria's harrowing stories, in their as yet unreflected states. I saw this as 'overwhelming-to-over-whelmed and angry'. This seemed to be depleting Sarah, who for her own survival needed to shut off a little, and keep her distance. This reminded me of Maria's mother's absence to Maria, through her depression, and her final abandonment in her suicide. So I thought of this as 'absent-to-abandoned'. I wondered if these were connected to her histrionic and attention-seeking behaviours: any 'absence' potentially threatening ultimate abandonment, and so, in potential grief, becoming anxious ('nauseous'), searching for her 'lost object' ('attention-seeking'). She seemed to be making a protest ('put self on floor'), which staff could not ignore, i.e. help was at hand (rescued, potentially to be spoilt as by grandparents). She had someone again to tell her story to (someone to 'hold' her in her trauma and losses again).

Ryle (1991) suggests that, 'In a minority of patients, the repeatedly enacted and experienced ability of the therapist not to collude with such

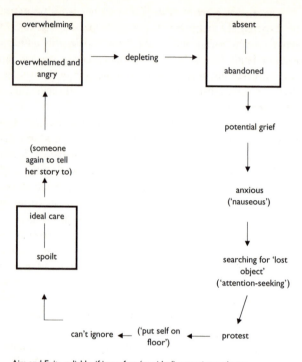

Aim and Exit: reliable, if imperfect (not ideal), attention and care

Figure 7.2 SDR in relation to Maria

procedures may need to precede the patient's capacity to use these tools for self-reflection, although even in such cases the descriptive tools are of value to the therapist' (p. 314). I felt that this would be the case with Maria. However, I was also aware that she may be developing memory problems. As Kitwood (1997) writes, what was once in childhood rendered individual and private – namely thinking – in severe mental impairment becomes once again external – 'held in mind' by others (Chapter 9). So I was not anticipating that Maria would need to make use of these tools directly herself. In other words, I did not think she had the resources needed for individual therapy. Given her traumata and unpredictable losses (including an unpredictable loss of memory) I felt that what she perhaps needed most of all was someone to be a predictable and reliable (that is non-collusive) human presence to her so she could tell her story. After all, it was this that she had an expressed wish to do. Sarah, although a most experienced practitioner, had no background in the therapies, so I considered that she might need the practised experience of the supervisor to hold the tools – in this case, the SDR – rather than expecting her to use these tools for her own self-reflection at first.

From a CAT perspective, the aim and exit to Maria's trap (Figure 7.2) would be to offer her reliable, if imperfect (not idealising) attention and care. The first step was therefore to encourage Sarah to offer Maria a regular time for them to meet; it had been '*ad hoc*' so far. Using CAT as a guide (usually either 16 or 24 sessions) Sarah committed to 24 sessions. Meanwhile, I saw my role as supervisor to keep an eye on whether Sarah was becoming overwhelmed, her response to this, likely in anger or absence, and to redirect as needed, using my 'mental SDR' to guide me. For example, in the early stages, Sarah seemed relieved when a holiday came up, such as Christmas. I thought that this 'absence' helped regulate the 'presence' of affect, so I wanted to allow for this, while gently encouraging Sarah at other times to reconvene if her sessions started drifting as they tended to do.

In the early sessions, Sarah did not share as much of what she was hearing from Maria of these harrowing times as I had expected. I felt that she was bound by their isolation, she the only one who could converse fully with Maria. I also wondered whether this also connected to another aspect of countertransference. Maria had a depth of need which Sarah seemed unable to extricate herself from. In one of her visits, her daughter had let us know that her mother had been retelling these accounts to her in this way throughout her life. Maria seemed to be relating to Sarah in the same way. This indeed seemed to speak to 'idealised' caring roles, here 'ideally caring-to-ideally cared for' – disconnected from the recipient's actual need for greater mutuality (to 'be in dialogue'). In CAT this relates to a dysfunctional intergenerational cycle (Ryle and Kerr 2002). At the same time, as a group we considered that Maria was inspired by ideals, as that part of her that perhaps had helped her to resist and to survive the war. I introduced Sarah to *Countertransference and Older Clients* (Genevey and Katz 1990). She found this helpful, with a release of some anxiety for her as she began to realise that many of her feelings and reactions were known and recognised by others. We had many examples in the supervision group of our own.

I noticed that there were other things that Maria was saying. For example reflecting on her own mortality, Maria voiced she would miss her daughter. Sarah seemed surprised when I pointed these out: she had not noticed that she *had* noticed that Maria mentioned other things (in CAT terms her own capacity for thinking had been temporarily overwhelmed). We felt in the supervision group that Maria was reflecting on the end of her life, quite naturally at eighty-seven (as she was then) and encouraged Sarah to validate this with her. I also wondered whether at another level this spoke to how important Sarah was to Maria, that Maria would miss her too if she weren't there to tell her the story of her life while she still had time. Maria often said things didn't matter (she was 'absent' to herself too), but I think they did.

Sarah could not see how she could ever discharge her (end the sessions). I felt this to be a countertransference, Sarah in the state of despair of an unimaginable end to the trauma (overwhelmed). I think this is common at this stage, and links to people's fear of the dependencies of clients: to their depth of need. Sarah was unsure as to what to do when Maria was silent or when she spoke of her fears for her memory: Sarah too was 'lost for words' sometimes. This I think is a different kind of absence. She was responsive to the idea from the group that when Maria was silent she need 'do' nothing, the group supporting her saying that as nurses they often felt the need to 'do' rather than 'be'. For Kitwood (1997), this links to 'relaxing' and 'holding', in the capacity to feel free to stop active work, and to allow the person with dementia their need for the other to slow down and allow both body and mind some respite, holding in mind the person's concern without having to intervene (Chapter 9).

Sarah and Maria were meeting more regularly. Sarah commented that she was starting to see Maria differently and became more reflective about her. It was about halfway through the 24 sessions, and she remarked that when she asked Maria something she seemed unable to elaborate or to reflect on it: Sarah had the potential to reflect on Maria's states, rather than only be in them with her. I said to her that the absence of reflective capacity can sometimes be because of the absence of this in early life. So I said it is simply about us recognising this rather than doing anything with it as such: 'letting her be'. Indeed, I feel that this is an area of difference when working with severe trauma compounded by early trauma or absence (deprivation), and indeed early memory problems. Whereas conventionally in CAT the aim is to map out effectively a person's emotional defences in order to challenge them, here I think this is a matter of holding them, without colluding with them. To Sarah, unsure of what to ask about the past and what is best to leave, I suggested she might think of archaeology: that the archaeologist may choose not to bring up a precious pot because she feels it might fragment with the disturbance of the soil around it, whereas she may decide to bring up other items because they look like they are intact enough; she knows where they all are though. She may well plot them out: in old age, the 'SDR' could represent the archaeology of the self. Sarah was beginning to develop the self-reflective position in relation to Maria: I was considering sharing the SDR with her.

Sarah started to tell us more in the supervision group of the detail of the harrowing experiences Maria described to her: she was beginning to be 'in dialogue' with us. This was alongside clearer descriptions of other aspects of Maria and her life, past and present. Maria herself began to talk less exclusively about these experiences, and to talk more about more recent and other past bereavements and also current-day aspects such as how her sister was doing or to talk about 'the youth of today' and the good French food. Sarah also said to us that Maria now attempted to speak to her in English at times. Maria recently said to her that she wished she could have given Sarah what she has given to her. We wondered whether this also spoke at some level to her relationship with her own daughter: whether she was saying to Sarah what she could not say to her daughter? Sarah encouraged her to say what she needed to say to her daughter.

One of the supervision group had joined us later, having known Maria previously, and was struck by the difference in her. This practitioner was experienced in grief work and considered that Maria had not 'let go' of her trauma so much as found some place for it in her whole story and that it was almost as if Maria now had some space to take an interest in Sarah. Sarah found Maria was more at ease, with further lessening of her somatisation. Although the hearing of the execution of her husband remained painful to remember, the intensity of Maria's PTSD associated with it had eased, to the extent that Sarah felt that she was no longer reliving it each time. Sarah also felt relieved of this enough, if of course at times still able to feel overwhelmed or distant. The group commented to Sarah on how she herself looked less strained, more at ease herself, when she talked about Maria. The experienced grief therapist commented that it seemed to her that Sarah had been something/someone constant in her life when this was changing for her, which is all we set out to provide.

Near the end of Sarah's work with Maria I drew out my 'mental SDR' for Sarah to help her 'debrief' on her experiences with Maria as they anticipated the end of their regular sessions. She was taken by this, saying it described the Maria she knew very well. I encouraged Sarah to share it with the day hospital staff. When the sessions were finished, Maria resumed some of her behavioural difficulties and Sarah also felt a recurrence of her feeling overwhelmed or distant: at the end of therapy it is usual to have resurgence of patterns; these were after all Maria's possible unreflected responses to loss.

In the follow-up period we would re-reflect with Sarah. Six months on from the end of therapy, Sarah said that when Maria talked of her trauma now it was less brutal in the telling, Maria looked happier, and more contented, as if the 'poison had been taken out'. Her story was much clearer to us, with increasing coherence and detail. Of the SDR, Sarah said that she could see herself in it now and would be inclined to use one with her next client. She also commented that staff in the day hospital could see their own reactions within it too. She felt that staff had more understanding of Maria's behavioural difficulties, that they were more able to empathise with her, were 'softer' with her, more able to approach her, and inclined to see her less as a psychiatric patient and more as a person. It sounded like staff had found an exit to a distancing procedure.

Overall, Sarah's work with Maria followed a similar process and outcome to the above: from an initial worsening or intensifying (due to 'exposure', from the 'response prevention' – specifically, preventing 'avoidance' – in the form of not colluding with a distancing procedural sequence), to a grief process, then more narrative detail and coherence; memories remained painful, but with a reduction of PTSD intrusive intensity, and some improvement, while incomplete, in somatisation. Maria's traumatic war experiences now appear more as part of her long life story, rather than overwhelming or occluding it. The SDR, representing non-collusion, may help the practitioner balance their own experiences of intrusion (being overwhelmed) and avoidance (numbing) which in turn is aimed at helping the client establish their equilibrium here that Horowitz suggests is important.

Implications for the treatment of complex and distant trauma

The existing approaches to treatment of the consequences of trauma are very successful for the treatment of short-term unexpected events such as those described by Terr (1991) as Type-1 trauma. Indeed, none of the randomised controlled trials of trauma-focused treatments addresses complex trauma. A review of the effectiveness of treatments for PTSD can be found in Foa et al. (2000). Few authors address the issue of treatments for complex trauma such as prolonged sexual abuse or prolonged captivity experiences. An exception to this is the work of Herman (1993). Similarly, there are few publications which address the treatment needs of older adults whose experience of trauma may be very distant. Exceptions to this are Hyer and Sohnle (2001) and Hunt et al. (1996). The description of the practice of CAT (Ryle 1995) has much in common but also much to offer trauma-focused treatment especially, in treating very complex or distant trauma. This is in the integration of an earlier developmental understanding which can help formulate the procedural restrictions and limitations on the capacity for self-reflection, which he sees as having their origins in trauma and deprivation. It is this, rather than the intensity of affects or behaviours, that is considered the key absence.

Ryle suggests that restricted experience that may be the result of narrow family role definitions, or beliefs about the world and its danger-ousness, may leave the individual with a small behavioural repertoire, which constantly receives confirmation from the world. Following trauma there is often extreme reduction of the behavioural repertoire, which limits the opportunities for testing out ideas about the dangerousness of the world. Restricted self-reflection and disjointed self-reflection may arise from the kinds of restricted or disjointed reflection afforded by others. Authoritarian parenting styles, for instance, may result in children who have no awareness or concepts with which to appraise their own subjective experience. As a consequence they may find integration of reciprocal role procedures very difficult.

Ryle discusses unmanageable experiences which are at the heart of PTSD. These experiences are seen as having the ability to overwhelm the capacity to feel, think or act and may become unthinkable or unspeakable experiences. Other people often reinforce this tendency towards avoid-ance, and procedures become adapted to avoid any stimuli which may lead to remembering. Silencing may occur as a result of overwhelming experiences when the perpetrator threatens punishment if the event is ever mentioned. Alternatively it is an internal representation of the perpetrator that threatens punishment even if in reality there has been no explicit direct threat. Defensive anxiety reduction may result from the internalised representation of critical parents. This entails avoiding the wishes or activities which may invite critical judgements.

The practice of CAT as described by Ryle (1995) offers a useful structure for working with complex trauma. Starting with an assess-ment phase, which identifies the appropriate match between a client's problems, the appropriate treatment model and therapist experience, allows the development of a treatment contract. By this means the client is placed in a position of adult responsibility. Initial sessions allow for the gathering of data and initial reformulation. The aim is to gain a thorough understanding of the client's experience and give some idea of what the therapist has to offer. This allows the possibility of forming a true thera-peutic alliance, defined as non-collusion with unhelpful procedural sequences, with a sense of control vested in the client: the therapist as a 'real other' while maintaining an intersubjective link to the client's often fragmented experience (Chapter 1). Following this with a reformulation session which includes a written reformulation cements this therapeutic alliance. During this phase identification of target problems and target problem procedures are pivotal to therapy. The explicit recognition of these processes allows clients as well as therapists to address them but also allows recognition of similar processes being played out in the transference–countertransference relationships (reciprocal role procedures).

Sequential diagrammatic reformulation offers an explicit way of viewing the sequential, self-maintaining nature of procedures. It also allows for a clearer understanding of how procedures are connected. As a technique it permits a clear reformulation as a constructive process between client and therapist. Many CBT therapists use diagrammatic formulation as part of their treatment, but with little consistency in both the content and the ways in which it is used. When used as part of CBT it is most effective when carried out as a collaborative process with the client rather than being something the therapist presents to the client fully worked through. It is also an element of treatment which has demonstrated great value in working with clients who may have limited use of English or whose therapy is being carried out via an interpreter. Constructs which may be very difficult to translate become more comprehensible when presented in diagrammatic format. One of the criticisms of CAT is that it is wrong to condense so much of life into a diagram. Ryle (2003a) noted that we do have to be careful and not be too persuasive in the use of these tools; however, good concepts help contain and access feelings or thinking that have not been available for reflection, and there is some evidence for the validity of the SDR (Bennett and Parry 1998; Ryle 2003b).

The essential aspect of CAT is the cooperative, respectful, non-collusive relationship with the therapist. Danieli (1988) describes the collusive nature of therapist–client relationships in addressing extreme trauma. Because of the extreme distress which addressing traumatic experiences engendered in both Holocaust survivors and their therapists, a 'conspiracy of silence' develops whereby the central issue of the experience itself is never addressed. CAT offers a structure and format for making many of the issues which may be implicit in other therapies explicit.

Conclusion

There is both a lack of recognition of the impact of distant trauma on older adults as well as few models of appropriate treatment. Most of the existing approaches to treatment are based on the treatment of sudden, unexpected single trauma which had occurred relatively recently. While these models enjoy a high level of success with their target population they may have less to offer for the treatment of complex or very distant trauma.

There are many similarities between CAT and CBT in terms of approach. CBT approaches to trauma focus on both re-exposure to the traumatic events as well as modification of maladaptive beliefs, attitudes and behaviours. CAT, in its explicit recognition of the latter and its formalised structure for addressing them in a way that is acceptable to clients and therapists, offers a means of addressing trauma. This means provides a sense of emotional safety as described by Herman (1993) as well as a way to proceed beyond the traps and dilemmas which are common sequelae of trauma.

It is becoming more common for psychodynamic concepts to be incorporated into CBT, but these modifications are occurring on an *ad hoc* basis. CAT, because of its origins, offers the possibility for integration of approaches in a rational way which has a theoretical framework underpinning it. A clear model is extremely important when working with distant trauma as the intensity of the experience can make the therapist work in a collusive fashion to avoid the pain of the trauma. Robbins (1997) provides evidence that trauma-focused treatments may be effective in addressing distant trauma. As this chapter has indicated, a synthesis of CBT and CAT approaches has much to offer therapists working with the complex issues surrounding the long-term impact of distant trauma.

References

Agger, I., and Jensen, S. B. (1990) Testimony as ritual and evidence for political refugees. *Journal of Traumatic Stress* 3: 115–30.

APA (1994) *Diagnostic & Statistical Manual 4th Edition.* Washington, DC: American Psychiatric Association.

Archibald, H. C., and Tuddenham, R. D. (1965) Persistent stress reactions after combat: a 20 year follow-up. *Archives of General Psychiatry* 12: 475–81.

Bennett, D., and Parry, G. (1998) The accuracy of reformulation in cognitive analytic therapy: a validation study. *Psychotherapy Research* 8: 84–103.

Bisson, J. I., and Shepherd, J. P. (1995) Psychological reactions of victims of violent crime. *British Journal of Psychiatry* 167(6): 718–20.

Blake, D. D., Keane, T. M., Wine, P. R., Ora, C., Taylor, K. L., and Lyons, J. A. (1990) Prevalence of symptoms in combat veterans seeking medical treatment. *Journal of Traumatic Stress* 3(1): 15–27.

Bleich, A., Garb, B., and Kottler, M. (1986) Treatment of prolonged combat reaction. *British Journal of Psychiatry* 148: 493–6.

Brewin, C. R., Dalgleish, T., and Joseph, S. (1996) A dual representation theory of Post Traumatic Stress Disorder. *Psychological Review* 103(4): 670–86.

Chodoff, P. (1963) Late effects of the concentration camp syndrome. *Archives of General Psychiatry* 8: 323–33.

Chung, M. C. (1993) Understanding post traumatic stress: a biographical account. *British Psychological Society, Psychotherapy Section Newsletter* 14: 21–9.

Cienfuegos, A. J., and Monelli, C. (1983) The testimony of political repression as a therapeutic instrument. *American Journal of Orthopsychiatry* 53: 43–51.

Danieli, Y. (1985) The treatment and prevention of long term effects and intergenerational transmission of victimisation. In C. R. Figley (ed.), *Trauma and Its Wake*. New York: Bruner Mazel.

Danieli, Y. (1988) Confronting the unimaginable: psychotherapists' reactions to victims of the Nazi Holocaust. In J. Wilson, Z. Harel and B. Kahana (eds), *Human Adaptation to Severe Stress: from the Holocaust to Vietnam*. New York: Plenum.

Ehlers, A., and Clark, D. M. (2000) A cognitive model of post-traumatic stress disorder. *Behaviour Research and Therapy* 38: 319–45.

Eitinger, L. (1961) Pathology of the concentration camp syndrome. *Archives of General Psychiatry* 5: 371–9.

Elder, G. H., and Clipp, E. C. (1988) Combat experience, comradeship and psychological health. In J. Wilson, Z. Harel and B. Kahana (eds), *Human Adaptation to Severe Stress: From the Holocaust to Vietnam*. New York: Plenum.

Fairbank, J. A., Langley, K., Jarvie, G. J., and Keane, T. M. (1991) A selected bibliography of PTSD in Vietnam Veterans. *Professional Psychology* 12: 578–86.

Fisher, J. V. (1999) *The Uninvited Guest: Emerging from Narcissism towards Marriage*. London: Karnac.

Foa, E. B., Keane, T. M., and Friedman, M. J. (2000) *Effective Treatments for PTSD*. New York: Guilford Press.

Genevey, B., and Katz, R. S. (1990) *Countertransference and Older Clients*. London: Sage.

Hamilton, J. D., Canteen, W., Beigel, A., and Yost, D. (1987) Post traumatic stress disorder in World War II naval veterans. *Hospital and Community Psychiatry* 38(2): 197–9.

Harvey, M. R. (1996) An ecological view of psychological trauma and trauma recovery. *Journal of Traumatic Stress* 9(1): 3–24.

Herman, J. (1993) *Trauma and Recovery*. New York: Basic Books.

Horowitz, M. J. (1986) Stress response syndromes: a review of post traumatic and adjustment disorders. *Hospital and Community Psychiatry* 37: 241–9.

Hunt, N., and Robbins, I. (2001a) The long term consequences of war: the experience of WWII. *Aging and Mental Health* 5(2): 183–90.

Hunt, N., and Robbins, I. (2001b) WWII veterans, social support and veterans associations. *Aging and Mental Health* 5(2): 175–82.

Hunt, L., Marshall, M., and Rowlings, C. (1996) *Past Trauma in Late Life: European Perspectives on Therapeutic Work with Older Adults.* London: Jessica Kingsley.

Hyer, L. A., and Sohnle, S. J. (2001) *Trauma Among Older People.* Philadelphia: Brunner-Routledge.

Janoff-Bulman, R. (1989) Assumptive worlds and the stress of traumatic events: applications of the schema construct. *Social Cognition* 7(2): 113–36.

Janoff-Bulman, R. (1992) *Shattering Assumptions: Towards a New Pathology of Trauma.* New York: Free Press.

Janoff-Bulman, R., and Frantz, C. M. (1997) The impact of trauma on meaning. In M. Power and C. R. Brewin (eds), *The Transformation of Meaning in Psychological Therapies.* London: John Wiley.

Kitwood, T. (1997) *Dementia Reconsidered: The Person Comes First.* Buckingham: Open University Press.

Krell, R. (1985) Therapeutic value of documenting child survivors. *Journal of the American Academy of Child Psychiatry* 24(4): 397–400.

Kuch, K., and Cox, B. J. (1992) Symptoms of PTSD in 124 survivors of the Holocaust. *American Journal of Psychiatry* 149(3): 337–40.

Macdonald, J., and Morley, I. (2001) Shame and non-disclosure: a study of the emotional isolation of people referred for psychotherapy. *British Journal of Medical Psychology* 74: 1–21.

Mazor, A., Gampel, Y., Enright, R. D., Ornstein, R. (1990) Holocaust survivors: coping with post-traumatic memories in childhood and 40 years later. *British Medical Journal* 307: 647–51.

Mollica, R. M. (1987) The trauma story: the psychiatric care of refugee survivors of violence and torture. In F. M. Ochberg (ed.), *Post-Traumatic Therapy and the Victims of Violence.* New York: Brunner Mazel.

Ochberg, F. M. (1995) *Post-Traumatic Therapy and the Victims of Violence.* New York: Brunner Mazel.

Orner, R. J., and Loos, W. S. de (1998) Second World War veterans with chronic post traumatic stress disorder. *Advances in Psychiatric Treatment* 4: 211–18.

Robbins, I. (1997) Treatment of war trauma in World War Two Veterans. In L. Hunt, M. Marshall and C. Rowlings (eds), *Past Trauma in Late Life: European Perspectives on Therapeutic Work with Older People.* London: Jessica Kingsley.

Robbins, I. (2000) Working with victims of war trauma. In H. Kemshall and J. Pritchard (eds), *Good Practice in Working with Victims of Violence.* London: Jessica Kingsley.

Robbins, I. (2001) Issues arising from the treatment of WWII prisoners of war. Paper presented to the European Association for the Study of Traumatic Stress. Edinburgh, May.

Ryle, A. (1978) A common language for the therapies. *British Journal of Psychiatry* 132: 585–94.

Ryle, A. (1990) *Cognitive Analytic Therapy: Active Participation in Change. A New Integration in Brief Psychotherapy.* Chichester: John Wiley.

Ryle, A. (1991) Object relations theory and activity theory: a proposed link by way of the procedural sequence model. *British Journal of Medical Psychology* 64: 307–16

Ryle, A. (1995) *Cognitive Analytic Therapy.* Chichester: John Wiley.

Ryle, A. (2003a) The history and use of the SDR. ACAT Conference, 8 March, Guy's Hospital, London.

Ryle, A. (2003b) History and use of the SDR. *Reformulation. Theory and Practice in CAT* 20: 19–21.

Ryle, A. and Kerr, I. B. (2002) *Introducing Cognitive Analytic Therapy: Principles and Practice.* Chichester: Wiley.

Speed, N., Engdahl, B., Schwartz, J., and Eberly, R. (1989) Post traumatic stress disorder as a consequence of the POW experience. *Journal of Nervous and Mental Disease* 177(3): 147–53.

Sutker, P. B., Winstead, D. K., Galina, Z. H. and Allain, A. N. (1990) Assessment of long term psychosocial sequelae among POW survivors of the Korean conflict. *Journal of Personality Assessment* 54: 170–80.

Terr, L. C. (1991) Childhood traumas: an outline and review. *American Journal of Psychiatry* 148: 10–20.

Zeiss, R. A., and Dickman, H. R. (1989) PTSD 40 years later: incidence and person situation correlates in former POWs. *Journal of Clinical Psychology* 45(1): 80–7.

Chapter 8

Borderline traits and dissociated states in later life

Jason Hepple

In this chapter I will consider the application of CAT principles to working with older people with personality-based problems, both as an individual and couple therapy as well as a theoretical model to inform discussion in a case conference setting – what I will call 'Systemic CAT'. The older people who may benefit from these approaches have problems stemming from their earlier lives, often as a result of emotionally depriving or abusive relationships in their childhoods, and have symptoms and behaviours that appear in the *DSM IV* definition of borderline personality disorder (APA 1994). This is not to say that these people have had long psychiatric careers with frequent admissions and self-harm; many seem to have coped through their middle years only to 'regress' back to more primitive ways of coping when faced with cumulative loss in later life. The distress for these people is often severe and destructive. Those who work in mental health services for older people will quickly recall people who fall into this group and how challenging, emotionally draining and resource-consuming is the support that they need. It is my hope that this chapter will at least draw together some common themes of working with this group of older people and provide an understandable theoretical base for this challenging work.

This chapter will be largely clinical in focus and will describe cases where CAT principles have been useful in helping the individual and system cope with severe self-damaging and destructive behaviours (borderline traits) and with the rare group of older people that retreat into an hysterical 'dementia' as a means of self-preservation (dissociated states). In order to ground these ideas I will briefly look at the literature around the concept of personality disorder in older people and the possibility that later life can see the resurgence of the more borderline personality traits. I will then discuss Ryle's development of CAT theory to provide a model of borderline personality structure before applying these principles to work with older people though clinical case discussion.

Borderline personality disorder in older people

> Despite the enormous amount of literature on the elderly, and on personality, there is a paucity of psychiatric literature on personality disorder in the elderly.
>
> (Kroessler 1990, p. 1350)

There has been an assumption, as is often the case when considering the mental health of older people, that what is not obvious is probably not there or is an inevitable part of the ageing process and is unlikely to respond to intervention. Depression, dementia and anxiety-based disorders in older people have a long history of under-recognition or therapeutic nihilism which has only been identified in recent decades. The tendency to label the 'difficult' older person as irredeemably 'confused' and thus beyond therapeutic help has led to the false belief that personality disorders (or more pertinently developmentally understood disorders) in older people are rare – presumably because the problem has 'burnt out' or the person has died before later life as a result of suicide, or self-destructive or reckless behaviours.

> The manifestations of personality disorder are often recognized by adolescence or earlier and continue on throughout most of adult life, though they often become less obvious in middle or old age.
>
> (APA 1987)

Part of the reason for this belief may be that the tools used to measure personality disorder are not sensitive to the changes in manifestation of personality traits in older people. In a striking study by Rosowsky and Gurian (1991) of eight cases of borderline personality disorder in older people diagnosed clinically by experienced mental health professionals, not one reached caseness for the condition using either the *DSM III-R* criteria (APA 1987) or the Diagnostic Interview for Borderlines (DIB, Gunderson *et al.* 1981). Despite the problems with the diagnostic tools used to identify the personality disorders in older people for research purposes (for a review of methodological issues see Mroczek *et al.* 1999) there is a growing consensus that personality disorder is at least as prevalent in older people as in those of all adult ages.

Reich *et al.* (1988) carried out an assessment of the prevalence of *DSM*

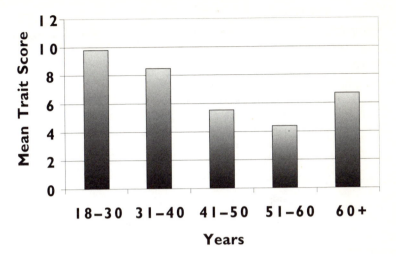

Figure 8.1 Prevalence of *DSM III-R* dramatic cluster traits by age
(from Reich *et al.*, 1988)

III-R personality disorder traits in a community-based sample of people of a range of ages. Given the probable under-reporting as a result of the methodological issues discussed above, it was interesting to see that prevalence of the dramatic cluster traits (which includes borderline traits) was actually higher in the sixty-plus age group when compared with those in midlife. See Figure 8.1.

In a meta-analytic review of the available literature on personality disorders in people over the age of fifty, Abrams and Horowitz (1999) found that overall prevalence rates for personality disorder in the over- and under-fifties were broadly the same: around 20 per cent of the patient populations in the included studies. Interestingly, the prevalence of some types of personality disorder was actually higher in the over-fifty group, notably the borderline, passive-aggressive and histrionic types, while the prevalence of the paranoid and narcissistic types showed the most decline with age. While these comparisons must be treated with caution due to the methodological issues discussed above, it seems that borderline and related personality traits are likely to show a resurgence in later life.

The explanation for this rise is likely to be multi-factorial. Morse and Lynch (2000) emphasise the link between co-morbid depression and personality disorder in older people. It is possible that a higher prevalence of depression and poorer response to and engagement in treatment by older people may exaggerate self-report of personality psychopathology,

Increased life events + Reduced coping abilities = Unmasking of borderline traits.

LIFE EVENTS

Loss of
- Partner, family, friends
- Job and financial status
- Social and family roles
- Physical / sensory skills
- Independence
- Mental abilities

REDUCED COPING
- Cognitive impairment
- Depression
- Reduced theatre for enacting psychological defences
- Reduced energy for enacting psychological defences

Figure 8.2 The unmasking theory for borderline personality traits in later life

due to low self-esteem and guilt. If one is to take a more developmental perspective, however, it is clear that older people face multiple losses (bereavement, retirement, physical and mental health) which are likely to provoke challenges to usual coping mechanisms and the possibility of regression back to more borderline or primitive defences in a vulnerable group with underlying character pathology.

> naturally occurring stressors of old age, such as retirement, widow-hood, and physical constraints may place too heavy a burden on individuals with character pathology and induce reactive, transient regressions. A narcissistic or histrionic character may present as a more primitively organised borderline personality during a regressed phase. This regression may account for the appearances of border-line personality disorder *de novo* in old age or after a quiescent phase during middle adulthood in persons who were diagnosed as having the disorder in earlier life.
>
> (Rosowsky and Gurian 1992, p. 387)

This explanation is appealing to the psychotherapeutically aware clinician and gives some hope that interventions may be beneficial and that under-standing and insight is achievable. It may be helpful, symbolically to

Table 8.1 Differences in the presentation of borderline traits in later life

DSM IV Trait	Differences in older people
Frantic attempts to avoid real or imagined abandonment	Fear of institutionalisation, overly demanding of caregivers' time
Unstable, intense interpersonal relationships	Powerful splitting of caregivers, highly critical and demanding of others
Identity disturbance	Lack of ability to engage in age-appropriate developmental tasks
Impulsivity	Less recklessness
Suicidal or self-harming behaviours	Less overt self-harm. More self-neglect, abuse of prescribed medication, food as control and somatisation
Affective lability	Present
Chronic feelings of emptiness	Expressed as hopeless resignation
Inappropriate intense anger	Often repressed and presented passive-aggressively
Transient paranoid thinking or dissociative symptoms	Accusatory and critical of others' motives, somatisation, pseudodementia.

think of this process as an unmasking of borderline traits that have been dormant or quiescent in the timeless unconscious since early life. When the mask that has presented a coping persona to the world for thirty or forty years is no longer sustainable, what is uncovered may not be exactly the same as when it last saw the light of day. The unmasking may reveal a new face (Hepple 1999).

Figure 8.2 lists some of the losses and disabilities that cause the regression back to borderline pathology. Of particular interest is the inability to sustain defence systems which may have been highly effective in earlier life. For example, a person who copes by being an idealised and placating carer (ideally caring relating to ideally cared for) to an abusive and critical partner may find their self-esteem unsustainable after the partner's death. Alternatively, a person whose self-esteem is sustained by their physical vigour, sexual attractiveness or mental agility (admiring relating to admired) may collapse into critical self-absorption when they feel others will 'see through' their usual persona. This latter group is explored in the earlier chapters on narcissism in later life (this volume, Chapters 5 and 6).

Table 8.1 looks at the component borderline personality traits as described in *DSM IV* (APA 1994) and suggests how their presentation is altered in later life. There is a general move away from the overtly dramatic (violence to others, suicidal acts, reckless behaviours, abuse of illegal drugs) to a more covert and passive-aggressive expression of distress (critical and demanding to caregivers with the generation of guilt in the other, to defend against the fear of abandonment). I am sure that clinicians reading this table will identify clients who have expressed some or all of these traits. The fundamental dynamic at work here is a profound hopelessness and fear that is defended against using the means left at the older person's disposal. Identifying the vulnerability and low self-esteem of the older person will help professionals and carers avoid enmeshment in the powerful reciprocal role dynamics that surface.

Later in the chapter I will discuss clinical examples of the treatment of resurgent borderline traits in older people using the CAT model. Here I will mention some related work using the model of Dialectical Behaviour Therapy (DBT) which gives some evidence that psychotherapeutic interventions may be useful in treating older people with depressive symptoms and co-morbid personality disorder. Morse and Lynch (2000) give a preliminary report on a trial of twenty-seven people over sixty years old with 'multi-problem elderly depression'. The group were randomised to either DBT (skills training plus medication) or TAU (treatment as usual, medication plus clinical management). The results suggest that the DBT group showed improvement over the TAU group in terms of adaptive coping, concern for being liked, self-criticism and need to control their environments.

Lynch (in Morse and Lynch 2000) describes three 'dialectical dilemmas for the elderly' clinically useful when treating older people with personality problems. The three dilemmas are: bitter vs acquiescent, brooding vs avoidant and autonomous vs dependent. There is some similarity here with a CAT understanding of personality disturbance, although the dilemmas described are not synonymous with the concept of reciprocal roles, in Table 8.2 I have attempted a restatement of the dilemmas in CAT terms for comparison.

Borderline personality disorder and CAT

CAT has developed a reputation for being a clinically effective model for helping adults with borderline personality disorder as described in *DSM IV*. On a small but growing evidence base that suggests that psychodynamically inspired therapeutic interventions are effective in the treatment of borderline personality disorder (for a review see Perry *et al.* 1999), Ryle and Golynkina (2000) report on a naturalistic study of 24-

Table 8.2 Lynch's DBT dilemmas for the elderly and comparative CAT restatement

DBT	CAT
Bitter vs Acquiescent	Contemptuous ↑↓ Contemptible / Guilty / Striving
Brooding vs Avoidant	Critical / Abusing ↑↓ Crushed / Hopeless or Passively Rebellious
Autonomous vs Dependent	Controlling / Contemptuous ↑↓ Controlled / Needy

session CAT. The results are encouraging in that at six months after therapy half the cohort no longer met the criteria for borderline personality disorder. At eighteen months several outcome measures showed benefits for the group as a whole although positive outcome was inversely correlated with initial severity. Although, at the time of writing, funding is still being sought for a larger randomised controlled trial of CAT in this group, evidence would suggest that CAT is an effective treatment for these people. Basic to the CAT understanding of borderline personality is the linking of physical, sexual and emotional abuse in earlier life with the emotional, unstable and destructive traits described in the *DSM IV* description of borderline personality (see Figure 8.2).

CAT practitioners and therapists have gained much experience applying the model to people with the more severe and self-destructive personality traits. CAT is a highly collaborative therapy where the written components of the model (the reformulation letter at Session 4, the Sequential Diagrammatic Reformulation (SDR) in the middle of the therapy and the exchange of goodbye letters) ensure that the therapist is listening to and has processed the client's material in a way that is shared by therapist and client. Negative transference and the likely reciprocal role play between therapist and client are discussed early and often in simple terms. The use of diagrams, art techniques and symbolic tools such as shells or buttons can help to engage clients who have poor self-awareness and limited verbal skills. With an emphasis on sharing analytic insights and theories as soon as they emerge in the therapy, CAT has

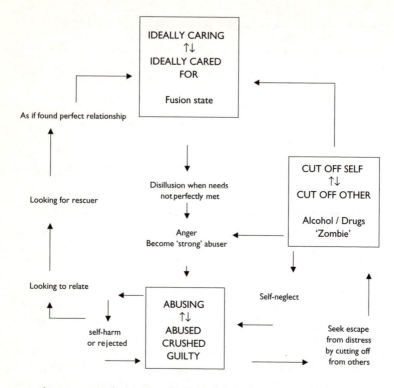

Attempts to escape from the core pain of feeling crushed and unloveable result in the fantasy that a perfect relationship is the only rescue. When care is not perfect, anger and disillusion lead to abusive behaviour and an ultimate return to the abused core. Cutting off from the pain through drink or drugs can lead to disinhibition and further abusive or idealised role-play or to neglect and self-abuse that further confirms the fear of unloveability.

Figure 8.3 Example borderline SDR template for a younger adult

shown itself to be able to engage and help people who have traditionally been hard to work with using other brief therapeutic and supportive models. As Ryle and Kerr comment:

> The collaborative construction of diagrams in the reformulation phase is a powerful experience for patients. Preliminary partial diagrams can be drawn from the first session, especially if therapy disrupting procedures are expected; the evolution of the diagrams as more evidence is collected is a positive collaborative map-making exercise which establishes a relationship which is 'off the map', that

is to say which provides the patient with a new way of being in relation to another.

(Ryle and Kerr 2002, p. 10)

Ryle (1997) has developed an elegant theoretical model of borderline personality disorder based on his earlier synthesis of object relations, personal construct and cognitive theory which is the basis of modern CAT. He describes a model of multiple split-off self-states based around idealised, abusive or cut-off reciprocal roles as the core of the model, with CAT's traps, dilemmas and snags forming the procedures that link the split self-states. Ryle and Kerr (2002) describe the model as being based on three forms of linked damage: harsh reciprocal role patterns, partial dissociation and impaired and interrupted self-reflection – each with a developmental basis in early life. There can be variable awareness of the existence of the other states when the client is experiencing the emotional intensity of the current state. For example, when in the idealised state of imagined fusion with another (the perfect relationship where all needs are anticipated and met, represented by the roles 'ideally caring relating to ideally cared for') there can be little or no awareness of how disillusion has previously thrown the couple from a state of idealised 'bliss' to one of angry disappointment, criticism and abuse ('abusing relating to abused / crushed'). Such 'state shifts', accompanied by extremes of emotion, prevent the client gaining an overview of the cycles they are repeating, leaving them with the experience of feeling disorientated, guilty and out of control, constantly running in a circle with no alternative way visible.

Figure 8.3 illustrates a borderline SDR with commonly found reciprocal roles, and basic linking procedures. This is something of a template – it is important to remember that in CAT each client's SDR will be unique and the words to describe the core beliefs and actions will be very personal to each client. Reciprocal roles commonly found in the narcissistic personality constellations described in the previous chapters are often found in the split-off self-states of the more borderline SDR (for example: admiring relating to admired, contemptuous relating to contemptible). When the dissociation is extreme the split-off self-states can form distinct (although often two-dimensional) multiple personalities with little or no awareness of the existence of the others at different points in time. Ryle thus puts forward a spectrum of dissociation with usual borderline pathology lying between healthy personality structures and the rare syndrome of multiple personality disorder.

By mapping out the split-off states in this way and demonstrating the thoughts, feelings and actions that link them, the client can begin to gain an overview of their ways of relating and can begin to predict, challenge and change these patterns by the development of exits. For example, an exit that could reduce the idealisation of a relationship in its early stages could read something like: 'Have realistic expectations, remember that no-one is perfect, work out what I can realistically expect from this relationship at this stage, negotiate the rules together.' Some clients describe the SDR as a map – although roughly drawn and not necessarily to scale, it at least shows the broad lie of the land and where the main danger areas lie. The reciprocal roles described on a client's SDR are often replicated in the relationship between client and therapist. The clarity and communicability of the SDR can be invaluable in keeping in mind how old, destructive patterns of relating are being replayed in the therapy and can prevent negative transference from encouraging lack of engagement or early termination of the therapy.

Ryle has thus established a clear model for working therapeutically with people who have experienced abusive or highly critical relationships in their early lives, who can find individual therapy exposing and frightening and who can sabotage the success of the therapy by acting out the very reciprocal roles that are at the heart of their distress and pain. The experience of the many CAT therapists in the UK and beyond suggests that CAT provides a valuable addition to the therapies available for the treatment of borderline personality disorder.

Treatment of borderline traits in older people using the CAT model

Bearing in mind the differences in presentation of borderline traits in older people when compared with younger adults, it may be helpful to provide an illustrative template SDR that incorporates some of these differences. Figure 8.4 highlights the main features: the search for ideal care, the cutting off from distress through somatisation (physical symptoms without an organic cause) or pseudodementia (seeming cognitive impairment brought on by psychological avoidance of anxiety) and the use of passive-dependent behaviour to exert abusive power on caregivers.

Somatic symptoms that do not have a physical origin present a particular challenge to those caring for the older person. The conversion of the emotional distress into the language of physical illness effectively prevents meaningful communication – cut-off self relating to cut-off other. The older person's agenda is usually headed by a discussion of the unresolved symptom with critical reference to those professionals who

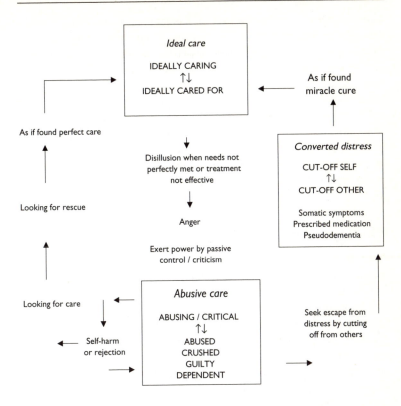

Some important differences in the type of SDR encountered when working with older people with borderline traits when compared with younger adults. The fantasy escape from a position of hopeless dependency involves the search for perfect care from family/carers professionals or a miracle cure for the cause of the dependency/disability. Inevitable disillusion results in the exertion of power through critical and passive-aggressive techniques. Cutting off from the core pain leads to a conversion of distress into somatic or dissociative symptoms that prevent meaningful dialogue with others.

Figure 8.4 Example borderline SDR template for an older person

have previously tried and failed to treat the symptom by medical means. The professional is in a difficult double bind. There is a need to rule out physical causes as far as possible due to the risk of misdiagnosis and justified criticism or litigation, but there is also the need to avoid collusion with the somatisation and putting the patient through unnecessary and potentially harmful investigations and treatment.

There is always a danger that a new professional will allow himself to be idealised as the saviour – the person who has finally made the right diagnosis when others have failed – and embark on new courses of investigation or treatment. Unless there really has been a hidden physical cause for the symptoms, the professional has a brief 'honeymoon' period where they engage in ideally caring role play with the patient (and bask in their praises being sung to all by the delighted patient), before the inevitable onset of disillusion and angry criticism when the new treatment does not take away the pain. Exits from the harmful procedures involve: excellent communication between professionals, the avoidance of splitting (idealising some, denigrating others) and the setting of firm boundaries around medication review and the seeking of further medical opinion or investigation. The following case illustrates the use of a systemic CAT model in such a situation.

The case of Mrs Jones

Born in the 1910s in the UK, Mrs Jones was the youngest of a large family and suffered from polio as a child, which necessitated long periods of hospital treatment, which the family could ill afford in pre-NHS days. She was criticised by her father for depriving her siblings due to her expensive hospitalisations. She learned that health care professionals provided the care that she failed to receive from her family, but only in the context and language of physical illness. Her experience of care at home was critical and overlooking: she recalled, as a child, being left in a wheelchair in the sun until she was badly dehydrated and sunburnt.

As an adult she married young to an abusive, alcoholic man who demanded perfect and unconditional care. Mrs Jones was able to divert her distress in attempting to provide this care to her husband. Striving to please him at the expense of her own needs left unexpressed anger and self-loathing which was stored up throughout the marriage. On her husband's death, after a long illness with chest disease, Mrs Jones decompensated, and the borderline traits that had been formed by her childhood experience and fuelled by the pent-up anger engendered by the ideally caring role with her husband, came to the surface with dramatic effect.

Mrs Jones claimed to have a rare rheumatological condition that could manifest as many diffuse and vague symptoms and for which no definitive tests were available to prove its existence. Most commonly she complained of intense pain in the middle of her body that she was sure was caused by the condition – or more pertinently, the lack of effective diagnosis and treatment of the condition. After several rounds of specialist opinions and second opinions at tertiary health facilities, Mrs

Jones was being treated with a range of potentially harmful medications on the basis that the diagnosis could not be ruled out, despite no investigations providing more than the mildest suspicion that the condition was present at all. One specialist even went as far as saying that he thought the condition unlikely, but still the treatment continued. Although Mrs Jones seemed contained by the ongoing medical care and often behaved like a 'model' patient, after the tests had been completed, disillusion set in as the 'pain' was still present and unbearable.

Next followed a difficult time for the primary care team who were being called out on a daily and nightly basis because of the pain, which resulted in the prescription of painkillers of escalating strength and the resultant opiate dependency. The doctors in the practice had differing views of Mrs Jones ranging from contempt and anger at the waste of professional time, to the assumption of the idealised caregiver role by one professional who was sure that a definitive physical treatment could be found, and continued seeking further opinions and trying new medications. In addition, Mrs Jones was arranging private sector opinions which were not connected to the work of the primary care team and which added more anti-depressants and tranquillising medications without awareness of the overall history. She engaged neighbours and friends to collude with her perceived 'misdiagnosis' and persuaded them to supply extra analgesics, although she was already harming her liver by chronic analgesia overdosing. At times of feeling crushed and abandoned Mrs Jones took to her bed, neglected her self-care and could be verbally and physically violent to caregivers. In the abuser role she threatened her GP with litigation and engaged an advocate from a national organisation.

Mrs Jones was referred to the mental health services and a systemic CAT model was used to try and contain the system which was increasingly out of control. A case conference was arranged involving over a dozen doctors, community nurses, social workers and home care staff who had been involved in the case as well as Mrs Jones or part of the meeting. Emotions ran high with staff exhausted and deskilled or critical and punitive towards Mrs Jones. One homecarer had slipped into idealised care and felt that other carers were insufficiently skilled to deal with Mrs Jones, while she had no difficulty. By writing down the feelings of the professionals in a brainstorming way on a flip chart it became clear and understandable to the group that we were engaged in reciprocal role play triggered by Mrs Jones's powerful psychodynamics. By the end of the first meeting catharsis and joint understanding had helped everyone gain a clearer perspective and had enabled a systemic SDR to be formed where simple exits could help clarify roles, confirm boundaries and

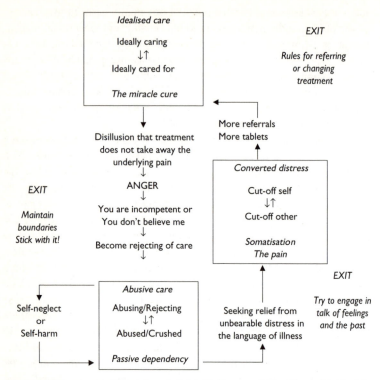

A systemic SDR for a person with borderline traits in later life. The core pain (abused/crushed) is defended against by somatisation and attempts to engage others using the language of illness. If further referral or new treatment is initiated there is the hope of idealised care. After a honeymoon period, however, disillusion sets in as the real pain has not gone away, leading to angry rejection of care. Without care Mrs Jones slips into self-neglect or self-harm which confirms the core pain.

Figure 8.5 Systemic SDR for Mrs Jones

support everyone in a sense of challenging but coordinated care. Figure 8.5 illustrates the basic systemic SDR for Mrs Jones.

As shown in this figure, Mrs Jones shifted between three reciprocal role states which can be named as: Compliant, grateful patient (Ideal care), Violent accuser (Abusive care) and Somatic distress (Converted distress). The main management problems occurred when Mrs Jones was operating out of either Abusive care or Converted distress. In the former, Mrs Jones could be violent and verbally abusive, attacking carers, causing damage to property and accusing carers of stealing and neglect. In Converted distress Mrs Jones would stay in bed for days or weeks, with poor self-care and rejection of all care other than promises of new medical treatments or interventions.

The main exits are described on the SDR. The community psychiatric nurse involved was given the task of trying to engage Mrs Jones in discussion of the more emotionally relevant material; her past, her feelings, her worries for the future; with an attempt to avoid prolonged dialogue around the pain and the illness which only ever led to angry criticism from Mrs Jones if new treatment initiates were not forthcoming. The general practitioner's task was to try and establish boundaries around the need for further medical investigation and to resist daily requests to alter or increase the analgesia. It is difficult in these situations to make cast iron rules around the need for medical care, as there is always the possibility of new symptoms and pathology emerging which does require a rethink and further assessment. With careful thought, a balance was achieved so that unless there was significant change in Mrs Jones's presentation, then medical review was set up for fixed dates in the future and the management plan should be stuck to until then. These measures were particularly helpful for other GPs who might be asked to assess Mrs Jones while on-call. Finally, the home care team was supported with the aim of sticking with Mrs Jones even when she became rejecting, hostile and critical to them. This did not mean doing things without her consent, but to stick to the times of her home visits, even when subjected to verbal abuse at the previous meeting, and then to offer help with practical tasks if Mrs Jones then wanted it.

The approach caused considerable benefit to the system as a whole. Mrs Jones was unable to engage in one-to-one dialogue on an emotional level on any other topic than the pain, which ruled out the possibility of offering her individual CAT or other therapy at that time. She was, however, able to build up a certain level of trust in the team charged with her care, and despite repeated cycles of the SDR and the emotional turmoil this involved, something of a therapeutic alliance emerged with key people in the system, which had the effect of containing Mrs Jones and helping the professionals keep a clear perspective and to feel supported in this difficult work.

Mrs Jones was invited to future case conferences which she sometimes attended (although often for short periods only). To avoid the inevitable dichotomy between a physical or psychological causation for the pain, attempts were made to agree a compromise: that Mrs Jones had both psychological and physical needs and that the team as a whole was charged with looking after both as well as they could. It was important to include any new personnel in case conferences as they became involved (for example an advocate from the voluntary sector), to avoid them being split off from the greater system. Finally, communication within the system of care and with interfacing agencies (general hospital staff, local pharmacists, etc.) was crucial to the maintenance of the treatment plan.

Over a period of several years the use of Systemic CAT has limited the damage and distress both in Mrs Jones and in the individuals in the extensive system of care that surrounds her. Recently, Mrs Jones has gone into residential care in a highly specialised nursing home using NHS continuing care funding. It is a challenge to the staff who have known her for a longer period to convey the nature of the management plan to a new staff group who are more experienced in the treatment of schizophrenia and affective disorders. It is important to convey that the seemingly random state shifts are understandable in terms of personality structure and traumatic earlier experience, and not by using the concepts of 'moods swings', psychotic illness, biological depression or dementia. With this understanding comes a move away from the use of tranquillisers and analgesics and an awareness that the storms are to be weathered rather than referred. Emotional support and supervision for the new staff group is essential for the success of the placement.

It is an interesting and perhaps worrying development that after a period of sustained violent and disruptive behaviour, Mrs Jones has developed new phenomena stemming from the converted distress role. Seeming deafness and most recently pseudodementia make communication almost impossible when Mrs Jones is in this state. This may mark a move away from somatisation (perhaps because new medical treatment has become less likely, removing this escape into idealised care), and a further and more prolonged retreat into a cut-off dissociated state that ends in physical dependency and seeming severe dementia.

In the next section I shall explore the nature and treatment of this rare from of hysterical dementia in older people, which can be understood using the CAT understanding of borderline traits in older people.

Dissociated states in older people

In my time working clinically with older people with mental health problems I have collected a small number of cases where the patient seems to have a progressive organic dementia with a progression towards social and physical dependency. Following extensive assessment, investigation and contact over an extended period of time, however, all intuitive senses suggest that the problem is psychologically caused and maintained. The psychiatric literature has thrown up a handful of these cases previously and the syndrome has been called, variously; 'a dementia syndrome of dependency' (Howells and Beats 1989), 'functional dementia due to hysterical behaviour' (Kirby and Harper 1987 and 1988) and 'severe and persistent regressive behaviour in elderly subjects without cognitive decline' (Padoani and De Leo 2000). Liberini *et al.* (1993) briefly report a further six cases, emphasising the need to make an early diagnosis to prevent institutionalisation and further deterioration. I have called this syndrome 'conversion pseudodementia in older people', in an attempt to move away from the word 'hysteria' (although the mechanisms are still the same), and to recognise the physical dependency which is part of the syndrome in addition to the seeming cognitive impairment.

Freud recognised the importance of hysterical mechanisms in symptom formation. The following extract is particularly notable for the accuracy with which it describes the concept of unmasked borderline and hysterical traits in older people as being a reaction to cumulative stress:

> our investigations of many, if not the majority of hysterical symptoms, have revealed cases which must be described as psychic traumas. Any experience which rouses the distressing affects of fright, apprehension, shame, or psychical pain can have this effect and it obviously depends on the sensitiveness of the person concerned whether the experiences acquire the importance of a trauma. We not infrequently find . . . partial traumas instead of one grand trauma, which can only achieve traumatic effectiveness by accumulation and which belong together only in so far as they form parts of a whole painful experience.
>
> (Freud 1957:25)

The essential features common to all the cases in the series are a syndrome of dependency and behavioural problems resembling dementia-related conduct disorders, but with stable cognitive performance over a period of years. The most common core symptoms are, in order of prevalence: verbally abusive, dependency in personal care, intrusive shouting, the need for institutional care long-term, incontinence, immobility, 'aggressive deafness', physically abusive and self-harm (usually scratching or falling). 'Aggressive deafness' is the seeming deliberate mishearing of the questioner's words in order to inhibit meaningful communication by making the questioner appear foolish or insensitive, usually in front of others (a likely humiliating relating to humiliated reciprocal role). An example is a man in his eighties who, when invited to attend the ward round shouted repeatedly: 'The wardrobe! What do you mean the wardrobe. I'm not going in the wardrobe. Help me! He's gone mad!'

Over the course of several years (the mean being seven), these patients

usually deteriorate in terms of physical dependency and require continuing hospital or nursing home care, although their flashes of lucidity make
carers realise their maintained cognition and awareness of their surround-
ings. It seemed to me that this unusual and terrifying state is best understood in terms of the CAT model of borderline personality disorder
applied to older people as explained in this chapter. The individuals did
not generally have previous psychiatric histories and developed these
symptoms in late middle age. Although it has not been possible to explore
the early life of the majority of cases, due to lack of informants and failure
to engage the person in meaningful reflection, it seems to be a useful
working hypothesis that borderline reciprocal roles are at the core of this
state and that the pseudodementia is an attempt to escape from the
distress of the collapse of idealised defences as later life brings cumulative losses. This understanding is gaining credence as we work with three
patients in the earlier stages of the process of dissociation who have been
able to explore their early experience of abandonment, emotional abuse
and highly critical care. One of these cases is discussed in detail below.
Figure 8.6 demonstrates a CAT understanding of conversion pseudodementia in older people.

The case of Mr and Mrs Brown

I report on a case that is still in progress, that demonstrates the connection
between early experience and later dissociation and the use of a couple
CAT approach where a supportive partner is available to engage in
therapy.

Mr Brown presented to a memory clinic in his mid-fifties with an
eighteeen-year history of cognitive impairment and functional disability
(unable to do finances, shopping and future planning), after extensive
investigation which had failed to establish an organic cause of pre-senile
dementia. On detailed cognitive testing his performance was highly
variable with most sub-scores indicating significant impairment but with
patches of performance in the top 2 per cent of the population. The
psychologist felt that Mr Brown could not help but show his true abilities
but seemed barely conscious of the obvious discrepancies that made an
organic diagnosis unlikely. On further assessment involving his caring
and supportive wife it began to be clear that psychological factors were
prominent in the presentation.

Mr Brown had grown up in a family where expression of any feelings
seemed dangerous and potentially harmful to fragile status quo. His
mother seemed to cope with her unhappiness by retreating into a world of

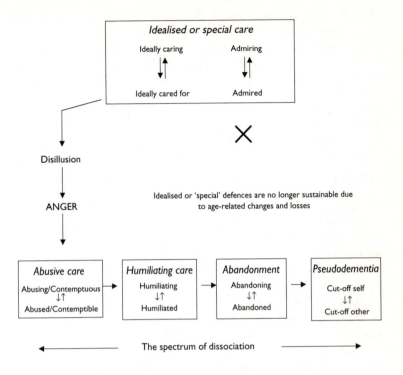

Figure 8.6 A CAT model of conversion pseudodementia in older people

her own. (It was striking that she was still alive in her nineties with a diagnosis of dementia although she could still finish cryptic crosswords.) His father was critical and demanding with a strong work-ethic and expected effortless success from his only son. Mr Brown had a success-ful early career, becoming a navigator in the armed forces and meeting and marrying his wife in his twenties while serving in Australasia. He was a devoted and caring father to their two children, although cautious in social situations. Problems began when he was suddenly made redundant in his late thirties and forced to leave the armed forces.

He and his wife took on the management of a shop, but Mr Brown became angry and dissatisfied with his situation, drinking heavily and becoming verbally abusive towards his wife and teenage children. He attempted accountancy exams, to forge a new professional career, but despite passing all the preliminary tests with flying colours, left the final exams complaining of amnesia and was unable to complete the course. It was then he began to slip into pseudodementia and social dependency on his wife, interspersed with angry outbursts.

Mrs Brown came from a larger family with a caring, striving mother and an emotionally closed father who needed attention and care to support his bread-winning role. Mrs Brown learned that keeping the boat afloat and putting your own needs second was the way to survive difficult times. Mrs Brown acted as a lock to Mr Brown's key and the two reciprocal role repertoires seemed to fit easily and ominously into a new pattern. Mrs Brown took on more and more of the tasks that her husband was now unable to do and was highly supportive of her husband's hospital appointments and investigations. As time passed, however, she became depressed and crushed by the reality of the retirement she looked forward to and became angry at her husband's abusive outbursts and inconsistent performance. For example, when his mother died he drove hundreds of miles alone and sorted out her affairs without any seeming problem – tasks he was unable to do at home. She had considered leaving the marriage but was wracked with guilt as most of the time her husband seemed like a lost and dependent child, needing her care.

In early sessions both Mr and Mrs Brown accepted a psychological approach and agreed to four individual sessions with separate therapists to come up with individual CAT reformulations. Mrs Brown talked easily of her life and upbringing and had great insight into her husband's isolated position and her role in it. Mr Brown struggled in individual sessions, cutting off from the conversation, being unable to remember the thread of the discussion and repeating stock phrases and recent experiences. Much information concerning his early life came from Mrs Brown in earlier joint sessions. The therapists then wrote a joint reformulation and presented to the couple as the beginning of a series of couple CAT sessions:

Couple reformulation (extract)

It seems as if Mr Brown, so disillusioned by the way he had been treated, felt that he had now lost all chance of achieving again the position of respect he had worked so hard for. He had been put on the scrap heap due to no fault of his own. He got in touch with his feelings of inadequacy and hidden anger but had learned that negative feelings could not be safely expressed so resorted to drinking and eventually to retreat into a world of his own, as his mother had done when faced with her own distress and disappointment.

Mrs Brown's response to her husband's difficulties was to try harder to be a supportive wife and put her own needs second – taking on more responsibilities and doing everything for her husband. This caring response seems to have had the effect of pushing Mr Brown further into a cut-off world where there was the safety of no strong feelings. He had learned, by expressing his anger explosively when drinking, that feelings like this may drive away his wife. It seemed safer to remain in the cut-off place where Mrs Brown took on the role of carer to a husband with a dementing illness. The effect of these changes in your life together has been devastating for both of you. You are not able to enjoy the retirement you have both worked for for so long.

The reformulation was received by Mrs Brown with tears and an expression of the frustration she felt. Mr Brown smiled benignly and seemed to want to support his wife but seemed unable to express any feelings or acknowledge that he understood what had been said. It was clear he was caught in a dilemma from which there seemed no escape. If he got better he risked being blamed for causing so much distress to Mrs Brown. If he stayed in the cut-off place he inhabited more and more of the time, he risked seeing his wife become progressively more crushed and hopeless and their retirement effectively a bad dream. The therapy is currently ongoing but to date Mr Brown is at least stable in his impairment and is having patches of more independent living. Exits are simple but hard to operate consistently. Mrs Brown tries to resist doing things for her husband, they try to spend time to share feelings with each other each day and each tries to develop areas of independent interest in the outside world. Mrs Brown is able to state clearly that she would not leave the relationship if Mr Brown improved and would not blame him for the years they had been in this dynamic. Mr Brown seems unable to hear or hang on to this message. Progress is slow but this may be the nature of work with such a high degree of dissociation in the identified patient. Figure 8.7 is a joint SDR in progress, for Mr and Mrs Brown.

Mr and Mrs Brown's case has allowed meaningful links to be made between early experience and later dissociation. It is only by the engagement of a caring partner that therapeutic work is possible, as Mr Brown cannot engage meaningfully in individual work. The case demonstrates the links between abusive reciprocal roles, fear of abandonment and progressive dissociation ending in the extreme cut-off state of pseudo-

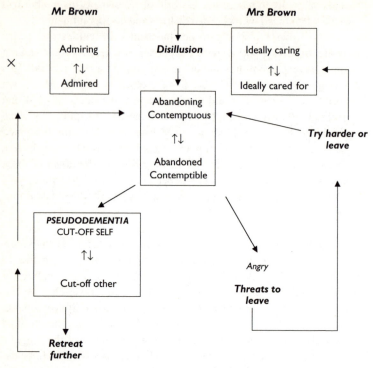

Mr Brown

Mrs Brown

The connection between the reciprocal roles and related procedures that result in Mr Brown's progressive dissociation and pseudodementia

Figure 8.7 Couple SDR for Mr and Mrs Brown

dementia. It gives some hope that the progression from the collapse of idealising defences to pseudodementia and physical dependency is not inevitable, as it seems in many of the cases in the series, but it may be that the syndrome needs to be identified in the earlier stages before real abandonment (by the withdrawal of all friends and relatives) occurs, if therapeutic approaches are to be effective.

Even in the more severe cases, it may be important to convey to carers that the person they are looking after does not suffer from a usual dementia, and lack of memory and awareness should not be assumed. This at least encourages carers to explain and communicate with the person as if they understood and helps to prevent 'talking over' the patient that reinforces humiliating care. Awareness of these factors and identification with the true distress at the root of the dissociation can be difficult for inexperienced carers to bear, and good supervision is essential to prevent staff becoming guilty and avoidant of the patient.

Conclusions

In this chapter I hope I have shown that borderline personality traits present much more commonly in older people than has previously been thought, and that the concept of personality disorder needs reappraisal as applied to older people. By applying a CAT model, it is possible to link reciprocal role procedures with the presenting symptoms – somatisation, self-neglect and dissociative phenomena – so that the individual and the system around them can gain insight into the psychological basis of the patients' distress and, if nothing more, acknowledge the human fear and existential anxiety that is at the heart of the symptoms and behaviours.

References

Abrams, R. C., and Horowitz, S. V. (1999) Personality disorders after age 50: a meta-analytic review of the literature. In E. Rosowsky, C. Abrams and R. A. Zweig (eds), *Personality Disorders in Older Adults: Emerging Issues in Diagnosis and Treatment.* Mahwah, NJ: Lawrence Erlbaum, 55–68.

APA (1987) *Diagnostic and Statistical Manual of Mental Disorders,* 3rd edn rev. Washington, DC: American Psychiatric Association.

APA (1994) *Diagnostic and Statistical Manual of Mental Disorders*, 4th edn. Washington, DC: American Psychiatric Association.

Freud, S. (1957) On hysterical mechanisms. In *Collected Papers*, vol. 1, ed. J. D. Sutherland. London: Hogarth Press, 24–41.

Gunderson, J. G., Kolb, J. E., and Austin, V. (1981) The Diagnostic Interview for Borderlines (DIB). *American Journal of Psychiatry* 138: 869–903.

Hepple, J. (1999) Borderline traits and dissociate states in later life: insights from cognitive analytic therapy. *PSIGE Newsletter* 70: 20–3.

Hepple, J. (2002) Cognitive analytic therapy with older people. In J. Hepple, M. Pearce and P. Wilkinson (eds.), *Psychological Therapies with Older People.* Hove and New York: Brunner-Routledge.

Howells, R., and Beats, B. (1989) A dementia syndrome of dependency? *British Journal of Psychiatry* 154: 872–6.

Kirby, H. B., and Harper, R. G. (1987) Team assessment of geriatric mental patients: the care of functional dementia produced by hysterical behaviour. *Gerontologist* 27: 573–6.

Kirby, H. B., and Harper, R. G. (1988) Team assessment of geriatric mental patients (II). Behavioural dynamics and psychometric testing in the diagnosis of functional dementia due to hysterical behaviour. *Gerontologist* 28: 260–2.

Kroessler, D. (1990) Personality disorder in the elderly. *Hospital and Community Psychiatry* 41(12): 1325–9.

Liberini, P., Faglia, L., Salvi, F., and Grant, R. P. (1993) What is the incidence of conversion pseudodementia? (letter). *British Journal of Psychiatry* 162: 124–6.

Morse, J. Q., and Lynch, T. R. (2000) Personality disorders in late life. *Current Psychiatry Reports* 2: 24–31.

Mroczek, D. K., Hurt, S. W., and Berman, W. H. (1999) Conceptual and methodological issues in the assessment of personality disorders in older adults. In E. Rosowsky, R. C. Abrams and R. A. Zweig (eds), *Personality Disorders in Older Adults: Emerging Issues in Diagnosis and Treatment.* Mahwah, NJ: Lawrence Earlbaum Associates, 135–50.

Padoani, W., and De Leo, D. (2000) Severe and persistent regressive behaviour in three elderly subjects without cognitive decline. *International Journal of Geriatric Psychiatry* 15: 70–4.

Perry, J. C., Banon, E., and Ianni, F. (1999) Effectiveness of psychotherapy for personality disorders. *American Journal of Psychiatry* 156: 1312–21.

Reich, J., Nduaguba, M., and Yates, W. (1988) Age and sex distribution of *DSM III* personality cluster traits in a community population. *Comprehensive Psychiatry* 29(3): 298–303.

Rosowsky, E., and Gurian, B. (1991) Borderline personality disorder in late life. *International Psychogeriatrics* 3(1): 39–51.

Rosowsky, E., and Gurian, B. (1992) Impact of borderline personality disorder in late life systems of care. *Hospital and Community Psychiatry* 43(4): 386–9.

Ryle, A. (1997) *Cognitive Analytic Therapy and Borderline Personality Disorder: The Model and the Method.* Chichester: John Wiley.

Ryle, A., and Golynkina, K. (2000) Effectiveness of time-limited cognitive analytic therapy for borderline personality disorder: factors associated with outcome. *British Journal of Medical Psychology* 73: 197–210.

Ryle, A., and Kerr, I. B. (2002) *Introducing Cognitive Analytic Therapy.* Chichester: John Wiley.

Chapter 9

Cultures of care in severe depression and dementia

Laura Sutton

The work of Tom Kitwood has become important in the field of dementia care. He addresses in particular cultures of care, their internalisation and the resultant unreflected enactments of others towards the person with dementia. CAT also addresses the internalisation of sociocultural activity. In this chapter I explore how Kitwood's work can be used within CAT in the case of severe depression, and how CAT can be used within the context of dementia care.

Kitwood's principal aim was to contrast a 'task-oriented' culture of care with a relationship-oriented culture of care. This arose because Kitwood, like many others, was horrified by what he saw when he first came across dementia care, in the way that others related to those who were dementing. He came to identify what he called the 'malignant social psychology' – MSP – surrounding people with dementia. He initially identified ten such parameters but later added seven more. This chapter draws on Kitwood (1997), which was the compilation of his work, published shortly before he died. The seventeen parameters of 'social malignancy' are covered there and are:

1.	Treachery	10.	Objecification
2.	Disempowerment	11.	Ignoring
3.	Infantilisation	12.	Imposition
4.	Intimidation	13.	Withholding
5.	Labelling	14.	Accusation
6.	Stigmatization	15.	Disruption
7.	Outpacing	16.	Mockery
8.	Invalidation	17.	Disparagement
9.	Banishment		

The 'malignant social psychology' speaks to ageism more generally. Kitwood's view was that people who have Alzheimer's disease or who acquire some such progressive neurological disorder later on in their lives attract to themselves a particularly severe form of such prejudice. Genevey and Katz (1990), who explore ageism through countertransference reactions, find for instance that people who are very much younger, such as in their thirties, who themselves contract a severely disabling condition may experience similar forms of such stigmatising.

From a CAT perspective, the recognition and desisting from re-enacting the MSP is effectively a recognition and noncollusion with harmful or limiting 'reciprocal roles'. For example, one of the seventeen parameters of social malignancy that Kitwood specified is 'outpacing'. This is where the other is 'providing information, presenting choices, etc, at a rate too fast for a person to understand; putting them under pressure to do things more rapidly than they can bear' (Kitwood 1997, p. 47). I find that this is not specific towards people with dementia because it is useful to keep in mind generally in working with people who may be very disabled psychologically, such as those who are severely depressed. In other words, 'outpacing-to-unbearably pressurised' would be a harmful 'reciprocal role' in CAT.

In CAT, without awareness or 'recognition' the practitioner may well be genuinely unaware of their lack of attunement with the person and not see the effect it has upon them. Without the 'reciprocal role' acknowledged or 'named' as such the client or patient may be left feeling floundering unaccountably with an untrustworthy inner commentary. If this 'transference and countertransference' is not acknowledged then it can only be 'acted out', rather than thought about and collaboration is not really possible. If it is named, then it can be thought about so reciprocal patterns can be recognised more clearly and revised: a practitioner, recognising that they are starting to talk too fast for instance, may take this as a cue to slow themselves down. In short, they may then 'relax'. 'Relaxation' for Kitwood is where 'The caregiver is free to stop active work, for a while, and even to stop planning. He or she positively identifies with the need that many people with dementia have: to slow down, and allow both body and mind a respite' (Kitwood 1997, p. 120). In other words, this identification shows that this need is true of both practitioner and patient or client. Thinking and feeling then become more possible, and through this, so does the connection of different states of mind. In CAT the therapist aims to hold in mind the different, sometimes fragmented, parts of the person, through the use of diagrams, called 'SDRs' (Sequential Diagrammatic Reformulations) which I think has relevance not only in the 'borderline' but also in dementia.

If relaxed, and so more able to keep the idea of the different parts of the person in mind, then 'facilitation' becomes possible. For Kitwood, in 'facilitation', 'a subtle and gentle imagination is called into play. There is a readiness to respond to the gesture which a person with dementia makes; not forcing meaning upon it, but sharing in the creation of meaning and enabling action to occur' (Kitwood 1997, p. 120). 'Relaxation' and 'facilitation' are two out of twelve parameters of what Kitwood (1997) calls 'positive person work', PPW:

1.	Recognition	7.	Relaxation
2.	Negotiation	8.	Validation
3.	Collaboration	9.	Holding
4.	Play	10.	Facilitation
5.	Timalation	11.	Creation
6.	Celebration	12.	Giving

In CAT, these could also be viewed reciprocally as 'relaxing mentally and physically-to-unpressurised and safe' and 'facilitating-to-enabled'. As thinking and feeling thereby become more possible, however rudimentary, so does the possibility of the co-creation of meaning, which in CAT is more familiarly known as 'joint activity' within the 'zone of proximal development' (Ryle and Kerr 2002).

Thus I find a fluidity between Kitwood's work and CAT practice especially for people with severer and/or chronic levels of distress or disturbance (whatever their age) in terms of understanding the conditions needed in order to develop the potential for a therapeutic (non-collusive) relationship. I would like to explore this with two case examples. First I would like to talk about how Kitwood's ideas along with those of CAT may combine helpfully for someone who is severely depressed. Then I would like to talk about how CAT with Kitwood's ideas may draw out a sense of the 'person' in 'person-centred' approaches to challenging behaviours in dementia, arguably so as to be less ageist.

Brian

Brian, who was in his early seventies, was severely depressed. Anti-depressant medication had helped to an extent but he remained very withdrawn, his movements slow. He was slow to talk and spoke virtually in monosyllables. It seemed hard for Brian even to think. His keyworker, Mike, a community psychiatric nurse, was interested in the therapies and wanted to work with him, having joined a supervision group that I run. Although Brian did not have a dementia, Mike was new to work in the therapies, so in order to help orientate him to the nature of working as a

Figure 9.1 Initial diagram for Brian

therapist to older people with serious and/or chronic mental health problems, I drew on Kitwood.

As Mike worked with Brian, he started to become aware of how he largely directed the sessions. This was not only in response to Brian's 'stuckness', although this was part of it. Mike was saying that it was to do with his nursing role. We began to realise that the discourse of 'being a patient in relation to being a nurse' was shaping the sessions in powerful ways. It was shaping Mike's behaviour. And 'in role' as the patient it was shaping Brian's. They had both come already with these potentials. This has shed light for me on what Kitwood means when he talks about how the 'cultures of care' prevent us and the person with dementia meeting 'person-to-person'. This led to a shift in Brian's therapy. He and Mike began, slowly and falteringly for Brian, Mike attentive but not outpacing him, to address other relationships of this kind in Brian's life. These included when he was in the army as a young man and at home as a child. The army offered a 'powerful-to-powerless' experience from others as sergeants to his status as private. His father had been in mental institutions with depressions at various points in his life, and died never having resolved his depression, and represented the 'powerless' side. We began to see Brian's 'stuckness' or 'involution' differently. Brian seemed more frozen than anything, if he weren't in his 'cocoon' of depression.

I introduced the group to the use of diagrams. Mike drew with Brian a picture of a cocoon. Brian very much related to this as his depression. This protected him from the outside world, but at the same time meant he could not learn to change from participation in the outside world. Outside the cocoon, Mike wrote the word 'frozen' and then drew an arrow from Brian's cocoon to the word 'frozen', drawing jagged edges around this (Figure 9.1). Brian also very much related to this. There was more to this than met the eye. Mike could see Brian breaking out into a sweat, becoming flushed at even Mike saying words like 'goals'. In short, Mike could see Brian having a panic attack. Brian then appeared to 'dissociate', that is, suddenly numb to feeling. He was back in his cocoon.

Mike neither panicked nor became (too) dismayed. He stayed as best he could with the 'bigger picture' – the drawing. He continued to attend to Brian, with reliable sessions, not outpacing him. Gradually, Brian was able to tolerate viewing the drawing a little and considering it. Sometimes he talked more now. Then went back in his cocoon. Mike's task was then to notice this: it was as though Brian sometimes was coming out of his cocoon able to tolerate his anxiety enough to say some things, but that this itself provoked panic, so Brian 'dissociated': he switched back into his cocoon. Other times he didn't venture out. I find it important in the supervision groups to encourage a standing back from both therapist and client/patient at these times. Standing back from both Mike and Brian it is easier to see how Brian might have been reacting in part to Mike as a 'powerful other' so froze often. It may have been that this kind of unnamed reciprocal process was what was making it difficult in part for Brian to talk. At the same time, Brian's moments now outside his cocoon as well as being in his cocoon were both aspects to him, the latter considerably more stable than the former. I think Brian needed Mike's reliable presence to hold this lack of integration for now, via their drawing. This is what is meant in CAT when it is said that the tools of CAT, their drawing being one of them, become shared tools which 'mediate' the as-yet tenuous therapeutic relationship (as Mike learned more about recognising, then revising, his procedure in being over-directing).

For Kitwood 'disempowerment' is one of the parameters of 'social malignancy' (see list on p. 201). Kitwood was clear that he did not mean malign intent on the part of the caregiver or loved one: instead, both parties are seen as influenced by the internalisation of a social discourse of care that shapes ways of relating; following the work of Buber, Kitwood considered that they are already 'in relation'. It is a discourse that is largely task-oriented so sets up the relationship in terms of 'doing for' the person. This may be well-intentioned. It has nevertheless potentially more invidious effects. Kitwood defines 'disempowerment' as 'not allowing the person to use the abilities that they do have; failing to help them complete actions they have initiated' (Kitwood 1997, p. 46). As a reciprocal role it may be expressed as 'disallowing-to-failing'. For Kitwood if the 'malignant social psychology' is addressed and avoided, then people's own capacities *however incomplete* become more evident, and new ways of relating to the person become possible such as 'relaxation' and 'facilitation'. Although this is difficult and frustrating in practice, Mike had the capacity to resist his procedure, in being 'over-directing and disallowing-to-dis-empowered and failing' enough in order to facilitate Brian in a relaxed enough way so as to enable Brian to tolerate the

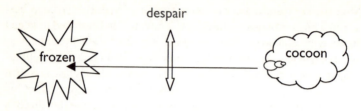

Figure 9.2 Developing Brian's diagram

anxiety of working with him through his fragmented state of mind. As Ryle says, the therapist needs to be able to stand by the person as the anxiety of change is faced and worked through (Ryle 1975).

As Brian got braver, he shared more of his fears and doubts. These included his suicidal feelings and thoughts. Mike had not known how to listen to these but now felt he knew how to more clearly. Anxiety in the face of not knowing how to listen can lead to a shutting off to the person in extreme distress. In CAT this may link to times in a person's life when others had been unable or unwilling to hear. Mike and Brian were discovering a different experience in being 'permitting-to-validated'. Kitwood defines 'validation' in PPW as 'The caregiver goes beyond his or her own frame of reference, with its many concerns and preoccupations, in order to have an empathic understanding of the other; cognitions are tuned down, and sensitivity to feeling and emotion is heightened' (Kitwood 1997, p. 120).

Mike was now becoming more able to stand back from Brian and notice different aspects. He noticed that Brian would be talking apparently comfortably about something then suddenly start talking about suicidal thoughts. I was wondering what occasioned the shift. It occurred to Mike that this was in response to panic, so he was able to write this sequence on his diagram. Then he drew a line in the other direction, to indicate that there may be other things he could do instead. The line itself is the symbol, of hope (Figure 9.2). Mike's response was important because otherwise the tendency now may be for Brian to seek rescue from Mike in the face of his feelings, so it would be important not to become over-protective at this point. Thus, rather than try and resolve or fix the shift (over-direct or over-care) Mike drew it out. This then enabled Brian to think about it, rather than be outpaced or disabled.

It can be difficult to appreciate how difficult the therapeutic process can be for someone such as Brian because it can be speaking to aspects not thought about: if the other had not wanted to hear then this is now repeated from oneself to oneself – it is a 'self-to-self' procedure in CAT. Brian was not fully aware of this and in his partial awareness I felt in him now a mixture of hope and despair, that is, in touch with feeling, yet ready to bolt, oscillating with panic and depression. How the person responds to this in themselves depends upon how this has been responded to in the past. If the person has typically had a lack of recognition or acknowledgement of feelings then they cannot know, or find it very difficult to know, what it is like to have the other recognise this, so it is hard for them to know that they can be held by the other in this way. This was also about session 17 of the 24 (plus follow-up) that he and Mike had agreed. I often find that around this point a sense of mourning comes through, and I think Brian needed Mike to 'stay with' this, neither bolting nor despairing and so numbing over himself. It is as if people are lamenting how life might have been, with a loss of dreams as well as revisiting of other losses, often parental (Knight 1996). This is why the newly developing experience of 'permitting-to-validated' needs to be maintained at this point (rather than repeating a procedure of shutting off as if not wanting to hear), especially in anticipation of the end of the main therapy sessions, as 'feelings' may well be prominent, for instance the anticipated end of therapy re-triggering feelings from other losses.

The wider team's reaction was important here. Brian was 'becoming depressed' again. Should he be admitted? Have ECT? Should his medication be increased again? Mike was at the meeting and was able to explain the therapeutic process more clearly. As a group, they decided not to intervene at this stage, and we always had that safety net if needed. This was heartwarming because our colleagues had avoided taking up the over-directing position too and maintained their attentiveness (we or Brian could go to them for their help if we needed). At this point, Brian asked Mike what he should do. Consistent with his colleagues, rather than slip into giving advice, Mike asked Brian who in his life he would have gone to for advice. Surprising us all, he said his father. This was his father whom he had seen as mentally weak. I find that people in these generations still speak to a moral discourse where 'weakness' is contrasted with 'being strong' as if a person can be in only one of two positions, either weak or strong and that this is linked to meanings of having 'moral fibre' (Pilgrim and Treacher 1992). There seem to be few words permitted or known for instance to express relationships such as 'critical and over-controlling-to-crushed'.

We had discussed the use of therapy letters generally in the supervision group. Creatively, Mike asked Brian if he might like to write a letter as if from his father to him now. Surprising us once again Brian came to his next session with such a letter. In it his father was saying that he realises that it is tough, that rewards are not here yet, but that he must continue. We were moved by this letter, reminding us of what Brian had said of his father who kept on going through his depressions, through the hardships of the 1930s Depression, to be able to feed his family. Just as Brian's respect for his father was growing, so too was ours for him. By remembering not to outpace him, and holding what can be viewed as his lack of integration in sight on the diagram, we became more able to relate to Brian in a different way. Rather than 'over-directing (strong)-to-disempowered and failing (weak)', it felt more 'enabling-to-enabled'. By not outpacing him Mike was able to draw out what was relevant and helpful to Brian at this point in time, and no more, which I think has enabled Brian to assimilate the ideas in a rudimentary way and work with them.

Brian was now more able to tolerate the idea of setting goals. Recently, when discussing a 'goal', which was to phone the shop to ask about getting his lawnmower fixed, Mike noticed Brian's characteristic reaction of panic. He decided to draw Brian's pattern to his attention rather than try and 'solve' it. Brian was then able to practice the alternative, in terms of breathing and resting until the panic started to wane, in the session. Again surprising us all, Brian came to the session after that having phoned the shop, who had sent someone out who fixed his lawnmower. Needless to say Brian was pleased, if a little nerve-wracked, at his effectiveness. At another level, as a metaphor, perhaps Brian like the lawnmower had not been working and Mike like the man from the shop had helped him get working again.

In CAT 'care' and 'containment' from an other are considered necessary conditions for becoming mindful (Chapter 1). The diagram, in holding his lack of integration together, enabled Brian to work with Mike's increasing awareness of the different parts of his 'self'; Mike neither colluding with Brian's partial view of his self (Brian believed that he was depressed because of his disposition – that is, that he was 'weak') nor intruding upon his (fragile) sense of self, for instance in the guise of offering advice or direction. I wonder if this is why Brian came to trust Mike so much. Now, he and Mike are talking about how it will be for him when he comes out of the cocoon of his therapy sessions, for which they are now preparing. Predictably, on coming out of his 'cocoon', Brian's initial reaction most likely would be to freeze, so he would need to practise his 'exit', namely breathing and relaxing in order to tolerate this exposure. Mike's most likely reciprocating action would be to over-protect, so he would need to be mindful of this. Although of course feeling unsure of his own abilities, with a tendency for others to over-protect, Brian is able to tolerate beginning to be more active in his therapy and to entertain the notion of goal-setting. However, it is important not to be too distracted by this at this stage. The follow-up period, which is seen as a part of the therapy itself in CAT, aims to consolidate Brian's use of the diagram. Then there is usually a review, with the possibility in Brian's case of referral for cognitive-behavioural therapy, where Brian is considering the possibility of working on assertiveness within his marital relationship.

What also helped in Brian's case I think has been the capacity of the wider team to be open to these ideas and ways of working. Brian's 'rementia', to use Kitwood's term, has required us as the professionals to address our 'stuck' places (our partial 'dementias') too. Our surprises with Brian spoke I think not only to underestimating Brian as an individual but to underestimating him because of his age and the depth of his mental health problems, as if in old age we believe that 'all is said and done' and 'it is too late now' (Sutton 2002).

Clearly this has been difficult and delicate work for Mike and Brian, with rewards still to come. I think that people in Brian's position may need this kind of help before they can engage 'collaboratively', that is, they need to have a real experience of non-collusion for the basis of trust which is needed for collaborative working. Having said that, Kitwood defines 'collaboration' as 'a deliberate abstinence from the use of power, and hence from all forms of imposition and coercion; "space" is created for the person with dementia to contribute as fully as possible to the action' (Kitwood, 1997, p. 119, fig. 2). The difficulties in achieving this can be seen with Geoffrey.

Geoffrey

Geoffrey was in his early eighties and had a diagnosis of multi-infarct dementia of moderate severity, diagnosed some five years previously. He had been in a variety of residential homes, each breaking down due to his challenging behaviours. He had been admitted to various in-patient units and was now awaiting continuing care. Esme, his primary nurse from one of the units, attended the supervision group and was interested in offering Geoffrey counselling.

Geoffrey typically would swear terribly at staff in these various settings, especially the women, some of whom would be intimidated by him, and he would attempt to hit any of the men (variously residents or patients) should they approach him too closely. He had been in the navy, with high rank. We could imagine that he perhaps attempted to maintain a continuity of identity through rank and hierarchy here. What struck me about him though was not actually his aggressive behaviours so much as how different he was at different times. I had occasion to meet him when I was on the unit for other reasons. Perhaps because of my 'rank' Geoffrey was most polite with me. It was as if he were 'in role'. Similarly he would sit in the office quietly, looking on sternly. I could imagine him at 'centre of operations' on the bridge. Yet when he walked down the corridor he looked lost and dishevelled.

I sat with him in the dining room and he started to tell me that he was '100 years old . . . er . . . 200 . . . er I don't want to live . . . well I do . . . I'm old'. Then he held his head. His hands holding his head reminded me of a chapter by Sinason called 'The man who was losing his brain' (Sinason 1992). This was her year's therapy with Edward, who had Alzheimer's disease. At one point Edward held his head in his hands. Sinason commented how hard it seemed for him to hold on to his thinking. So I now said to Geoffrey, 'It looks like it is hard for you to hold on to your thinking.' He looked at me, so I said, 'You feel 100 years old? Would you like to live to a ripe old age?' His face relaxed and he smiled. He said that he would but that it's hard '. . . these people' he said, looking over to the other patients.

Because he could speak and converse to an extent, staff would try and reason with him, letting him know that his behaviour was unacceptable. It made me think how Geoffrey's 'inner world' and the 'outer world' of his unit were so different. They seemed to be relating to his more competent parts, and not to his incompetent parts, so it would be hard for him to sustain their instruction. They did not seem to have a model which could help them keep the two aspects to Geoffrey in mind. At the same time, Geoffrey was not an easy person to be with. Or, perhaps more helpfully, how were we to make sense of Geoffrey with whom we must relate? (Ryle 1975). He reminded me very much of 'narcissism' (Chapters 5, 6). For this 'split egg' diagrams have been used in CAT (below): there is typically an 'admiring-to-admired' aspect and a 'contemptuous-to-contemptible' aspect to the person, and the area between the split may be seen as an emptiness. Typically in narcissism the person finds the recognition of their own neediness unbearable and humiliating, so switches to anger if the other is not able to sustain them in their admiring attention.

Geoffrey showed an 'admiring-to-admired' aspect (his role of high rank) and a 'contemptuous-to-humiliated and needy' aspect (from which he looked out onto others with disdain). I wondered whether Geoffrey was partly finding the reflection of the other patients a too painful reflection of his own demise now (Figure 9.3). Ennis and Loates (Chapters 5, 6) explain how ageing itself can be experienced as a narcis-

High rank

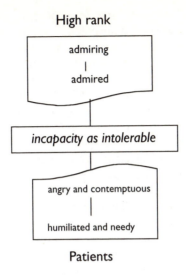

Patients

Figure 9.3 Geoffrey's struggle

sistic wound because it threatens one's self-image. I felt that Geoffrey was perhaps raging against the loss of power and status that Ennis and Loates convey, compounded by his awareness of 'something wrong' with his thinking now which was hard for him to grasp and hold on to, a predicament made all the more difficult to bear I think because of potentially internalised ageism, to which people with dementia, says Kitwood, are particularly subject (Chapter 2). Kitwood and others explore the tendency in Western societies to admire youth and look out onto ageing with disdain, and Geoffrey after all had talked with me about his dilemmas of ageing, seeming to find it hard to associate himself with those who were also dementing.

In narcissism, if the other person fails to provide the much-needed admiring attention, this threatens a potential dissolution: there is no comfortable self-definition now available to them, so anxiety sets in with an uncontained rage towards this failure of the other. It may be that Geoffrey always was potentially guarding himself against such experience, and that this is now doubly difficult; Geoffrey's relatives remarked that the diagram was so like he always was and explained more of his life to us. The unfamiliar sensations of loss of memory and thinking effected by his series of strokes may then give rise to disturbing feelings of disintegration, the very things so guarded against, so the potential for anxiety and depression in Geoffrey is high (he did not know if he wanted to go on living), but with little personal development in terms of emotional competencies to get him through. We see the contrast between his 'competent parts' – his stern gaze – and his 'incompetence' – his dishevelled state – more clearly now. He is, furthermore, now dependent upon us, when once he had been centre of operations.

Thus massive losses may be sustained. Seeing Geoffrey's loss of familiar sources of control and his struggle to comprehend his experiences in this way led us to feel more empathic towards him. We were more able to see Geoffrey as a 'person', struggling to survive psychologically and to maintain connection with others in known ways, largely alone and unsupported. Kitwood refers to this as 'unattended dementia'. He views much of 'challenging behaviour in dementia' arising because life is set up for people on impossible terms. Stokes (2000), who has integrated Kitwood's work into his person-centred approach to challenging behaviours in dementia, says that over his time working with people with dementia he has come to be impressed with how much people with dementia are struggling to survive, to remain a part of the human milieu, how unsupported they can be, and how much we misunderstand and blame them. He writes:

> isolation is the norm for those with dementia. It is not that we simply fail to engage them in conversation, as for many the ability to converse and understand speech will have been lost, but we actually deny them our presence. The need for human contact may be met by eye contact, a smile in passing or just by sitting alongside somebody, even though nothing is said
>
> (Stokes 2000, p. 109)

Potentially, the most significant factor underpinning our belief that we can reduce our understanding of dementia to neuropathology, and thereby neglect the fact that we work with people who have dementia, people who are struggling to survive and communicate, is our dread of dementia. We must address the phenomenon of *social distance*, the distance we place between ourselves and any group of people we fear, or feel threatened by. This distance is a barren land, yet fertile ground for the creation of myths, stereotypes and prejudice. As we never get close to these people, we do not, cannot know them. Hence we can make up any stories we wish, promote any beliefs we want, with little prospect of their being challenged and contradicted

(Stokes 2000, p. 48, Stokes's emphasis)

Stokes (2000) does not see that the 'person has gone' in dementia. He suggests instead that getting to know someone with dementia is a double-edged sword because it brings the awareness that they were once 'just like me', and if that is true, then one day 'I might be just like them'. He invites us to consider that we might. Have you ever had the experience of going up the stairs and then forgetting what is was you went upstairs for? What if that happened again? And then it happened again. How would you react? What would you do? What if you lost your capacity to remember that you are forgetting. This happens because most recent memories are lost first, a phenomenon called 'Ribot's law'. Then you cannot, even if you wished, remember that you have just gone up the stairs. Because your most recent memories are lost, what if you find yourself in an unfamiliar room with other people, some of whom you vaguely recognise and who look official as if they are in charge. Are you in your office? Or perhaps you have gone to a friend's house on the way to pick up the kids. Would it occur to you that you are in a residential home and that the official looking people are staff? Would it occur to Geoffrey when he is in the office that he is not 'on the bridge'?

Stokes (2000) uses his empathic approach to orientate to the idea that people may be reacting to their circumstances now, including their dementia, in ways familiar and known to them. He gives the example of a woman who on arriving on a ward resists and spits at staff. This was a woman who had been known as such a gentle person. He asks whether her behaviour is at odds with her known self and considers, yes. But a person lost to herself, no. It turns out that this person was terribly insecure and had led a sheltered life. Stokes wonders whether because of her insecurity she had organised her life in such a way so as to avoid the anxiety of facing the vicissitudes of life. She had never before had a dementing illness, nor been removed from her familiar lifestyle and contained on a ward. No longer sheltered, and given the loss of some of her conceptual abilities, she was now highly anxious and self-defending, perhaps in the only way now available to her, namely spitting. Stokes (2000) challenges us to consider if any of us would be any different: and how we would like the other to respond to us.

In CAT there is a 'psychotherapy file' which is a questionnaire about people's characteristic ways of relating, both to themselves and to others (Ryle and Kerr 2002). It has recently been prepared in diagram form. One of the 'dilemmas' is, for instance, the 'upset feelings dilemma'. This reads: 'Feeling upset, I *either* bottle up my feelings, others don't notice I'm upset, others ignore me, take advantage of me, or abuse me, I feel that bottling up feelings doesn't work [I am still upset], *or* I express my feelings explosively, others feel hurt, attacked, overwhelmed, threatened, others respond by attacking me or rejecting me, I feel expressing my feelings doesn't work [I am still upset].' Analogously, for this person, her life dilemmas might have been something like, 'Feeling insecure, I *either* hide these feelings by staying home, so feel safe and in control but limited, *or* I am exposed.' For this person it may have been that the latter option seemed too anxiety-provoking so she stayed in her life at the other side of the dilemma, limited, but safe. Now, through her dementia, she was unable to remain at home, so she no longer has her shelter over her feeling exposed and unsafe. Without her more developed conceptual (reflective) capacities available to her now she may express this anxiety in an unreflected, that is, explosive way: spitting. This may lead others to draw back from her, so she has no other to provide her with the emotional shelter she was once able to provide for herself.

For Kitwood the MSP effects a denial of life experience, of connection to one's continuity. He then drew on the work of social psychologists like Harré, and the psychotherapist Winnicott (see Chapter 1) to contrast the development of a 'social self' over one's life and what he calls the 'experiencing self' respectively, in order to begin to address the question of why some people appear to fragment in the face of their dementia whereas others seem to be able to find some rapprochement (reconciliation) to it, in the context of their lives. This is the same process of storying the self that is a part of therapy for anyone. In the above example this woman's 'social self' would have been the part of her that has been able to construct her own means of security. Her 'experiential self' would be her anxious and fearful part. In object relations theory in CAT the former may be in part 'parentally derived' (originally perhaps an over-protecting parent keeping her shielded from life, so safe but limited), the latter aspect child-derived (the 'fragmented child withheld from life', cf. Leiman 1997). Kitwood is saying that often people's 'social selves' are more developed than their 'experiential selves' and that personal development is about gaining more of a balance, especially in dementia where one's capacity to work with intuition and feeling is paramount.

The former for Kitwood links to the notion of the 'adaptive' self and the latter to realms of play and the imagination. He is arguing that as the 'adaptive' self is increasingly lost with increasing dementia, because of the loss of conceptualising ability on which it depends, so the realm of the experiencing self becomes ever more significant. He considers that those who were free to play in early life, amidst secure 'attachments' and who have taken this into their adulthood alongside needs for work, for which the social self is adapted, may have more emotional development to hold them through their dementia. Similarly in CAT the suggestion is that as people grow up and become adult most are able to break free of parental injunction, especially if they have been free to play and to explore, but that some people find this hard if their sense of 'self' is too weak. For the above person (Stokes does not give her name), her potential here seems to have been unrealised in her life. Kitwood says it is not too late to realise it, Stokes (2000) integrating Kitwood's work with the 'resolution therapy' that he developed with Goudie, aimed at the resolution of need.

Stokes (2000) remarks that it used to be thought that the passivity that some people with dementia show after initial resistance on being admitted into care was a sign that they have 'settled in', but comments how wrong we have been. With contemporary eyes, these states of quiet unresponsiveness are now being taken as signs of coping in isolation and the lack of the other in their lives (Stokes 2000). Kitwood (1997) is saying that these absences of attention are signs of our cultures of care, tracing this to the rise of institutional care in the rise of industrialisation. This links to a way of relating between 'us' and 'them' – 'distancing-to-abandoned' – which necessitates very basic coping mechanisms in the recipient such as withdrawal. Kitwood's view is that the diminution of persons has become the norm in industrialised societies, which was why he became interested in these social processes, in the subtle exercises of social power, in remarks tinged with mockery or cruelty and so on that carry on in everyday life – the MSP as he came to refer to these processes – that often pass unnoticed at a conscious level (Kitwood 1997). Ultimately, suggests Kitwood, the person withdraws to a kind of cocoon to preserve some sense of life:

> When the external environment has largely failed to provide security and occupation some people retreat, so to speak, into a 'bubble that occupies little more than their own body space. Within it they create a place of minimal safety, and make their last desperate bid to remain psychologically alive.
>
> (Kitwood 1997, p. 75)

From a CAT perspective, such states of detached resignation, in partly reciprocating our own detached roles, are deeply dialogic events, in relation to how some persons are positioned with respect to others.

Kitwood (1997) defines 'labelling' as 'using a category such as dementia, or "organic mental disorder" as the main basis for interacting with a person and explaining their behaviour' (p. 46). In Geoffrey's case, to 'label' him would be to repeat the malignant social psychology (see list on p. 201). It would be potentially to retraumatise him by repeating his own defensive position towards others who hold up a mirror to his own incompetences. A different way to understand him may be in terms of his 'social' or 'adapted' and 'experiential' self. His 'social self' or 'adapted self' would be his 'admiring-to-admired' and 'angry and contemptuous-to-humiliated and needy' aspects. In this respect, narcissism as such is healthy: we need the esteem of others to know we are held in esteem, that we are safe in the group. Geoffrey's 'experiencing self' would be the part of him that rages and panics when others are not reciprocating his need for external reminders of his admirable qualities. Geoffrey I think would be viewed in Kitwood's terms as having had an over-developed social or adapted self and a poorly developed experiential self. In order to help him, therapy, or a therapeutic approach – as for anyone with similar dilemmas – would need to make neediness honourable and deserving of care.

By recognising the reciprocal role procedures supplied to us via the discourse of 'malignant social psychology', and then desisting them – such as not outpacing Geoffrey – this is effectively not re-traumatising him through our own unwitting 'internalised ageism': it is effectively not to repeat with him a 'contemptuous-to-contemptible' position of our own as a result of unreflected internalised ageism, in order to allow his neediness to be recognised in an honourable way via PPW, extended by Stokes (2000). The therapeutic aim for Geoffrey is then to maintain for him a sense of his own identity externally, by ensuring he is able to have some of the recognition that he seeks without repeating shaming messages of society back to him (Figure 9.4). This may enable him to bear his own ageing and illness less shamefully, and so relieve his depression and anxiety as much as possible, and so want to live to a ripe old age.

Through these explorations in the supervision group, we are developing ways of formulating these therapeutic practices more clearly. Esme developed her understanding of when she switched into task-oriented mode in relating to Geoffrey as a result of her role, as we became more aware of these processes generally for us. At the same time she was trained in counselling and I was impressed with her observational skills in terms of non-verbal communications, her lack of need to be over-cognitive, and her use of therapeutic touch ('timalation', see list on p. 203, is a neologism by Kitwood derived in part from the Greek *timao* meaning 'I honour, i.e. do not violate personal or moral boundaries . . . [to] provide contact, reassurance and pleasure, while making very few demands. It is thus particularly valuable when cognitive impairment is severe', Kitwood 1997, p. 90). In being open to recognising and avoiding or revising the MSP *and* offering Geoffrey counselling sessions using her evident PPW

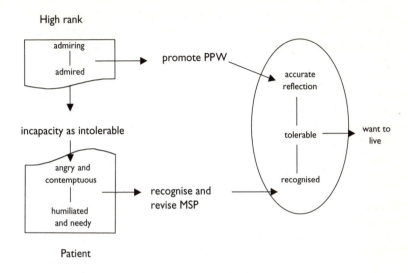

Figure 9.4 A therapeutic approach for Geoffrey

skills, Esme found that Geoffrey came to share with her aspects of his life that he had found difficult to talk about for reasons of shame.

One of the differences though which Kitwood (1997) remarks upon in caring for people with dementia is that these therapeutic needs must continue to be sustained via the interpersonal milieu:

> In dementia, many aspects of the psyche that had, for a long time, been individual and 'internal', are again made over to the inter- personal milieu. Memory may have faded, but something of the past is known; identity remains intact, because others hold it in place; thoughts may have disappeared, but there are still interpersonal processes; feelings are expressed and meet a validating response.
>
> (Kitwood 1997, p. 69)

He makes the point that this is the reverse of what happens in infancy, where, as in the theory that informs CAT, 'meaning' is held to be medi- ated through the conceptual development of the other from the very first (Chapter 1): here, to the very end. For Kitwood, as dementia advances, we as the 'more cognitively competent other' must then have concepts to help in sustaining those who are losing theirs. From these explorations in the supervision group I have come to appreciate how CAT's position on the development of the 'self' can help bring into view the 'person' more visibly in person-centred approaches to challenging behaviours. Mapping out some of the different aspects to Geoffrey I think helps to hold together his degree of fragmentation in mind now. This may help staff to reduce their expectations of him, that is, from over-identifying with his over-developed competent part, and help them to recognise his now exposed less competent parts, with his steadily increasing loss of conceptualising ability, revealing a struggle now to hold him-self together. Then Kitwood's 'relaxation' (see list on p. 203) potentially becomes more possible, because Geoffrey would then need less to have to hold himself together, as the integrating function (the 'eye' to see the 'I'), is now held more safely by others.

This is not easy, though, because it is hard to see such incapacitating decline. Sinason (1992) remarks that in dementia the progressive decline from knowing, possessing words, concepts, to 'not knowing' is the difference between being 'normal' and being profoundly mentally handicapped, experienced in the 'mind and the heart of a single being'. She suggests that in the face of such incapacity there is no easy position and that the wish for ignorance is strong, but that 'ignorance is not bliss, and neither is knowledge' (Sinason 1992). She shows though how we might listen to someone expressing their feelings of disintegration with less anticipated dread. Meanwhile, Kitwood makes the point that the disintegration of the embodied person that we witness as a slow process in dementia is after all something that will happen to us all eventually. For him, dementia triggers fears about existence and mortality, and about fears of frailty and dependency, a long drawn-out death or personal annihilation. Kitwood questions how far we are able to bear this. He asks, if people with dementia are undermined, to what extent is their loss of adaptive resources and disconnection from an experiencing self in part a consequence of the lack of adaptive and subjective development so far in the assumed more-competent other.

He says that dementia will always have its tragic aspect but that there is a world of difference between bearing it alone and someone 'bearing with' you (Kitwood 1997). This can be difficult to do though when we, as the 'more competent other', are still developing, and, often as younger practitioners to much older people, being exposed to late life issues 'before our time' (Knight 1996). Robbins and Sutton (Chapter 7) point out the lack of research on the effects of complex traumata into late life and draw out some of the ways in which CAT understandings may be helpful because its model helps the practitioner to bear the complexity and overwhelming nature of the disconnected presentations of some clients, and to help bear what they have endured and witnessed without numbing unduly. I find that these ideas from 'positive person work' can also help the practitioner when supporting those who present in severe involutional states, when the borderline between depression and 'dementia' is difficult to discern.

Conclusion

In this chapter I have looked at work in progress, particularly at how supervision groups can help in developing awareness of therapeutic issues in later life, encouraging and supporting staff in spending more time engaging in psychological work with older and elderly people, including in severe mental impairment. In particular I have looked at how Kitwood's notion of the malignant social psychology alongside the notion of reciprocal roles may be helpful in developing awareness of potentially ageist countertransferences, along with guidelines for positive person work, to further support those who have severer forms of mental distress or disorder when the borderline between the functional and the organic is difficult to discern. It is difficult to sustain these kinds of approaches, however, and the temptation for a sentimental approach or nihilism can be strong in the face of such difficulties. However, Kitwood's work on the cultures of care and the work more generally on how to approach challenging behaviours within a cultural context lends helpful direction.

Acknowledgements

I would like to thank Brian, Geoffrey's relatives, Mike and Esme for their kind permissions to draw on their material for this chapter. All names and some details have been changed in order to maintain anonymity. I would also like to thank Dr Anthony Ryle for his comments on previous drafts of this chapter.

References

Genevey, B., and Katz, R. S. (1990) *Countertransference and Older Clients*. London: Sage.

Kitwood, T. (1997) *Dementia Reconsidered. The Person Comes First*. Buckingham: Open University Press.

Knight, B. (1996) *Psychotherapy with Older Adults*, 2nd edn. London: Sage.

Leiman, M. (1997) Procedures as dialogical sequences: a revised version of the fundamental concept in CAT. *British Journal of Medical Psychology* 70(2): 193–207.

Pilgrim, D. and Treacher, A. (1992) *Clinical Psychology Observed*. London: Tavistock/Routledge.

Ryle, A. (1975) Self-to-self and self-to-other. *New Psychiatry* (24 April): 12–13.

Ryle, A., and Kerr, I. (2002) *Introducing Cognitive Analytic Therapy: Principles and Practice*. Chichester: John Wiley.

Sinason, V. (1992) *Mental Handicap and the Human Condition. New Approaches from the Tavistock*. London: Free Association Books.

Stokes, G. (2000) *Challenging Behaviour in Dementia: A Person-Centred Approach*. Bicester: Winslow Press.

Sutton, L. (2002) Introduction: contemporary views – a duel with the past. In J. Hepple, J. Pearce and P. Wilkinson (eds), *Psychological Therapies with Older People: Developing Treatments for Effective Practice*. Hove: Brunner-Routledge.

Afterword

I heard the old, old men say,
'Everything alters,
And one by one we drop away.'
They had hands like claws, and their knees
Were twisted like the old thorn trees
By the waters.
I heard the old, old men say,
'All that's beautiful drifts away
Like the waters.'

(W. B. Yeats,
'The old men admiring
themselves in the water'.
Printed by kind permission of
A. P. Watt Ltd. On behalf of
Michael B. Yeats.)

Index

abandonment 15, 84, 97, 165; borderline personality traits 181, 182; dissociated states 194, 197, 198; marriage breakdowns 82

Abraham, Karl 55

Abrams, R. C. 179

abuse 106–7, 158; borderline personality traits 177, 183, 186; marriage breakdowns 82; object relations theory 56; physical 89, 90, 91, 93, 183, 193; sexual 147, 151, 153, 165, 170, 183; verbal 90, 91, 92, 189, 190–1, 193, 195; *see also* trauma

ACAT *see* Association for Cognitive Analytic Therapy

activity theory 13, 32, 33, 34, 36, 154

adaptive self 107, 214–15, 216

Adelman, J. 115, 122, 127–8

Adler, G. 111

affects 23, 24

ageism *xv, xvi*, 3, 4–5, 39, 45–66, 154; biological approaches 101; dementia 102, 211; internalised 211, 216; malignant social psychology 201–2, 219

Agger, I. 157

aggression: indigenous communities 70; narcissism 114; passive-aggressive strategies 89, 181, 182; *see also* anger

'aggressive deafness' 193

agreeableness 19

alienation 150; *see also* isolation

'aloneness' 111, 116

Alzheimer's disease 42, 95, 97, 101, 201–2, 210

American Psychiatric Association (APA) 178

anger: abusive backgrounds 106–7; borderline personality 89, 111, 181, 195–6, 197; Michael's case 136, 137, 138; narcissism 210; war veterans 154, 157; *see also* aggression; rage

Anouilh, Jean 53

anti-depressants 85, 89, 144, 163, 164, 189, 203

anxiety: ageism 54; borderline personality traits 199; castration 118; CAT clinical examples 85, 87, 95, 97, 205–6; defensive anxiety reduction 171; dementia 213, 214; different reasons for 84; existential 57; group work 62; 'holding' role of therapist 21, 22; management methods 160; narcissism 211; 'narrow-band' functioning 78; persecutory 28; positive person work 216; pseudodementia 186; under-recognition 178; *see also* fear

APA *see* American Psychiatric Association

archetypes 56, 70, 73–4, 81

Archibald, H. C. 151

Arden, M. 61

arousal 147, 148, 164; *see also* hyper-arousal

Association for Cognitive Analytic Therapy (ACAT) *xv*

assumptions 8, 148, 149

attention-seeking 164, 165

avoidance 148, 170, 171

'bad objects' 28, 29

Bakhtin, M. 13, 18, 58

Bandura, Albert 23